Write to Learn

Write to Learn

EIGHTH EDITION

DONALD M. MURRAY

Professor Emeritus

The University of New Hampshire

THOMSON

WADSWORTH

Australia   Canada   Mexico   Singapore   Spain   United Kingdom   United States

Write to Learn, Eighth Edition
Donald M. Murray

Publisher: *Michael Rosenberg*
Acquisitions Editor: *Dickson Musslewhite*
Development Editor: *Laurie K. Runion*
Editorial Production Manager: *Michael Burggren*
Marketing Manager: *Carrie Brandon*
Associate Marketing Manager: *Joe Piazza*
Senior Print Buyer: *Mary Beth Hennebury*
Compositor: *GGS Book Services, Atlantic Highlands*
Project Manager: *GGS Book Services, Atlantic Highlands*
Cover Designer: *Dutton and Sherman Design*
Printer: *Webcom Ltd.*

Printed in Canada
   4 5 6 07 06

For more information contact Thomson Wadsworth, 25 Thomson Place, Boston, Massachusetts 02210 USA, or you can visit our Internet site at http://www.thomson.com

ISBN: 1-4130-0173-4

Library of Congress Control Number
2004106097

To Minnie Mae

Who made soup of old bones and mailed out
manuscript in which I had no faith

Contents

CHAPTER 22
Writers Help Writers   199

CHAPTER 23
Learning from Writers   207

CHAPTER 24
Revive A Dead Draft   258

CHAPTER 25
Revise   261

CHAPTER 29
Explore Creative Nonfiction   316

CHAPTER 30
A Lifetime Apprenticeship   320

Preface

Many of us intend to keep travel journals when we return to the country of our ancestors, hike the Appalachian Trail, tour Thailand. We buy fancy travel journals or they are given to us by friends and relatives. Our intentions are good but the journal pages remain blank—at least mine do. When I began this edition of *Write to Learn*, I realized that this and the previous seven editions are my travel journals that have recorded an intellectual voyage as I have tried to understand and practice the writer's craft.

Twenty years ago when the first edition was published I could not have imagined an eighth edition, but when I have faced each new edition, I have felt the excitement of possible new insights, new ideas, new connections, new understandings—and each possibility has been fulfilled. I have continued between editions to write daily—well, almost daily. At 79 I am still an apprentice to my craft.

New to This Edition

Although the length of the book is the same, this edition has more and shorter chapters because those instructors who reviewed the seventh edition suggested this. I found that in writing shorter chapters, I have made discoveries, as well as created an edition that students may find more available as they are able to get through chapter topics more quickly.

A major emphasis in this edition is on the writing that is done in the head before a word appears on the screen. In a real sense, when I am at my computer I am harvesting a crop of specific details, thoughts, ideas, questions, answers, connections that have grown in my mind while I have been away from the writing desk, and I share this insight with students.

I have again changed the writing process to a sequence of sections: Write Before Writing, Research for Writing, Begin Writing, Keep Writing, and Finish Writing. I have never seen the writing process as an absolute, but as a way of working that will change according to the experience of the writer, the writing task, and the work method of the writer. I hope this new order will help students as they write their way toward meaning.

I have written a new chapter on reviving a dead draft, a problem that we all face from time to time. I have also given new attention to meeting deadlines, to seeing within the draft, and other topics that have grown from the concerns of colleagues, students, and my own efforts to develop my craft.

I have also added a new chapter, written by Lisa Miller of the University of New Hampshire, on using the Internet, and a new chapter that allows students to hear famous writers of the past and present talk of their attitudes and techniques while they are making writing.

In addition, the "In the Writer's Workshop" activities—which offer students a wealth of ideas for exploring chapter topics in more depth—now appear at the end of parts and have been thoroughly revised and reorganized into new parts: On Your Own, With a Writing Partner, With a Group, With Writing Mentors, and On the Internet. Also at the end of each section are "Shoptalk" questions that provide answers to common questions that beginning writers might ask.

Acknowledgments

I have always been indebted to those who have reviewed each edition, but this year I was honored that a very busy fellow writer and inspiring teacher agreed to make suggestions for this edition. Her name was Wendy Bishop and she was diagnosed with leukemia on August 8, 2003, and died on November 21, 2003. We have all lost a friend and a colleague who always gave more to her students, colleagues, readers, and friends than we gave her.

I am indebted to the insights of other reviewers:

Bruce Ballenger, *Boise State University*

Eileen Donovan-Kranz, *Boston College*

Mark Harris, *Schoolcraft College*

Vanessa Johnson, *Roosevelt University*

Gail Robinson, *Clark College*

Lisa Shuchter, *Naugatuck Valley Community College*

Doug Waugh, *Muskingum Area Technical College*

My own understanding of how effective writing is produced has been inspired and challenged by Don Graves of Jackson, New Hampshire; Chip Scanlan of the Poynter Institute in St. Petersburg, Florida; Tom Newkirk of the University of New Hampshire who lives across the street; Brock Dethier of Utah State University; Tom Romano of Miami University in Ohio; Ralph Fletcher of Durham, New Hampshire; Joe Hight of the Department of Labor of the United States Government; and far more than I could list here. I am especially indebted to the many contributions of Lisa Miller of the University of New Hampshire.

My editor and friend Laurie Runion has made so many contributions that it is really our book, not mine alone. Other editors and designers who have used their professional skills to produce this edition include: Dickson Musslewhite, Acquisitions Editor; Michael Burggren, Editorial Production Manager; and Heidi L. Allgair/GGS Book Services, Atlantic Highlands.

About the Author

DONALD M. MURRAY is Professor Emeritus of English at the University of New Hampshire where he inaugurated a journalism program, designed an advanced composition course, helped establish a graduate program in composition studies, and served as director of freshman English and as English department chairperson. He twice won awards for his teaching and was awarded an honorary doctorate by the University of New Hampshire in 1990, Fitchburg State College in 1992, and New Hampshire College in 1997.

As a journalist, Murray won a number of awards, including the Pulitzer Prize for editorial writing with the *Boston Herald* in 1954. He was an editor at *Time* before freelancing as a magazine writer in New York City for seven years. He served as writing coach for the *Boston Globe*, the *Providence Journal*, and other newspapers. In 1991 he was selected best columnist in Boston by *Boston* magazine and in 1996 he earned the same honor from *Improper Bostonians* magazine. In 2003, the Special Interest Group in Creative Nonfiction (a subgroup of the National Council of Teacher's of English) established "The Donald Murray Prize" to be given to the writer of the best essay published on teaching and/or writing.

He has published more than a dozen books, including *The Craft of Revision*, Fifth Edition (Wadsworth); *Read to Write*, Third Edition (Wadsworth); *A Writer Teaches Writing, Revised Edition* (Wadsworth); *Shoptalk: Learning to Write with Writers* (Heinemann); *Crafting a Life in Essay, Story, Poem* (Heinemann); *Writing to Deadline* (Heinemann); *My Twice-Lived Life: A Memoir* (Ballantine); and *The Lively Shadow* (Ballantine).

Above all, Don Murray is a student and practitioner of the writing process who still considers himself an apprentice to his craft. In addition to studying the processes of other writers, he continues to write novels and poetry, and a weekly column, "Now and Then," for the *Boston Globe*.

The View from the Writer's Desk

What I've found and what I believe is that everybody is talented. It's just that some people get it developed and some don't.

STEPHEN SONDHEIM

How do I know what I think until I see what I say?

E. M. FORSTER

The hardest thing I had to do even to become a writer was believing that I had anything to say that people would want to read.

ALICE McDERMOTT

CHAPTER 1

Craft . . . not Magic

As you read these opening pages, try to imagine how I wrote them. Did I plan out each page? What problems did I encounter in writing them? How many drafts did it take to solve them?

You can't. Like the skillful criminal, the experienced writer knows how to remove fingerprints and footprints, to leave no trace at the crime scene. You can't know that I wrote more than a dozen beginnings, first finding what I wanted to say, and then rewriting to find out how best to say it.

And you certainly can't know that I felt no sense of failure when I wrote sentences that did not work, did not read clear, did not clarify and communicate what I had to say. It was a grand delight to write and rewrite, finally seeing and hearing these lines run clear. Each draft is an experiment, an exploration, and, if I am lucky, a discovery.

Most books on composition are written by readers who imagine writers know what they are going to say and how they are going to say it. But such texts may not help beginning writers who face a blank screen with a blank brain. This book is written by a writer who does not know what he is going to say or how to say it before the writing begins.

The writer's ignorance is essential. It leads us to new topics and new ways to make the topics clear to ourselves—and our readers. Even experienced writers feel a sense of emptiness and ignorance before the first draft, but beginning writers believe their panic is a lack of talent and of knowing. The experienced writer knows this *unknowing* is the beginning of all effective writing and they have developed a craft that allows them to discover what they didn't know they knew. This textbook reveals the secrets of the writer's craft so that students can develop the writer's ability of discovering and sharing what they know.

I am a student [fan with large lungs] of ice hockey and have played a little pond hockey and street hockey with roller skates. The University of New Hampshire—where I taught for 24 years—has nationally ranked women's and men's hockey teams, and when I talk to players and coaches about a game I have watched from the stands, I am struck by how different a game they have seen at ice level. I note how a player made a pass, but they comment on how another player, away from the puck, made an unexpected move to get where the pass would arrive. We do not agree on the most important plays, the turning points, even the strategies of each team. Sitting in the stands "reading" the game has little relationship to what a player "writes" when he or she has the puck on the stick and faces the speeding, ever-changing movement of offense and defense.

The same thing is true of my son-in-law, Michael, who is a composer, orchestrator, and conductor. We both listen to music but he hears it far differently than I do. He begins with silence and creates melody; I listen to the recorded melody but have little idea of the interplay of instruments that combine to create the melody.

I go sketching with my other son-in-law, Karl. We look across the same field that slopes down into dark woods with a glimpse of a river's edge, but our visions are different and what he sees as an experienced painter and I see as an amateur are greatly different. Studying a masterpiece in a museum to understand it and facing your own blank canvas to create a painting are two vastly different challenges. One is to know what the artist has done on the finished canvas, the other is to know what to do on an empty canvas.

When beginning writers study a piece of writing, they may not have an accurate idea of what the writer did to produce the final draft they are studying. Trying to figure out how a piece of writing is made is like trying to imagine a pig from a sausage.

Michael begins to make music with silence, Karl begins to paint on a blank canvas, I face the empty computer screen. This book looks at writing from the point of view of the writer when the screen is blank. We do not know what we will say or how we will say it. We write to learn, to discover, to find out what we didn't know we knew, to make readers think and feel in response to our writing.

Our tasks are not to imitate but to create what was not there before we began, to create what is, if we are lucky, far different than what we planned. Of course we want to produce work that communicates, but the first communication is to ourselves.

As far back as I remember, I wanted to be a storyteller. My Scottish grandmother, with whom we lived when I was growing up, made sense of her difficult life through narrative, and each story she told that bound her to the old country had a moral. Sunday mornings and evenings our Baptist preacher delivered sermons that were documented with stories. Riding in an uncle's car—we never owned an auto ourselves—in the days before car radio, we sang songs like "I've Been Working on the Railroad," recited poetry like "Gunga Din" or told stories. I was read to by Uncle Will who lived with us. I only remember him reading to me, but Grandma, Mother, perhaps even Father on the rare evenings when he was home from work or church read to me—"The Little Engine That Could," "Billy Goat's Gruff," and "Winnie the Pooh."

Hearing stories, I began to tell myself private stories before falling off to sleep. The stories created a life better than mine. I was always the hero. I wanted to become a word magician who knew the trick of using words to transport readers into other lives where writer and reader could both be heroic.

I thought writing was magic and I was told that writers, like painters and actors and composers and singers and baseball players, had to have talent. What was easy for them was hard for me.

I knew it would never be easy for me. I believed I had been born without talent, but writing was what I wanted to do more than playing first base for the Red Sox, more than being a pirate, an Indian scout, a polar explorer.

Since my teachers confirmed my lack of talent, I decided to search for the magic formula that would turn my ordinary days into adventures. I began my search in elementary school, continued it in junior and senior high school, for three years in the Army, in college, and when I got a job as copy boy on a city newspaper. I studied the best writers on the newspaper for whom I was getting coffee, reading over their shoulder, reading their early drafts and their published stories. Asking them questions, I discovered they did not believe they practiced magic. They were simply workers who knew their craft. And I figured craft was something I could learn.

I invite you to join me as I continue my apprenticeship to the craft of writing. Come on in. Join me in the pool of language. You can make a belly flop, edge in a toe at a time, make a racing start, just dive off the edge. There is no right or wrong in beginning to use language to explore your world—what you know that you didn't know you knew, what you need to know, what you need to stand back and reconsider, what you need to share.

Of course writing the final draft is different—like the swim meet with rules and traditions—but now you should only be having fun. My way of writing is not usually to jump right into the pool but walk around it until a word, a phrase, an image makes me want to see where it will lead. Then I slide into the pool of language and write fast, my fingers getting ahead of my brain, until I see something that needs attention, focus, research or memory, development.

As I walked around the pool today, "sauerkraut" came to mind. I had dinner last night with our only friends who ever serve sauerkraut, and I recently heard from my high school friend who spent two days in a huge crock of sauerkraut hiding from German soldiers in World War II. He has never eaten sauerkraut since. It is a favorite food of mine that came late in life. I see a pile of sauerkraut, smell it, taste it in my mind and then find myself writing.

> Sauerkraut. That's what was missing in my childhood. And pizza and Shitaki mushrooms, General Gao's chicken, corned beef, sushi, salads and yogurt and cheese—we never once had a smelly cheese in our kitchen. I had a childhood deprived of all that was strange, smelly even stinky and surprisingly tasty. We ate meat with ketchup and potatoes with butter and were proud of it. Nothing foreign for us. Of course my family was deprived of more than food. No ideas, no arguments, no disagreement. We didn't talk religion and politics, only appearance and behavior, my folks were strong on behavior, and dress and haircuts and . . .

This is going to be a fun piece to write. Of course it's only my way of writing and my subject. You will have to find your own sauerkraut, but that's part of writing to learn, so let's begin.

CHAPTER 2

Make Writing Easy

Whew. What a relief. You don't have to think you have talent to write. There is no secret society of writers you have to join. There is no mystery. Now let's start writing.

Write what?

I don't know. I don't need to know what I am going to write and neither do you. Writing produces writing.

I have come to accept and respect, even welcome the terror and emptiness I used to fear when I faced the blank computer screen and the insistent demand of the blinking cursor. Not knowing what I will write, or even if I can write, means I will not write what I have written before. I have begun a voyage of *discovery.* The initial satisfaction from writing is *surprise:* we say what we do not expect to say in a way we do not expect to say it.

Surprise is also essential when I come to my desk with a writing assignment. I know the topic but not how I will approach it or what I will learn from the assignment. After sixty years of being published, I am still an apprentice to the writer's craft, taking instruction from each morning's draft—the experiments in meaning writers use to discover what to say and how to say it.

All writers are self-taught. Your instructor can help, your classmates can help, this book can help, but you still have to write to learn how to write in your own way—and that way will change as you gain writing experience, see the world in a new way, switch to a new topic or genre. As you read this book, stop the moment you feel you have something to say, an itch you can scratch by writing, an opinion, a doubt, a belief and write. This book should be a collaborative experience as we write together. If you write as you read, you will better understand what I am saying—and you will have the satisfaction and fun of discovering what you did not know about your life.

When I begin, I sit back and let my mind drift. This is not the time for hard thinking, for concentration, for purpose, but the time for the drifty kind of creative reflection that school does not teach, time for patience, for accident. What the poet William Stafford wrote has sustained and inspired me year after year:

> . . . one should lower his standards until there is no felt threshold to go over in writing. It's easy to write. You just shouldn't have standards that inhibit you from writing. . . . I can imagine a person beginning to feel he's not able to write up to that standard he imagines the world has set for him. But to me that's surrealistic. The only standard I can rationally have is the standard I'm meeting right now. . . . You should be more willing to forgive yourself. It doesn't make any difference if you are good or bad today. The assessment of the product is something that happens after you've done it.

I have presumed to write books to tell others how to write, but I have to remember that I must be willing to write badly to write well, that what I accomplished yesterday may be of no help today.

You mean you haven't learned to write and you write books on how to write? Yes, and I flunked out of high school and became a professor, was a fearful kid and was in combat as a paratrooper, said I'd never get married and have been married twice, never imagined I'd be a parent and am now a grandfather. Life is always unexpected and writing should be as well.

School emphasizes straight-line thinking, but writers and artists, scientists and marketing managers also practice circular, associative thinking that connects what the logical mind would never connect. In beginning to write, I have to remind myself not to think too hard but relax, listen to what drifts through my mind.

Sometimes a stimulus—a sound, a smell, something I see—stirs memories. I see the moonlight illuminate the woods behind my house and remember how much we hated moonlight in the Battle of the Bulge in World War II when what would be a lovely night in peacetime exposed us as we tried to hide from the enemy. I hear an oboe being played on the radio and imagine it is my long dead daughter practicing her oboe in the next room. I smell the pine Christmas tree and travel in memory to the summer woods I visited years before.

If those connections interest you, if they seem to hold a mystery, a problem, a question, then write—but the topic does not have to be that clear. I particularly delight in the connections without immediate explanation. I sit back, try to make my mind blank when I remember a newspaper story I read the night before about the possibility of restoring passenger rail service through our town. The phrase "train to college" drifts into mind.

Try it yourself. It is impossible to have a blank mind. Something will drift out of your memory or experience, something you see or hear, smell or touch or taste will come into your head. The important thing is not to strain at it but remain in a relaxed state, making notes on what appears on stage in the theater of your mind.

Now let's stop talking about writing and write together. As Gertrude Stein said, "Any time is the time to write a poem." And I'd add, to write anything else. Let's get writing.

I start by making a list. Lists are powerful. They harvest memory, remind us of what we know and need to know, connect, reveal the beginning of an emerging pattern of meaning, move us to a new point of view toward the familiar, create a writing itch that may have to be scratched. My lists very rarely have sentences because sentences attempt to clarify and limit thought in the beginning. I list fragments, words and images that come to mind.

> Train to college ... doesn't run anymore ... north station ... boston bruins ... montreal train ... prep school kids ... how they dress, talk. . .move ... walk up hill ... suitcase ... tie Windsor knot ... escape ... map on ceiling ... football ... high school flunk out ... away from home at last ...homesickness at home ... no away ... sickness ... trip to beg for father's pay ... war on ... roommate ... fist fight ... navaho blanket ... editor newspaper ... Mort Howell ... my second good teacher ..."you seemed to know how the world worked" ... draft notice ... no designer jeans ... designer person ... made myself up ... and didn't ... became what I was ... clipped on kick-off ... knee still hurts ... mort howell gives me papers ... Christian Science Monitor editorial ... you'll be a writer.

Try it. Don't worry about spelling, grammar, mechanics, rhetoric—not yet. And don't worry about revealing yourself. No one will see what you've written— not yet.

Next I look for the fragment in the freewriting I just did that surprised me or caught my interest at the moment. "My second good teacher" reminded me of my first good teacher in the sixth grade and my third good teacher in college after World War II, and that made me realize that three good teachers were enough. That leads me to want to figure out what made these three teachers good for me.

I hope you are moving between your draft and my page, moving back and forth, often discovering something unexpected, interesting, surprising, confounding, curious that may be worth exploring in writing. People—many teachers included—make writing a big deal. It is, on many levels, a very complex intellectual issue, the way designing a new downtown hotel, office, and shopping plaza can be for an architect. But I'm just a worker, a carpenter of prose, and my job is obvious and easy. Now I will write about my first good teacher and work my way to my third, and I will start with description, making myself re-see (and eventually my reader see) that first teacher. In writing a specific description I often find revealing details appear that will lead toward meaning.

Where do I start? In the beginning.

When I walked into my sixth grade classroom in September ...

> *What do I say next? It is obvious. Each line we write tells us what the next line has to be. I describe going into a classroom for the first time. What did I see, feel, do? What surprised me?*

... I saw a young man with glasses standing at the front of the room.

> *Now I am back in that classroom and my writer's memory has locked in. I think what I must have thought when I was twelve years old.*

He must be a new principal. The only men in the Massachusetts Fields School were the principal or the janitor. This man wore a brown suit.

> *How do I write? Line by line. I am in a conversation with the reader. What does the reader want to know? What was a man doing in the classroom? I tell them. No mystery. The sentence written usually tells me the sentence that must be written next.*

"Good morning. I am Mr. Hamilton, your new teacher."

> *Now the reader needs to know why he was one of my best teachers. I have no choice. I can't go off and write about getting glasses that year, or beating up Walter Almeda whose father played for the Red Sox, or paying a bribe to get a paper route and then having to fight a grown man who had paid the same bribe, or what it was like to live during the Great Depression. I used to write like a puppy, running after every new scent, but now the evolving draft tells me what I have to write next.*

The first thing that surprised me was that Mr. Hamilton let us know him as a person. He was married to a teacher and he talked about her. He was young and we didn't seem to learn from him as much as learn with him. His enthusiasm about learning was contagious and he was tough.

He demanded more of me than any teacher had before but he somehow communicated to me that he saw in me what no one else had seen, not at home, church, or school. He shared my secret ambition that I would be successful, possibly even be a published writer—if I worked hard—and I did work hard for him.

> *It is time for me to move on to the next teacher who made a difference in my life. It was six years later and grade 13, my first year of college, before I met another teacher, Mort Howell, who connected with me. I realize the reader is going to say, "What? There were no good teachers from grade seven through twelve?" and I have to ask the question the reader asks when the reader asks it. If I don't hear the reader's questions I get someone to read my draft and ask them what questions they would ask and where would they answer them. What do they need to know that I haven't told them?*

Of course there were other good teachers. North Quincy Junior and Senior High Schools had a good reputation, but the teachers I had didn't make a difference to me. Classes were large in the Great Depression of the 1930's, 45 to

60 in a classroom, and if you didn't learn the way the teacher taught, too bad. I was an A/F student doing well in the courses I liked, poorly in the ones that bored me. I didn't know I was bored. I thought I was stupid. But that didn't bother me.

I had good jobs for a teenager outside of school and I thought hard work would do it for me. And the future showed I was right in part. Hard work works.

I worry that I have gone off on a tangent, but to reveal my good teachers, I have to expose their challenge.

I dropped out of school in the spring of my tenth grade, did it again next year, and in my senior year when I never went to school on Thursday but went to Boston to attend the 10 AM and noon shows of the big bands at the RKO in Boston.

Now I have to get myself to college and that is a story I have told many times. I don't want to get into it here but the reader will wonder how a high school dropout got to college. I'll plunge on, realizing I may have to do some cutting in this section but I can't cut until I know the length of the essay and can judge how much the reader needs to know against how long the reader will be patient and stick with me through the explanation.

Mr. Howell came out from behind his desk and sat beside me in the empty classroom. We were colleagues, not teacher and student as we read the lead editorial I had written. He did not lecture me on the writer's craft, we read what I had thought was a final draft together, pausing to consider and reconsider each paragraph, sentence, word, working back and forth, cutting, adding, reordering, making a comma a semicolon, then a period as a long sentence became two sentences—for emphasis.

There was always a reason for each change and if I didn't see it, I could ask him and he would bounce the question back to me, listen to my answer, modify it, agree with it or give his own answer.

We read aloud, listening to the music of each line. We stood back and considered the line of logic that ran through each editorial. We played the role of reader to see if the meaning was clear and we read it as the subject to see if we were fair.

We sat side by side at the workbench practicing the craft I was to dedicate myself to for the rest of my life. Writing about this fifty-eight years later I am there and Mort Howell is here, still at my side as I write and rewrite these sentences. He never lived to see a computer, but I am not practicing electronics on my Dell; I am practicing the craft of writing he demonstrated hour after patient hour at my side.

Note the process or steps I went through during this writing session, then write down the steps you went through as you wrote. They may not be the same as mine. That's fine. I don't write like me every time. My process changes according to the writing task, what I am trying to say and to whom I am trying to say it.

I don't want you to write like me. I do want you to see that writing is a logical craft that you adapt to each writing task. No mystery. Craft.

CHAPTER 3

Unlearn to Write

Those mornings when I sit at my desk and no words come, when the draft staggers and stumbles to a halt, or I read what I have written with shame and disgust and punch "Delete," I often find I have been following the rules drilled into my skull by Miss Leavitt, the high school teacher I had in the eleventh and twelfth grade.

They were the rules I had first been taught in elementary school, retaught in junior high school, and the first two years in high school. They were absolute, unquestioned, always followed by the writers we studied. When I wrote outside of class, I often broke the rules or simply ignored them, but they sounded so certain, so logical, so authoritative—pun intended—that years later, like a forest fire that travels underground and suddenly bursts out unexpectedly, I find I am following one or more of them. I have to stop and once more unlearn the rules guaranteed to produce ineffective and graceless writing.

My teachers were well intentioned but they were readers who did not write themselves.

Later in this chapter you will be introduced to a process that published writers use to write and that you will be able to adjust to your way of thinking, your experience with writing, and to the writing task itself. But first you—and I—have to unlearn to write.

It might be fun for you to stop right now and write down the absolute rules you have been taught about writing to see if they match what I was taught and had to unlearn.

What I Had to Unlearn

1. KNOW WHAT YOU WANT TO SAY BEFORE YOU SAY IT

When I wrote in school, the teacher would march up and down the aisles repeating, "Know what you want to say before you say it." Most of the time she would require that we write a thesis statement at the top of the page, telling what the writing we hadn't yet done would say.

Writers are writers, however, because the act of writing is a voyage into the unknown; it's an adventure in discovering what you know, but didn't know you knew; in connecting in ways you haven't connected what you know before; in discovering what you need to know.

Once in a while I do know what I am going to say or have an assignment that limits discovery. In those cases I have to *unknow* to find my own way to the predicted meaning. The best writing is traitor to intent. It grows, line by line, from a terrifying emptiness when there is no purpose, no topic, no clear meaning.

Writers write and discover what they have to say as drafts. It is the writing, not the writer that speaks. Novelist and short story writer Donald Barthelme explains:

> Writing is a process of dealing with not-knowing, a forcing of what and how.
>
> We have all heard novelists testify to the fact that, beginning a new book, they are utterly baffled as to how to proceed, what should be written and how it might be written, even though they've done a dozen. At best there's a slender intuition, not much greater than an itch. Art is not difficult because it wishes to be difficult, rather because it wishes to be art. However much the writer might long to be, in his work, simple, honest, straightforward, these virtues are no longer available to him. He discovers that in being simple, honest, straightforward, nothing much happens: he speaks the speakable, whereas we are looking for the as-yet unspeakable, the as-yet unspoken.

People ask, "Where do you get your ideas?" I answer, "I don't have ideas." I am terrified of ideas. I may have a shard of ancient Indian pottery, a fragment of bone that may be dog or dinosaur, a burr under the saddle, an answer that has not yet met its question, a contradiction to a certain belief, a fragment of language that contains a tension, a hint that there is an as-yet unseen world around the next turn in the road that I must explore. As Graham Greene said, "The novel is an unknown man and I have to find him."

When I am lucky, I don't even have that. I have a panic nothingness and I start to describe something that I caught in the corner of my eye, not knowing I saw it, and as I write the barely remembered scene becomes clearer—draft by draft—the way blank photographic paper slowly reveals its image in a tray of developer.

I have the world—memory and vision—and words. That is enough. I write and what I find myself saying reveals what I have to say.

2. FORM COMES BEFORE CONTENT

My teacher would assign the form—a literary essay, a personal essay, an argument before the topic. Now I know the form should grow organically as the writer writes to discover what to say and how to say it. The blueprint for an argument may come from a textbook as a blueprint for a bridge comes from a textbook on building bridges, but it must be adapted to the width of the river, the current, the makeup of the banks and the river bottom, the traffic it will bear. The form of the argument should grow according to the facts on both sides, the proponent and opposition, the place the case is being argued and the audience. The argument evolves as the writer gathers the facts and anticipates the reader's doubts and questions.

Writers should not build a form and then pour concrete into it, but write and then see what develops. In school we build walls between fiction and nonfiction, narrative and exposition, poetry and argument, but the writer breaks down those walls using dialogue and scene in nonfiction, argument and logic in fiction.

3. CORRECT SPELLING, GRAMMAR, MECHANICS ARE ESSENTIAL IN THE FIRST DRAFT

Ernest Hemingway said, "Prose is architecture not interior decoration." It is important for the accurate communication of meaning to follow the traditions of language on the final draft. They are the conventions reader and writer share. Most of the time, in fact, we will follow these conventions, but if we concentrate on them while writing, our language becomes stiff and meaningless.

I am a terrible speller. I use a bad speller's dictionary, a word list book, my computer spell check, and my wife to correct my spelling before I submit a draft to an editor, but if I stop to spell well as I write, I may lose the river of thought that is carrying me towards meaning.

The same is true of grammar and punctuation. In fact, if I am writing what I have not written before, my language often becomes awkward as I struggle to find what I want to say and then how to make it clear to me and then my reader. In fact, the breakthrough into a new meaning often comes when the syntax collapses and I find myself saying badly what I will later make clear.

4. LONG IS BETTER THAN SHORT

My teachers had good reason to teach us vocabulary through the grades, introducing us to longer and more complex words. They had to help us escape the limitation of brief subject-verb-object sentences, introducing clauses and complex sentence structures. The same thing was true of paragraphs and beyond. The un-intended message was that longer is better and, in fact, those students who used big multisyllabic words, long mountain trails of sentences, huge overpacked paragraphs, page upon page saying what could have been said in a few words were rewarded with praise and A's.

When these students, partly because they have gotten such good grades, try to become writers, they discover that short is better than long. Writers use the shortest words, shortest sentences, and shortest paragraphs they can. Since the ideas they have to communicate are often complicated, the shortest words that contain the appropriate meaning may be long ones and the shortest sentences may be full of clauses.

5. DON'T WRITE AS YOU SPEAK

I was taught NOT to write as I spoke. I was instructed to follow the writing style of the previous century and write in a formal manner. Speech and writing were taught to me as separate subjects by different teachers. We live, however, in an informal, dress-down age. We appreciate writing that gives the illusion of speech, good writing as conversation. Of course it isn't realistic—uh—it isn't like—you know—uh—what I sorta, you know—uh—mean.

Graceful and effective writing today sounds like idealized speech, flowing naturally toward meaning. Readers want to hear the individual voice of the writer, the writer's way of speaking tuned to the meaning of what is being said and the audience to which it is aimed.

I write aloud as most writers do, hearing what I am writing before I see it. I can write with the screen turned off. Try it yourself. You should be able to write as well or better than when it is turned on.

6. ALWAYS OUTLINE FIRST

Not always. You can't draw a map of a country you have never visited. If you are using writing to explore a new territory, you probably can't write an outline until after the first draft, when it may be very helpful.

It depends, of course, on the form you are writing as well as your familiarity with the subject. In writing this edition of *Write to Learn*, my editor and I had to agree on an outline. But even then the outline is not the rigid plan I was taught in high school, but a sketch. Later, I will introduce ways to outline, but it does not have to come before the first draft.

7. THE FIRST DRAFT SHOULD BE THE LAST DRAFT

Sometimes that does happen. I have been writing a weekly newspaper column for sixteen years. I know the form, the length, the audience, my persona, and voice. Most of the time I revise and edit as I go along and when I finish, but last week the editor—who was right—demanded three major revisions. For years when I wrote magazine articles I wrote three drafts of each one and revised each draft ten times. I went through the article thirty times.

Most of the time I have to write a *discovery draft* to find out what I have to say, a *development draft* to fill out and document what I have discovered, and a *clarifying draft* to make it clear to myself and the reader.

In school, I was only required to rewrite when I wrote a bad paper. If I was singled out to rewrite it was because the teacher felt I had failed. The same was true when I started working on a newspaper, but when I graduated to magazines and books, the first thing I had to learn was to rewrite. Not just because my first drafts failed—and they did—but because it took many drafts to discover and communicate my subject. For writers, writing is rewriting and I learned to enjoy the craft of cutting, adding, and moving around so the subject became clear to me and, eventually, to my readers.

8. THERE IS ONE RIGHT WAY

I believed longer than I like to admit what my teachers seemed to believe: There is one right way. If I could find the one right word, the single right sentence, the only right paragraph, I would become a writer. What I have learned as a writer is that there are many wrong ways and many right ways. The way of the writer is selection and choice; the method, trial and error. Writing is an experimental science.

There are no rights and wrongs in writing. You can be absolutely correct and write badly, or you can write well, but not be correct according to the "rules."

The writer confronts—word by word, line by line, paragraph by paragraph— the demanding questions: Does it work? Does it advance the meaning? Does it fit within the context? Is it accurate? Is it graceful? Is it clear? These questions are principles of effective writing. They must be asked draft after draft.

James Thurber commanded, "Don't get it right, get it written."

When I fail, I go right back to first grade. Miss Kelly jams me in the wastebasket, my feet sticking out by my head like rabbit ears. I am humiliated. I despair. I want to quit but I have to remind myself that failure is essential. If I am not failing, I am not writing. I am repeating what I have said before—in the way I have said it before.

The wrong word leads to the right word, the broken syntax points toward the phrase that clarifies. Writing is not stenography. Writing is thinking, a process of trial-and-error experimentation in which failure reveals what we cannot yet say, but where the saying may lay hidden. Novelist John Fowles tells us, "Follow the accident, fear the fixed plan—that is the rule."

9. REVISION AND EDITING ARE THE SAME

In school I was told that when I finished a draft, I was to check the spelling, grammatical usage, and punctuation. Correctness was all.

As a writer I learned that writing was a search for a significant meaning and then communicating it. Correctness was the last part of the writing process, patting your hair in place, straightening your tie.

Revision is literally the process of re-seeing. When writers revise they reconsider the subject, the genre, the focus, its development, its voice. Writers revise first to discover and develop what they have to say and then to shape it so readers who have no interest in reading the message will read it.

Editing is the process of clarification. Writers go through the entire piece line by line, again and again, to make sure each detail is accurate, that every word or phrase that needs to be defined is, to cut what is unnecessary, to add what is necessary, to move words around to make the meaning clear, and to follow the conventions of language if they help the reader receive and understand the meaning.

10. SAY WHAT YOU ARE GOING TO SAY, SAY IT, SAY WHAT YOU'VE SAID

I can hear my teacher repeating this counsel again and again and again. She demanded an introduction, a repetitive body of prose, and a conclusion. It was once good advice, and in fact such an organization may be required in certain situations, in writing scientific papers, for example. But the general reader today does not have the patience to read the same thing three times.

In this book we will demonstrate the lede, or lead, that propels the reader right into the subject in the first paragraph, in the first sentences, in the first words. And the book will also show the conclusion that implies the meaning without insulting readers by telling them what to think or how to feel.

11. WRITE IN GENERALITIES FOR A GENERAL AUDIENCE

Makes sense, but it doesn't work. Universal writing rises from the specific, the resonating detail that sparks emotions, memories, thoughts in the mind of the reader. As novelist and essayist James Carroll says:

> The law of particularity forces fiction writers, poets, and dramatists to obsess over details, instances, and concrete images, while treating the experience of one or two characters as if it matters as much as the sum total experience of the entire human race. To writers, a moment in time, properly rendered, is worth all time—a single, vividly imagined place is worth the cosmos.

The more particular I am—writing of my Scots Baptist grandmother, for example—the more readers read the memories of their Russian Jewish, Irish

Catholic, Chinese Buddhist grandmothers. Accurate, resonating specifics makes readers read—and trust what they read.

12. TALENT IS RARE

Talent is common. I once wrote with a class of elementary students so talented I asked them how they were chosen. They had IQs between 80 and 85—and a teacher who respected the stories they had to tell and their potential to tell them. Every class I taught had students that were more talented than I was. I did not have a freshman English class that had a student who could not become a professional—if they worked at it. I have had students who have careers in writing and editing with verbal scores in the 300s on their SATs.

What most of my students did NOT have was the desire to be published and the work habits to make it possible. The distinguished short story writer Andre Dubus declares, "Talent is cheap. What matters is discipline." Novelist E. M. Forster testifies, "The act of writing inspires me," and Graham Greene says, "I have no talent. It's just a question of working, of being willing to put in the time. . . . If one wants to write, one simply has to organize one's life in a mass of little habits."

13. EASY WRITING IS BAD WRITING

Writing should be easy. The cliché states, "easy writing makes hard reading." Just the opposite. Hard, constipated writing makes difficult reading, writing that is not read. We make writing hard out of displaced virtue.

I work hard to make writing easy, remembering the times when the writing went well and repeating those attitudes and conditions.

14. STUDY WHAT IS PUBLISHED AND IMITATE IT

Wrong. It is logical, but what is being published can be reproduced by staff members or experienced freelancers. Editors are looking for the voices they haven't yet heard telling the stories they don't know exist in ways they have not yet imagined. As Doris Lessing says, "You have to remember that nobody ever wants a new writer. You have to create your own demand."

How do you do that? By respecting your own vision of the world. Sandra Cisneros says it best:

> Imagine yourself at your kitchen table, in your pajamas. Imagine one person you'd allow to see you that way, and write in the voice you'd use to that friend. Write about what makes you different.

I have found that all the things that made me strange—even frightening— to my family, my neighbors, my pastor and my church members, my teachers and schoolmates, and continue to puzzle my wife and my children, colleagues and friends, and even myself are those things that I have to offer the world.

As my writer friend Chip Scanlan says, "Do the writing only you can do."

15. DON'T MAKE MISTAKES

Failure is essential to the writer. It is the failures that reveal the possibilities for good writing. We have to write badly to write well. Writers take risks, they take chances.

Be promiscuous—as a writer. Write in as many forms and voices for as many readers or publications as possible. Write what you know and what you need to know and what you will know only by writing. As Annie Dillard advises,

> One of the few things I know about writing is this: spend it all, shoot it, play it, lose it, all, right away, every time. Do not hoard what seems good for a later place in the book, or for another book; give it, give it all, give it now. The impulse to save something good for a better place later is the signal to spend it now. Something more will arise for later, something better. These things fill from behind, like well water.

John Jerome says, "Perfect is the enemy of good."

16. YOU CAN'T TEACH WRITING

Of course you can. My students taught themselves to write better in my classes than they wrote before the class. Take instruction from the writer Ursula Le Guin:

> If you want to be a tuba player you get a tuba, and some tuba music. And you ask the neighbors to move away or put cotton in their ears. And you probably get a tuba teacher, because there are a lot of objective rules and techniques to both written music and to tuba performance. And then you sit down and you play the tuba, every day, every week, every month, year after year, until you are good at playing the tuba; until you can—if you desire—play the truth on the tuba.

It is exactly the same with writing. You sit down, and you do it, and you do it, and you do it, until you have learned how to do it.

The Writing Process

This book has been built on a single process. That sequence of writing tasks is based on my continuing study of the process of published writers in many different genres and a great variety of student writers, all tested against my own daily experience at the writing desk.

The writing process in this eighth edition of *Write to Learn* is:

WRITE BEFORE WRITING
RESEARCH FOR WRITING
BEGIN WRITING
KEEP WRITING
FINISH WRITING

WRITE BEFORE WRITING

The writer circles the subject before beginning the draft, searching memory, playing with language, connecting and disconnecting facts, studying images, making notes, writing beginning drafts in the mind so the writer comes to the writing desk full of material that may be used or may lead to new ideas, facts, memories, connections, voices.

RESEARCH FOR WRITING

Writers write with information and then use words to connect and communicate that information. The raw material of effective writing is discovered on the Internet, in the library, from memory, from observation, from interviews. The research may be formal for an academic report or informal for a personal essay, but the writer must have the material with which to build effective writing.

BEGIN WRITING

Beginning the draft is the hardest part of the writing process. There are many, perhaps hundreds of ways to begin and once a word or two is out on the screen, all the other choices disappear. The writer has only a few seconds—I've timed this with students—to connect with the reader. With an effective beginning the reader keeps reading; with an ineffective beginning the page is put aside.

KEEP WRITING

The writer is the first reader, developing what is being said, delivering just the right amount of information at the right pace so that writer and reader are having a conversation with the reader's questions anticipated and answered as they are asked. Give readers too little information and they will lose interest; too much information and they will also lose interest.

FINISH WRITING

Many begin but few finish. This is much more than a matter of ending. The effective writer rewrites, then revises and edits. They are separate processes and they are motivated not by rules but by the writer's desire to complete the adventure of the draft and report what has been found to the reader.

Why Use the Process Approach to Writing?

We take the mystery out of the craft of writing and reveal a process that writers use to produce their drafts. Here is why I use the writing process approach to writing.

TO WORK IN AN EFFECTIVE PATTERN

We may imagine that we just sit down and write, but we usually follow a process of preparation and execution based on our thinking style, our working habits, and our experience with the task. We should know and keep refining that process. If we do not know what we do and why, we may follow a procedure that is confused and inefficient. We may make writing harder than it needs to be and even practice a process that produces bad writing.

TO AVOID PANIC AND DESPAIR

When we sit down to write, the task seems so overwhelming that we need a proven procedure, attitudes and habits, sequential acts, that have worked in the past so that we move into the unknown in a way that has brought us to the known in the past.

TO SAVE TIME

If we do not have a process, we jump around and perform tasks out of order that have to be done over. If we have no focus, then our research may be wasteful; if we correct the grammar before we have discovered a meaning, we are wasting our time.

TO WRITE EFFECTIVELY AND EFFICIENTLY

Following a process that we have used successfully before increases our effectiveness. We will, for example, have the documentation in inventory that we need when we develop what we have to say.

TO TALK EFFECTIVELY WITH COLLEAGUES, STUDENTS, TEACHERS, BOSSES

Most conflicts between writers and their readers—classmates or colleagues, teachers or bosses—come when the writer is at one stage in the process and the reader is in another. The writer may be seeking a focus and the reader may not be helping with that search but correcting spelling. A common understanding of the writing process will allow the reader to respond to writing in a way that is effective.

The Process Is Circular

Since we have introduced the writing process as a sequence or list, it appears linear with the writer following the first stage, then moving on through the second, third, fourth, fifth stages, following a straight line toward meaning; but, in practice, the process is often circular. At each point the writer may move back through an earlier stage of the process.

- The need for a new focus may be revealed while you are doing research.
- As you write a draft, a new focus may be needed or you may need to do more research.
- When you revise you may have to re-focus, re-research, or re-draft.
- Even when you are editing, you may need once more to focus, research, draft, or revise.

Sometimes you may even start by researching, drafting, or revising something you have written before. The writing process should not be a series of rigid commands but a flexible strategy. As in war or sports, an effective strategy must change as it confronts reality. Writing is never boring to me because I always find new opportunities and challenges when I begin to write and all the way along the road to meaning.

Why the Process Will Change

Writers' processes will change for three principal reasons:

1. *The way the writer's head works.* I was just reading a book by a famous artist who pointed out that some painters will begin a portrait by sketching the whole head, others will start with a particular such as an eyebrow, and others

will switch back and forth, according to how they see the subject. I write in the morning, other writers work at night; I write fast, others work slowly; I have to get the beginning right before I go on, others plunge in and write the final beginning later; I like to discover the end, others have to know the end before they begin.

2. *The writing task.* A newspaper article produced on deadline is a different task from a scholarly article written for a distant deadline. The recommendation letter requires that the audience be considered first while in writing a lyric poem, the reader may be considered last. A book written over two years is a far different task than a blue book exam finished in an hour.

3. *The writer's experience with the task.* In writing my first newspaper columns, I wrote many drafts, trying to feel my way into a new task. Now I usually write one draft, having rehearsed most of the writing that was once done on paper in my head. As we become familiar with a topic, a form, an audience, a voice, our writing process may change.

Remember: there is not one writing process.

Repeat: THERE IS NOT ONE WRITING PROCESS.

I often make the mistake of applying the writing process or strategy that worked on the last writing project to a new one. It may work but it also may not work. Remember what I said earlier, the process will change according to the writer's way of thinking and working, the writing task, and the writer's experience with the task.

I have built this book on the writing process that my research and experience tells me is most often used by writers and is also a process that is easy to learn. It is not THE way to complete a writing task but A way. Once you become experienced with this process you have a basic approach to writing that is practical and logical. When you are stuck in writing you can go back to basics and begin the process anew, but as you continue to write you will keep adjusting the process to the challenge on the page.

Sometimes I write with a river flood of fluency, other days I build a draft slowly like a bricklayer. No matter. I am a writer. I write. And you should as well. The trick is to find the process that works and I find the one in this book—write before writing, research before writing, begin writing, keep writing, finish writing—works most of the time.

CHAPTER 4

Write Beside Writers

When I was in ninth grade I had read my way through the Wollaston branch of the Thomas Crane Library and would take the trolley car that passed our flat to the great stone main library in Quincy Center. One day when I was probably looking for anatomy books—no *Playboy* in those days—I found myself in the stacks, looking at the low 800's in the Dewey Decimal system and I found a book by Burton Rascoe telling of his adventures as a reporter. I took it out and read it, then reread it to discover the life I would lead when I became a foreign correspondent for a major newspaper.

When I returned that book I went back in the open stacks to the same section and found other autobiographies, essays on the writing craft, writer's journals, letters, and how to write books. Since Miss [No Ms. then] Chapman had told me in the fourth grade I was going to be class editor, I knew I was going to be a writer. I started to copy quotations on the writing life and craft from writers—not readers, scholars, or critics—but men and women who wrote their own books. I designed my own apprenticeship.

I didn't know that centuries before when books were rare, people often kept "A Commonplace Book" in which they would copy fragments of wisdom and humor to which they could refer as a help to make their way through the mysteries of life. I continued to copy fragments of wisdom about the writing craft in high school, the Army, college and when I went to work at Burton Rascoe's trade. I haven't stopped yet.

At one time my quotation collection filled 24 three-inch thick notebooks, but when I started using the computer I collected the best on my hard drive, and I published many of the quotations in a book called *Shoptalk: Learning to*

Write With Writers. These writers, living and dead, from all over the world are my colleagues. They surround my writing desk and when I am stuck I read their collections which instruct and inspire me. I am not alone. I am a member of the great community of writers who have tried to understand and share their very different worlds with readers in novels, TV and movie scripts, poems, argument, plays, reportage, memoir, nonfiction books, essays, and every form of written communication. I have found that we share the same fears, problems, and delights and in this chapter I will give you a start on your own Commonplace Book so that you can join the community of writers.

Recently I was asked to list the quotations that had influenced me the most in chronological order and explain how they influenced me. These were not to be the best quotations on the writing craft but the ones that influenced me at the most crucial points in my career. My teachers could point the way, but writing is essentially a self-taught affair.

- *nulla dies sine linea,* never a day without a line

This quotation by Horace in 658 BC is the habit I've tried to live by ever since I first found it. Try it. This simple command, more than anything else, will help your writing. You may write a chapter, a page, a paragraph, a sentence, but it is more than you had before you sat down.

- Daily word count

I learned that William Faulkner, Ernest Hemingway, Graham Greene, and many other writers counted words and kept a written record. There are several reasons this is a good habit:

1. Counting words gives you a tangible goal: 150 words a day, 500 words a day, 1,000 words. The amount is not as important as the regularity.
2. Counting words delays the question of quality. At the end of the morning's writing, I have often felt I had written well. The next morning's reading proved me wrong. Other mornings I thought my draft worthless and the next day discovered it was good.

- Patience

This quotation by Flannery O'Connor in a *Paris Review* interview published in 1958 taught me patience. The writer lies in ambush like the soldier, waiting for the moment when the writing flows:

> Every morning between 9 and 12 I go to my room and sit before a piece of paper. Many times I just sit for three hours with no ideas coming to me. But I know one thing: If an idea does come between 9 and 12, I am there ready for it.

- "Write easily, quietly"

In 1978 I read an article by Janwilliam van der Wetering which has supported and inspired me ever since. Ever since I have tried to write "easily, quietly."

To write you have to set up a routine, to promise yourself that you will write. Just state in a loud voice that you will write so many pages a day, or write for so many hours a day. Keep the number of pages or hours within reason, and don't be upset if a day slips by. Start again; pick up the routine. Don't look for results. Just write, easily, quietly, after you've done it.

- Lower your standards

In the early 1980s Chip Scanlan brought a quotation from the poet William Stafford whom I later met. His counsel has been a comfort to me ever since:

I believe that the so-called "writing block" is a product of some kind of disproportion between your standards and your performance . . . one should lower his standards until there is no felt threshold to go over in writing. It's easy to write. You just shouldn't have standards that inhibit you from writing. . . ."
I can imagine a person beginning to feel he's not able to write up to that standard he imagines the world has set for him. But to me that's surrealistic. The only standard I can rationally have is the standard I'm meeting right now . . . You should be more willing to forgive yourself. It doesn't make any difference if you are good or bad today. The assessment of the product is something that happens after you've done it.

- "Write about what makes you different"

Again it was Chip Scanlan who led me to *American Voices—Best Short Fiction by Contemporary Authors*, selected by Sally Arteseros, Hyperion, 1992. And in it I found this quotation from Sandra Cisneros that explained my work and the fact that what my parents, uncles, teachers, ministers, classmates found strange was what connected me with readers. I didn't try to write like someone else. I tried to write like myself.
Here are some other quotations from writers who have entered my workshop of mind and shared the joys and struggles of the writing life.

SELF-CONFIDENCE

The hardest thing I had to do even to become a writer was believing that I had anything to say that people would want to read. *Alice McDermott*
It is easy to work when the soul is at play. *Emily Dickinson*

WRITING WHAT YOU DON'T KNOW

I never know what my stories are about until they are finished, until they choose to reveal themselves. I merely feel their power, how they breathe on me. I try not to write them. I prefer the rush of having them write me. *Kate Braverman*

I believe that fiction feeds on itself, grows like a pregnancy. The more you write, the more there is to draw from; the more you say, the more there is to say. The deeper you go into your imagination, the richer that reservoir becomes. You do not run out of material by using all that's in you; rather, when you take everything that is available one day, it only makes room for new things to appear the next . . . You don't need to know a whole book in order to write the first page. You don't even need to know the end of the first page. You need only the desire to create something that will say what you feel needs to be said, however vague its form at the beginning. You need a willingness to discover the wealth and wisdom of your own subconscious, and to trust that it will tell you what to do and how to do it—not all at once, but as needed, step by step. You have to take a deep breath, let go of your usual control, and then begin walking in the dark. *Elizabeth Berg*

CREATIVITY

That is the pure pleasure of creation—the not knowing that leads you to the knowing. *Bobbie Ann Mason*

TALENT

What I've found and what I believe is that everybody is talented. It's just that some people get it developed and some don't. *Stephen Sondheim*

Writers create themselves. They are pulled from potential to realization, discovered not taught. To educate—educere in the root Latin—means quite literally "to bring out." The process of being brought out, of developing an innate capacity, of realizing that you harbor an overwhelming impulse to write things down, is touched on again and again by writers in this book. If you are willing to be led from within—if you are willing to allow your most rigorous teacher to a clear, well-written page—perhaps you will discover the spark of talent that was there all along. *Marie Arana*

For the longest time I didn't realize I was creative—I just thought I was strange. In art classes, in elementary school, I would be criticized for coloring trees the wrong colors and not staying inside the lines. I understand now that what the teachers were trying to do was help me: The more average they could encourage children to be, the better chance they had to fit in and lead reasonably normal lives when they grew up. No one ever suggested to me that I might be part of a community of people extending across time and space who are artists. I just knew I was different from my playmates—I saw things in more detail than they did. I wrote about this in the introduction to *The Moon by Whale Light*—about the first time I realized that I had a metaphorical mind. I was walking with my schoolmates through an orchard on the way to school, I looked up at a tree and saw plums hanging there in a way that made them look like bats. When I told my playmates, they recoiled in horror. They weren't afraid of bats; they were afraid of me—that I saw bats when I looked at plums. *Diane Ackerman*

WRITING BEFORE WRITING

For a couple of years I was waking up at five every morning to write for a few hours before going to work. That was when I knew what I wanted to say but didn't know how to say it. When I finally found the right voice, it took me only a month to write the novel. I'd take my eight-month-old son out in the stroller for a walk, and while he was looking around at the trees and grass in the park, I'd be thinking about what I was going to write next. Then I'd come home and write when he napped. I did exactly what a friend once told me to do—I never used my child's nap time for anything but writing. *Eve Horowitz*

It was with that book [*The Alleys of Eden*] that I finally figured out where a literary writer has to write from. That is, where I dream from, instead of where I think from. The hardest thing for me to learn as a writer was that I could not will my work into being. I learned I should not think about it. I should not abstract it and try to understand it in an intellectual way. I had to go to the dream place, into my unconscious, my artistic unconscious, and focus on the moment to moment flow of sensual experience to art iculate my vision of the world. This was the fundamental thing and once I figured out how to go to that place consistently, everything else followed. *Robert Olen Butler*

SURPRISE

I don't plan my writing. What comes out is usually quite surprising. I write to find out what I'm thinking. *John Ashbery*

SEEING

As great architects and others have said, God lies in the details. I would say that art lies in the details and that the best skill that a writer can develop is an openness, a receptivity to life, at its most basic level, its most intricate details. There's almost nothing that can go wrong in a book that you can't fix with fascinating, riveting details of one sort or another. That's what life is; life isn't general. Life is texture, process, complexity. The intimate, sometimes terrifying, details of life are to my mind what make life so unexpected and breathtaking. If you can convey a scene in sensory detail, not only can you enter that scene yourself in your imagination or memory, but you can allow readers to walk into that scene also at the level of their senses. *Diane Ackerman*

The law of particularity forces fiction writers, poets, and dramatists to obsess over details, instances, and concrete images, while treating the experience of one or two characters as if it matters as much as the sum total experience of the entire human race. To writers, a moment in time, properly rendered, is worth all time—a single, vividly imagined place is worth the cosmos. History is the record of the causal link between human choice and consequence, and as the very word implies, history in that sense is the ground of story itself. *James Carroll*

The more particular, the more specific you are, the more universal you are. *Nancy Hale*

NOT KNOWING

When you first start writing—and I think it's true for a lot of beginning writers—you're scared to death that if you don't get that sentence right that minute it's never going to show up again. And it isn't. But it doesn't matter—another one will, and it'll probably be better. . . . I write out of ignorance. I write about the things I don't have any resolutions for, and when I'm finished, I think I know a little bit more about it. I don't write out of what I know. It's what I don't know that stimulates me. I merely know enough to get started. *Toni Morrison*

A novel searches and poses questions. . . . The wisdom of the novel comes from having a question for everything. It does not prescribe or proscribe answers. *Milan Kundera*

FINDING WHAT TO WRITE

There is in you what is beyond you. *Paul Valéry*

I replied that I could no more define poetry than a terrier can define a rat but that I thought we both recognized the object by the symptoms which it provokes in us. . . . Experience has taught me, when I am shaving of a morning, to keep watch over my thoughts, because, if a line of poetry strays into my memory, my skin bristles so that the razor ceases to act. *A. E. Housman*

THE WRITING HABIT

Happiness is going to bed knowing you will write in the morning. *Shelby Foote*

I write every day, in the early morning. I become melancholy if I don't. Writing is really more of an obsession than a habit. *William Trevor*

If you want to be a writer, you have to write every day. The consistency, the monotony, the certainty, all vagaries and passions are covered by this daily reoccurrence. . . . The act of writing is a kind of guerrilla warfare; there is no vacation, no leave, no relief. *Walter Moseley*

I have the feeling that if I don't write, the previous day disappears . . . one writes to recover what has been lost. *Isabel Allende*

I go into the workroom and shake the black ball and wait for something to surface. If I don't recall it, then it probably wasn't worth remembering. I have faith that the good things will resurface, will rise, if given the chance. I merely have to be faithful enough to the task to provide it with that chance. And that means showing up for work in the mornings: Doing, each day, this day's work. That's what I keep saying to my students: to recite that mantra and live by it. No other questions asked, no other thoughts, no worries about outcomes or the future or what the next writer is doing. Just: This day's work. "Did I work today?" That is the only question you allow yourself, and you aim to be able to answer "Yes" on most days, and then leave it there. *Richard Bausch*

WHERE WRITING STARTS

I wanted to quit my job writing promotional copy, but I had a wife and two kids to support. I wanted to do another novel but had no ideas. I was worried. Then two sentences came to me: "In the office in which I work, there are five people of whom I am afraid. Each of these five is afraid of four people." In a dream, a kind of controlled reverie, I quickly developed the characters, the mood of anxiety, the beginning, the end and most of the middle of Something Happened. And I knew Bob Slocum, my protagonist, intimately. Eventually, a better opening line came to me: "I get the willies when I see closed doors," and I wrote the first chapter around that line. But I kept the original to lead off the second part. *Joseph Heller*

All I ever know is the first line, the first sentence, the first page. *Erskine Caldwell*

I had a line—"I wonder will it strike us over here"—that I thought would be the last line of As If It Matters. When I had that line, I knew the book was finished, but I hadn't got the poem to go with it. So I kept mulling that over, and then eventually I sat down and pushed around a poem. It works like that, by accretion. You turn yourself into some kind of magnetic field so that things stick, and then you sit down—and the hard part is—push it out, and then you revise it. *Eamon Grennan*

I remember that I started writing Sleepless Nights because of a single line. The line was: "Now I will start my novel, but I don't know whether to call myself I or she." *Elizabeth Hardwick*

When my writing is going well, I know that I'm writing out of my personal obsessions. *Bharti Mukherjee*

DISCOVERY

How do I know what I think until I see what I say? *E. M. Forster*

[A]s you continue writing and rewriting, you begin to see possibilities you hadn't seen before. Writing a poem is always a process of discovery. You discover things about yourself as a poet, about language, about the nature of poetry. I think it was W. H. Auden who once said to me that writing a poem is like solving for x in an equation. *Robert Hayden*

That's not what writing is—writing what you know. You write in order to find things out . . . it's an act of discovery. *Garrison Keillor*

To be a writer does not mean to present a truth, it means to discover a truth. *Milan Kundera*

For me, writing poetry is a series of bewildering discoveries, a search for something that remains largely unknown even when you find it. *David Wagoner*

In travel you discover something and then go home and write about it. In fiction the discovery comes at the moment of writing. Halfway down the page you suddenly meet something unexpected. It's the surprise in writing that is the sustaining factor. *Paul Theroux*

BEGINNING

It's like being on a high board, looking down to a cold, chilly pool. Then I give myself a little push. The water isn't as cold as I thought. *Neil Simon*

WRITING

Planning to write is not writing. Outlining . . . researching . . . talking to people about what you're doing, none of that is writing. Writing is writing. *E. L. Doctorow*

WHY WRITE

In a very real sense, the writer writes in order to teach himself, to understand himself. *Alfred Kazin*

KNOW TOMORROW'S TASK TODAY

What I do at the end of an afternoon's work is write two or three lines on what I think is the direction of the narrative, and where we might logically go the next day. *Camilo Tose Cela*

At the end of each day of writing, I leave myself with a technical question I can come back to the next day. By technical question, I mean maybe there's a passage of dialogue I want to look at because it sounds stilted or it doesn't sound realistic. Maybe I notice that the voice isn't strong—there are some bobbles—and I want to look at diction. I want to look at the consistency of my word choice and begin there, by trying to work with particular words to see what isn't quite authentic to the character. Maybe I've noticed four or five or six really heavily connected words that are suggesting a theme that I wasn't aware of in the work, and so I'm going to begin with that problem. Maybe I'm going to look at the way in which I'm motivating flashback, because if I'm using the same device [over and over] there's a problem. Maybe some of those flashbacks don't need to be there. *A. Manette Amsay*

VOICE

You have to keep working to find your voice, then have the grace or good sense to recognize it as your voice and then learn how to use it. *John Guare*

The American oral language is very musical, and if you read a lot and get involved with language, you can get a feeling for how the lines wish to proceed, how the words wish to follow each other, how the sounds work together in a kind of music. *Lucille Clifton*

The voice is the element over which you have no control: it's the sound of the person behind the work. *John Hersey*

Just to write a good sentence—that's the postulate I go by. I guess I've always felt that if you could keep a kind of fidelity toward the individual sentence, that you could work toward the rest. *Richard Ford*

The language must be careful and must appear effortless. It must not sweat. It must suggest and be provocative at the same time. *Toni Morrison*

English usage is something more than mere taste, judgment, and education—sometimes it's sheer luck, like getting across a street. *E. B. White*

Working at sentences and rhythms is probably the most satisfying thing I do as a writer. I think after a while a writer can begin to know himself through his language. He sees someone or something reflected back at him from these constructions. Over the years it's possible for a writer to shape himself as a human being through the language he uses. I think written language, fiction, goes that deep. He not only sees himself but begins to make himself or remake himself. *Don Dellilo*

When it comes to language, nothing is more satisfying than to write a good sentence. It is no fun to write lumpishly, dully, in prose the reader must plod through like wet sand. But it is a pleasure to achieve, if one can, a clear running prose that is simple yet full of surprises. This does not just happen. It requires skill, hard work, a good ear, and continued practice. *Barbara Tuchman*

STYLE

You always play the same way. You can't play different from who you are. Maybe you growl now, but your personality, intelligence, feeling, they don't change. I think it was Matisse who said, people have one idea and they're going to deal with it forever. *Wynton Marsalis*

FAILURE

FAIL.
FAIL AGAIN.
FAIL BETTER. *Samuel Beckett*

The beautiful part of writing is that you don't have to get it right the first time, unlike, say, a brain surgeon. You can always do it better, find the exact word, the apt phrase, the leaping simile. *Robert Cormier*

Of *The House of Five Talents*, I wrote the first draft in longhand, with a pencil, on Saturdays, Sundays and vacations; had it typed, triple spaced; and then carried it around in a briefcase. Thus I was able to work on it very easily not only evenings but on the subway or any other time when I had a few minutes to spare. You have to be fresh for the first draft of a book, but I find that once I get to work on the second or third draft; it's like knitting. *Louis Auchincloss*

REWRITING

I've done as many as twenty or thirty drafts of a story. Never less than ten or twelve drafts. It's instructive and heartening both, to look at the early drafts of great writers. I'm thinking of the photographs of galleys belonging to Tolstoy, to name one writer who loved to revise. I mean, I don't know if he loved it or not, but he did a great deal of it. He was always revising, right down to the time of page proofs. He went through and rewrote War and Peace eight times and was still making corrections in the galleys. Things like this should hearten every writer whose first drafts are dreadful, like mine are. *Raymond Carver*

Write it out as verbose as you want. Have verbal Diarrhea. Then cut the unnecessary words, but keep the plot. Then rewrite and cut again. Then rewrite and cut again. After three times, you have something. *David Mamet*

I began to write essays, one a month for Esquire magazine, and I am not exaggerating when I say that in the course of writing a short essay—1,500 words, that's only six double-spaced typewritten pages—I often used 300 or 400 pieces of typing paper, so often did I type and retype and catapult and recatapult myself, sometimes on each retyping moving not even a sentence farther from the spot I had reached the last time through. At the same time, though, I was polishing what I had already written; as I struggled with the middle of the article, I kept putting the beginning through the typewriter; as I approached the ending the middle got its turn. (This is a kind of polishing that the word processor all but eliminates, which is why I don't use one. Word processors make it possible for a writer to change the sentences that clearly need changing without having to retype the rest, but I believe that you can't always tell whether a sentence needs work until it rises up in revolt against your fingers as you retype it.) By the time I had produced what you might call a first draft—an entire article with a beginning, middle, and end—the beginning was in more like forty-fifth draft, the middle in twentieth, and the end was almost newborn. For this reason the beginnings of my essays are considerably better written than the ends, although I like to think no one ever notices this but me. *Nora Ephron*

I work not by writing but by rewriting. Each sentence has many drafts. Eventually there is a paragraph. This gets many drafts. Eventually there is a page. This gets many drafts. *William Gass*

I've always been highly energized and have written poems in spurts. From the godgiven first line right through the poem. And I don't write two or three lines and then come back the next day and write two or three more; I write the whole poem at one sitting and then come back to it from time to time over the months or years and rework it. *A. R. Ammons*

I write very impulsively, so terribly fast only I can decipher my scrawl. But only one quarter of this first outpouring, at the most, is usable, so actually I work very slowly. It's mostly pacing, researching, brewing endless cups of herb tea while I think of how to annotate these terrible earlier drafts. Hours are spent figuring how to rewrite one single sentence—I've never managed to write anything, even a book review, in fewer than three or four drafts. *Francis de Plexis Grey*

EDITING

There is a sort of basic law about everything for me, and that is that you have to pay attention. You've got to pay attention, as a writer, to the structure of language. You've got to pay attention to the sounds. *Barry Lopez*

LANGUAGE

(i) Never use a metaphor, simile, or other figure of speech which you are used to seeing in print.
(ii) Never use a long word where a short one will do.
(iii) If it is possible to cut a word out, always cut it out.
(iv) Never use the passive where you can use the active.
(v) Never use a foreign phrase, a scientific word, or jargon word if you can think of an everyday English equivalent.
(vi) Break any of these rules sooner than say anything barbarous. *George Orwell*

CONCENTRATION

The problem of creative writing is essentially one of concentration, and the supposed eccentricities of poets are usually due to mechanical habits or rituals developed in order to concentrate. Concentration, of course, for the purposes of writing poetry, is different from the kind of concentration required for working out a sum. It is a focusing of the attention in a special way, so that the poet is aware of all the implications and possible developments of his idea, just as one might say that a plant was not concentrating on developing mechanically in one direction, but in many directions, towards the warmth and light with its leaves, and towards the water with its roots, all at the same time. *Stephen Spender*

BOREDOM

I think I'm trying to keep myself from being bored. When I think about why I would be a writer, why I should continue to be a writer, it seems to me one of the few things you can do where you're never bored. *Gish Jen*

■ SHOPTALK ■

I just wrote what came into my head and it looks like squashed bugs, run-over skunk and upchuck.

Ah, you think like a writer. I've often felt the same way. Those are good, strong images. If you can write like that you'll be able to write vigorous, interesting writing.

What I do with a discovery draft that doesn't seem to discover anything is to hold my nose and look for anything that surprised me, that I didn't think I would say. It may be a line, a word, an image, or just an attitude toward something, a feeling that may point to a topic you should explore. The hint of what you may have to write may also come from your tone of voice, the music you hear feebly rising from the ick as you read it out loud.

And you may have to start over, but I find that most upchuck drafts contain something that runs against what I have believed, thought, or felt, something that I need to think about—by writing.

> I keep writing the same thing. I don't mean just the subject, but the same attitude toward the topic. It is borrrrrring. Does this happen to you, and if it does, what do you do about it?

It does and I have some tricks to jar me out of the rut.

A. I change the point of view. If I've been writing about my grandson, I turn around and write from his point of view. How does he see the visiting giant with the white beard? I do this with ideas. I'm against capital punishment. What are the arguments for it? The story of a crime, for example, can be told from the point of view of the victim, the arresting officer, the officer who failed to arrest the perpetrator, the criminal, the EMT, an onlooker, the prosecuting and defense attorneys.

B. I move back in time or ahead to put the topic in a different historical perspective.

C. If the story is long, I write it short, which causes me to dig more deeply into it. If it is short, I write it long, which causes me to extend myself into an area of new knowledge.

D. I try a different voice, sounding angry, sad, amused, nostalgic, frustrated, doubting, believing, naive, experienced.

> Do writing tools make a difference in finding a subject to explore?

They sure do. The dip pen, the fountain pen, the typewriter, the dictating machine, the computer, and now the voice-activated computer all make it easier to write, to record the flow of information and language. Ease is important. If you have to focus your attention on getting each word down you will not develop the momentum that will carry you from what you know to what you may know that you don't know you know until it appears on the screen.

> Does reading help in finding something to write about?

Of course. There is a whole genre of critical essays and reviews of books, but more than that reading allows you to find subjects that interest you and shows you how different writers view the same subject. My good writing friend Chip Scanlan will copy pages of another person's writing to better hear the writer's voice, to discover how that writer paces the text, how details are introduced, how language is used.

It is plagiarism if you put your own name on it, but good artistic practice to use imitation as a form of instruction. Most museums have many students making copies of great works, and musicians will study other performances by imitating them.

Someone has said that writing is a visual art. How can I improve my seeing?

I'm one of those someones. Seeing will improve your writing—and writing will improve your seeing.

I increased my ability to see by listing hundreds—thousands—of specific details. I made myself consciously see, looking for details that revealed how people's actions betrayed their words, revealed false fear, documented bravery in the face of limitations, exposed a conflict between people.

I not only looked for what was done, but what was not done. The unsaid often tells more than the said. I watched the world out of the corner of my eye, aware and alert to all that entered the increasing range of my vision. And the more revealing specifics I saw and used them in writing, the more I saw.

There's one big side benefit to the relationship of seeing and writing: I am rarely bored. Waiting in the doctor's office, ticket line, in the parking lot, air terminal, I concentrate on seeing. I watch how people walk, how they treat each other.

I'm not especially happy about it, but I seem to live life on the sidelines. I don't star on any team or get elected president of anything. Since I'm not on the inside with any group, how can I find something to write about?

Writers live on the sidelines. When others bustle about—busy, busy, busy—writers observe and reflect. Writers connect. Writers record and celebrate and analyze and explain.

I'm an engineering student, not one of those artsy people. Why do I have to write?

A study a few years ago revealed that engineering graduates wrote more than any other group of students. We live in a small world connected electronically. Writing isn't just novels and poems, writing is memos and proposals and reports and plans and agreements. Information is power and the people who can communicate information clearly and accurately will exert that power.

I have good ideas but they run down and I have nothing to say. Anything I can do?

Of course you can try another idea but if this is happening regularly I suggest you just force yourself to keep writing. That is what I do. When I can't think of what to say next, I realize I am thinking ahead of the writing. Writing is thinking and if

I keep writing new ideas, new questions, interesting problems appear in what I am saying.

> **I have always been told I have to have a firm thesis statement before I can begin to write. Is that true?**

No. In fact, writing a thesis statement first can produce bad writing, writing in which there is no discovery. There are times when it may be necessary to write from a firm conclusory statement, but I can't remember when I have had to do that. The thesis statement has been taught in traditional English classes because teachers who are not writers have been taught it is important. And writing a good thesis statement AFTER you have finished writing can be a challenging and productive intellectual exercise.

We write not to say what we know, but to learn, to discover, to know. Writing is thinking, exploring, finding out. The thesis statement imprisons the writer in previous thought.

> **Be honest. Isn't writing just hard work?**

It sure can be. The famous sports writer Red Smith said, "There's nothing to writing. All you do is sit down at the typewriter and open a vein."

But it doesn't have to be. I used to make writing hard, thinking it was virtuous, that writing should be a struggle. I bragged about how hard I worked and so did the other writers I knew. But they had all chosen a life of writing because it was easier than math or languages or science and, most of all, because it was fun. I became bored with their moaning—and with my own.

I studied what I did when the writing did come easily and then followed those methods to make it easy for me to write so that my writing would be easy for my readers to read.

■ IN THE WRITER'S WORKSHOP ■

ON YOUR OWN

1. Use a different sense—hearing, smell, taste, touch—to describe a place or person important to you. You will not only increase your sense awareness—and use other senses than visual when you write—you will stimulate your awareness in every sense.

2. Pick a news story—a basketball game, an election, a shooting—and put yourself in the story, telling it from your point of view to see how point of view can give you new ways to look at the world.

3. List the most important events or people in your life, then see how they connect, what the relationship is between, say, learning to swim and teaching

handicapped children to swim and becoming an education major. The best writing comes when two events or people or ideas collide, sparking a story or essay.

4. We live in a movie/TV age. Turn yourself into a screenwriter for a day and look for dramatic scenes in your life, places of conflict, change, resolution. Seeing the screen story you will discover a subject. Remember that movies and TV shows are written, and it is the quality of the writing as much as the acting, direction or photography that makes fine drama.

5. Take a sketchbook or some art paper and draw a familiar place or location. You don't have to be good at art, but the discipline of trying to catch line, form, color will sharpen your visual skills for writing.

6. Writers, with their particular vision of the world, make me look at my world so that I see something to write about where I had seen nothing before. Become your favorite writer—I might choose Alice Munro or Sharon Olds—and tell your story in the writer's voice, using the way the writer looked at the world, what the writer said, how it was revealed.

7. Take a film, digital, or video camera and use it to focus at the familiar world around you—perhaps your bedroom, a courtyard, a piece of countryside, a street corner. Zoom in close, move back to a distance shot, then zoom in close again. Write down the things you noticed that you hadn't seen before: the many colors in "ordinary" brick or a tree's bark, the pattern or roofs or windows, the casual way a seagull rose on an invisible wave of air, the wobbly step of a young teenager wearing grown-up shoes, how the fur of a frightened dog rose when someone approached.

8. Go to an art museum and study the paintings, drawings, photographs, sculptures to see how the artist saw and revealed the word. What line, touch of color, shadow or shape revealed the character of the person portrayed? Students at Cornell Medical School take part in a program at the Frick Museum that increase their powers of observation by careful study of works of art.

Imagine how Rembrandt, Munch, Degas or other great artists would look at your world and you may see something to write—and a way of writing it. I recently visited an exhibition of portraits by Alice Nell, a powerful American painter, and learned a great deal about art, vision, the people she painted—and about writing. I again realized the importance of the dominant impression in writing, giving priority to the revealing detail.

WITH A WRITING PARTNER

9. Team up with a classmate and visit a familiar spot—the library, a hangout, a game, a coffeehouse—and point out to each other what you see and what it reveals. You won't see the same things in the same way, and in the difference there may be a subject. As Sandra Cisneros said, "Imagine yourself at

your kitchen table, in your pajamas. Imagine one person you'd allow to see you that way, and write in the voice you'd use to that friend. Write about what makes you different."

INTERVIEWING OTHERS

10. Interview a family member, neighbor, friend to find out the turning points in their lives or what they have learned from life experiences. Interview me and you might find that I wanted to go into battle with cowards, not heroes. By exploring what I mean you may realize you have a story to tell from your own life.

ON THE INTERNET

11. Check out a World Wide Web site about a subject or process that interests you. Go to the Librarian's Index to the Internet at <http://lii.org>, and do a search for your subject or browse through the index's categories. You'll find information on almost anything you can come up with, such as inventors and inventions at the Invention Dimension, <http://web.mit.edu/invent/>, the Egyptian pyramids at the British Museum's Ancient Egypt exhibit, <http://www.ancientegypt.co.uk/menu.html>, censorship at the Free Expression Policy Project, <http://fepproject.org/>, or electric guitars at the Rock and Roll Hall of Fame and Museum, <http://www.rockhall.com/>. Check out the data on these sites and you might find a subject to explore further in your writing.

Write Before Writing

. . . I don't think I've ever "tried" to find something to write about. The things I write about come at me—while I am walking in the woods, driving the car, reading my mail, any time at all. Since I don't start with an idea, but with a visual image or a voice, I need to be "listening" all the time.

ELIZABETH COOKE

Everyone thinks writers know more about the inside of the human head, but that is wrong. They know less, that's why they write. Trying to find out what everyone else takes for granted.

MARGARET ATWOOD

The writer. . . sees what he did not expect to see . . . Inattentive learner in the schoolroom of life, he keeps some faculty free to hear and wonder. His is the roving eye. By that roving eye is his subject found. The glance, at first only vaguely caught, goes on to concentrate, deepen; becomes the vision.

ELIZABETH BOWEN

CHAPTER 5

Write Before Writing

When my friend Don Graves studied the writing of elementary school students in 1973 he observed that the best writers came to both first drafts and revisions after having "rehearsed" their writing in their head. They came to the blank page prepared to write. The drafts would change as they were written, but the best students never arrived at their desks empty-headed, but had a mental inventory of lines, patterns, sequences, images, specific revealing details, voices ready to be called upon when they began to pencil words on the page. Don Graves's significant observation changed much of the writing instruction in this country and others.

When teachers taught rehearsal before writing, the students were not just ready to write, they needed to write. The material in their heads insisted on being explored, ordered, understood, shared—now. The great poet T. S. Eliot described this feeling rather bluntly when he said years ago, "What stimulates me to write a poem is that I have got something inside me that I want to get rid of—it is almost a kind of defecation."

I was interested in Don's findings but not surprised. It seemed, in fact, a bit ordinary to me. I had always rehearsed before writing. When I finish my morning's pages, I decide the next day's writing task. I don't know what I am going to say, but I do know what I am going to explore in writing the next morning. My subconscious and unconscious accept this assignment and go to work gathering and connecting specific memories, observations, stray facts, images and voices so my brain is ready to write. I do not understand this invisible process of mental play, but it has worked for me all my life.

I hadn't, however, emphasized rehearsal in my teaching. It was too obvious. Teachers often teach what they had difficulty learning since they had to figure it out. What they always have done instinctively they ignore, thinking that it must be instinctive with their students as it was for them. Don Graves's findings taught me to pay attention to what happens before the writer writes.

What was insignificant before Don's studies was revealed as extremely significant. Don's demonstration of the importance of rehearsal was in my brain when I became a writing coach for *The Boston Globe*, *The Providence Journal*, and other publications. I asked the reporters as we studied their drafts if they rehearsed. I had believed all would say yes, but I was surprised that many did not.

The reporters on these papers were all consummate professionals. They all had worked their way up to these newspapers by being the best reporter/writers on smaller publications. They knew their craft and practiced it five days a week, yet I found that the best writers ALL rehearsed what they were going to write after they left the press conference, interview, political or sports event, fire, shooting, or flower show opening. ALL the poorer writers did not rehearse but came to their writing desks empty headed, panicked by the black screen and imminent deadline, then trying to think what to write.

I did the same survey with my students and found the same difference. Good writers rehearsed; poor writers did not rehearse. I began to teach the important but invisible writing that precedes the first written draft. The best students had their instinct to rehearse reinforced and they could improve their writing by increasing their writing before writing. The students who did not write effectively discovered the importance of writing before putting words on paper or screen and their writing improved. I also gave more time and paid more attention to what I should rehearse before I began my own writing. I found I had many ways of rehearsing and I developed more as I appreciated the significance of this phase of the writing process. I studied how musicians, actors, football and field hockey players, engineers and scientists, doctors and sales persons rehearsed before they faced the next day's or next week's problems.

I rehearse the next day's writing as soon as I leave my writing desk. I assign the topic to my subconscious and conscious, "Tomorrow we are going to start the chapter on Writing Before Writing." That's all. I don't want to think formally at this time. I do not want to think about the topic as I felt before. The novelist Graham Greene said, "Isn't disloyalty as much the writer's virtue as loyalty is the soldier's?" I do not want to be loyal to what I have thought or written before. I wrote this chapter without looking back and reading what I have written on this subject before.

I am aware of the play that is going on in my head as I drive, wake in the night, watch television, shop, read other books, eat, walk, sit. I do not usually hear these fragments of languages and images when I am busy and surrounded by other voices, but occasionally in the middle of a party or a hockey game,

I will see or hear fragments of language or images pass through my mind like a shooting star.

It is tempting to lock on to this fragment and start to think formally about it, but I tell myself, "No thinking. Do not interfere with the subconscious." I allow these fragments to float along in the river of my mind like a flooded river in which logs, roofs, bridge spans, trees, and cars rise into sight and then sink. Let them go. I tell myself "Do not micromanage your subconscious, do not think. When I am back at my desk I will think by writing."

I may make mental notes, even write a few words in my notebook, on a napkin, on the three-by-five cards I keep in my shirt pocket, on the screen of my PDA. These notes are in a private code and they are never sentences. The sentence fences in the glimpse of what I may write. Some of the notes for this chapter were "Graves," "associative," "tension," "side effects." Before I began the chapter I didn't know what most of these code words really mean and I did not want to know—not then. Mostly I believe what is forgotten deserves to be forgotten; what is remembered deserves thought by writing.

When I come to my desk after 24 hours of rehearsal I never have problems finding what to say. I write to unleash a draft that I hope will NOT be what I intended to say but something that surprises me and shows me a new way to explore the topic.

I have found that writing before writing is the best way to find something to write about and also the best way to begin and the best way to approach an assignment. This invisible writing is where ideas for poems, reports, essays, proposals, short stories, research papers, novels, case histories, scholarly articles, plays, appeals, film scripts all come from.

Some of the ways my conscious and subconscious write:

PAY ATTENTION

The most important event in the history of humankind lies not in great events, but the ordinary life of individuals. The writer is the member of the tribe who says, "Look at what you are walking past. Stop. See. Listen. Watch what we are doing to each other." Purpose sees what others pass by and overlook. All writers in all genre are saying to the reader: "Stop, take account, pay attention."

"The importance of a writer . . . is that he is here to describe things which other people are too busy to describe," says James Baldwin. "I remember standing on a street corner with the black painter Beauford Delaney down in the Village, waiting for the light to change, and he pointed down and said, 'Look.' I looked and all I saw was water. And he said, 'Look again,' which I did, and I saw oil on the water and the city reflected in the puddle. It was a great revelation to me . . . . He taught me how to see, and how to trust what I saw."

We are all trapped in the commonplace, accepting the familiar and not examining it or looking beyond it. Then the writer points out examples of love, hate, caring, loyalty, disloyalty, kindness, violence, what is not said as well as what is said, what is done and undone, what should be and is—or isn't, all the many acts we commit upon each other. As important as it is, the first rule of writing is not getting the rear end on the writing chair, but paying attention.

WELCOME SURPRISE

Writers seek surprise. They revel in contradiction, irony, the distance between what should be and what is, problems, questions and answers without questions, even when their own beliefs are challenged. As we move images, facts, phrases around in the playground of the mind, we hope to surprise ourselves. What we do not expect to think or write is usually the focus of new—and surprising—topics we need to explore. And unexpected ways of writing to explore these topics come in the same way as surprises that may not or may work. The other day as I was helping my wife who suffers from Parkinson's, I became aware of the increased loneliness in a marriage when you become a caregiver. It was not a happy thought, but a surprising insight that made me write. And then I thought of how much I gloried in displaying my virtue as a caregiver and that gave me two more pieces, one about the arrogance of virtue and the other the very real danger of too much care giving that robs the person who receives the care of independence and self-respect.

Writers are not loyal to what we have thought, felt, believe, but accept the ever-changing world and greet the changes that others so often fear.

PRACTICE ASSOCIATIVE THINKING

Most teachers instruct us in linear thinking. A is always followed by B, iii always comes before iv. The writer practices associative thinking as well as logical, straight line, predictable thinking. Watch a dog tracking a bird or a criminal on the run. They stay on the track or off, circling as they move ahead.

In associative thinking, two plus two doesn't necessarily add up to four. Sitting at my desk I look into the woods behind my house. A shadow looks for a moment like a German soldier I fought a lifetime ago. They were good at hiding in the woods. So are the deer that live near our houses yet are rarely seen. We look like a suburb but if you add up the wood lots we have preserved as back yards, you become aware that we live in a broken up forest with animals who were here before we came and who will be here after we leave. My thinking was zigzaggy as I hopped from topic to topic, but it gives me an idea for an essay or two.

CONNECT

One of the most repeated quotations on writing came from the British novelist E. M. Forster: "Only connect." Pay attention to those things that connect in your mind. The bridge over the river that reminds you how to resolve a dispute. The fear of not being loved and the fear of being loved. The unhappiness of loneliness and the joy of solitude. The development of systems engineering in the design of the first intercontinental missiles and the writing process on which all my books on the writing process was built.

DISCONNECT

Separate those things that are usually connected. Disconnect drinking and driving and teenagers and you will discover the problems of elderly drivers, elderly drinkers, elderly drinkers who drive. Disconnect patriotism from war and you may discover the real forces that bring a nation to war: natural resources, territorial control, religion. Disconnect the Bible from religious belief and you will discover a great literary document.

LOOK FOR TENSIONS

Tensions are caused by forces that are bringing elements together or forcing them apart.

There is the tension I have experienced three times in wanting to keep my father, my mother, and my middle daughter alive and then wanting to relieve their suffering with the gift of death. There are tensions in every human relationship—forces that draw us together and drive us apart. The tension between needing to learn to write like an academic and yet keeping the writing in your natural voice. The tension between wanting to save our natural resources and wanting to use the technology that is using them up.

TRY DIFFERENT POINTS OF VIEW

When I taught, I sat at the end of a great rectangle of tables. I didn't feel comfortable standing up and lecturing. Sitting at the table, we were fellow writers working at our craft. Once or twice a semester I would sit at the other end of the table or in the middle of one side. This always surprised and worried students. They saw me from a different point of view and I saw them differently. We are selling the house we lived in for 40 years. After the real estate agent commanded "Declutter!" it became a different, unfamiliar, picked up, neat house and it was different to me, less a home, more a piece of property for sale. And I saw in memory the land on which our house was built before it was built, when I walked the river edge as a student after I came home from war, where I had feared woods and also sought them as places of refuge. Looking at the world as son or daughter, in-law, grandson or granddaughter, brother, sister, cousin, ex-spouse, new spouse each gives a new vision of what you thought was familiar and that leads to ideas for stories.

THINK LIKE A READER

Ask the questions a reader will ask as you examine potential subjects. What do they need to know? What will they demand to know? What questions will they ask? What will make them read on? What do you have to do to earn their trust? How much will they want to know about the subject? How little? Looking at the subject as a reader BEFORE YOU WRITE may sharpen or change your approach—and give you new ones.

STUDY IMAGES

Writing is a visual art. The novelist Joseph Conrad said, "My task . . . is, by the power of the written word, to make you hear, to make you feel—it is, before all, to make you see." Our ideas come from images and are developed with images that make the reader see. It is by images that I move back to World War II: a lieutenant I liked sitting erect in a jeep at the top of a telephone pole where a land mine had propelled him; a major heading back from the front lines dragging an olive blanket that gave as much comfort as his baby blanket had, a friend carefully holding his head in his lap. Look for the images in the subject you intend to explore—the professor that builds a fortress of books to hide behind as he lectures. The classroom that had a professor at the lectern and his three students in the back room of an almost empty classroom. The student who comes to her first teacher conference with a clipboard and a list of questions attacking the instructor's lecture. Each image may initiate a subject or help develop one.

CONSIDER IMPLICATIONS

Every event we witness, every change we make in our lives, every change those close to us make in their lives, any choice, any decision has implications that may be worth exploring in writing. My high school had 13 tracks—a system that separated students by their potential ability in high school. These tracks ranged from 1–3 college tracks, to 13 shop tracks. This was good for teachers who could deal with students as groups, not as individuals. The students, however, were tracked for life—bright, dumb, and in between. And there were students such as myself who bounced between 1 and 13 and thought myself stupid.

Tracking can also be mysteriously assigned because of test scores, school records, or social-economic-racial-ethnic background. My wife who was her class valedictorian was placed in secretarial classes because she was a woman, and her father who was a good baker made little money and had no social standing. Once you were labeled, it was almost impossible to move up—or down—escaping your track. In thinking about implications we discover how to approach our subject or find one.

BE DISLOYAL

When a person used to be proposed for sainthood in the Catholic religion, a Devil's Advocate was appointed to challenge the proposal. The Devil's Advocate attacked all that is believed by others, all that is virtuous and celebrated, all the reasons sainthood is a possibility. Before the first draft I am Devil's Advocate to my ideas and my approach to the subject, challenging them in my head. Later I will challenge them as I draft and especially when I revise and edit.

When thinking of writing or actually writing, I am disloyal to what I have written on the subject before, disloyal to my own beliefs, disloyal to how I have written. I must be disloyal to what I intended to write and NOT resist the questions other students or colleagues, teachers or editors who are critical of my ideas or writing style.

LOOK FOR PATTERNS

The writer is always a seeker of patterns. Cause and effect, event and implication, act and result. The childhood beatings I received should be put in a context of a "spare the rod and spoil the child" generation, of stern parents born in sin as their Calvinist church taught; of immature parents who felt inadequate and overreacted and made the child the tail end of a sequence of events—grandma criticizes mother who criticizes father who spanks little Donald.

The writer imposes order on disorder. The story—fiction or nonfiction—explains what needs explaining. Life may not be rational but the artist always attempts an explanation.

THINK OF THE FUTURE

To find a subject, imagine the effect of time on a situation. Forty years ago a small town near us was surrounded by fields populated by cows. Then the land was bought and turned into mini-strip malls, then they were abandoned to become an urban slum in the city and big malls were built in a ring outside of the strip malls. What will this town look like 40 years in the future? What patterns of behavior are likely to repeat themselves?

THINK OF THE PAST

And what can we learn from the pattern of strip malls replaced by larger malls? How did the village start? As you ask that you have a story of how the river dam brought power and factories that have become condos, fancy shops, restaurants. The colonists did not design the towns for the beauty we now see. They were built to harness the river power to operate the mills and the mill owners built small homes so the workers could live within walking distance of the mill.

CHANGE YOUR VOICE

The music that comes from my lines as I write out loud tell me if I am amused, irritated, angry, nostalgic, sad. Try a different voice to see if it fits you and brings a new realization about the subject.

> "The wetlands outside my new condo protect me from more building."

> "The wetlands outside my condo are wasteland to us, a haven to many birds."

> "A streak of red flashes up from the wetland outside my condo and I run for the bird book."

> "I am learning that the wetlands outside my condo are filled with life. I wonder, looking in our wall of windows what they think of us."

> "I continued to feel guilty that my new condo is on a strip of preserved wetland. I have pushed nature into the bushes of the wetlands."

> "I wonder who my nature neighbors will be when I move into our new condo. I hope they will welcome me, but I doubt it."

Each line has, for me, a different tone and each tone reveals a different voice as I think about living next to the wetlands.

TAKE A NAP

When I don't see how I should approach a subject, I assign the problem to that part of my brain where dreams originate and take a nap. Sometimes I have a dream that reveals an insight. I have actually dreamt my draft as it was written or as it should be written. I read the pages in my sleep. Other times I wake after a ten-minute nap and a solution to an unsolvable problem is there, in my head, solved.

When the Nobel Prize-winning author, Ernest Hemingway, was asked where he worked he answered, "In my head." I am a very amateur artist with little productivity, but attempting to draw and paint has made me see what others do not see and I can delight myself watching, as I often do, the winter sun coming up behind the lacework of black trees, the anxious happiness many feel while shopping, the revealing tension between a parent and a child. Writing has taken me into the cave of my brain where I can play with ideas, images, contradictions, memories, words, lines, mysteries, fears, facts, hopes, allowing unexpected material to connect and disconnect if I am relaxed, and keep my head trapped in linear thinking, everything in its place leading to what I already know. Writing before writing will reveal your subjects and your individual way of seeing them. And when you can retreat to the grand playground of the brain you will never again be bored.

The Writer's Memory

You have a better memory than you think. You may—or may not—have a good quiz show or short answer test memory. I don't, but it is not important. I have a writer's memory. This memory doesn't work *before* you write, but *after* you begin the first draft.

When the page is blank so is the writer's memory. We can only recover fragments: a line, rarely a sentence, a snapshot image, an improperly cropped photograph. In fact, I write in ignorance having faith I will write what I didn't know I knew. I follow Grace Paley's wisdom, "We write about what we don't know about what we know."

The writer's memory is a powerful telescope to the past. When I write, the flow of language takes me back to places I haven't visited in years. As I started to write in an earlier chapter about Mort Howell who was my freshman English teacher in 1942, the words on the screen surprised me by describing the editing sessions I had forgotten, when he came out from behind his desk and sat with me when we worked together on the school paper.

Those moments when we worked at the writer's craft together introduced me to editing for discovery not just correctness. Each of us would suggest words, phrases, sentences, paragraphs that might replace—improve, develop—what I had written and I was not introduced to failure but possibility. The English language and the writer's craft was our play.

In 1963 when I became a freshman English instructor, I didn't remember Mort Howell. I wasn't writing about him then, but I came out from behind my desk just as he had, and entered into the game of writing with my students.

The inventory of life experience, thoughts, questions, facts, dreams, descriptions in your brain is enormous. You already have the concerns—the obsessions, fears, pleasures—that will color your life and your writing. As Willa Cather wisely said, "Most of the basic material a writer works with is acquired before the age of fifteen." I remember trying to write words with a stick in the dirt before I could read. I have had a lifelong fascination with stories. My grandmother with whom my family lived and who really brought me up had a "shock" (a stroke) and was paralyzed when I was a child. I helped care for her and became interested in chronic disease. I was a medical writer at one time, and the process of aging is often the topic of my weekly columns in the *Boston Globe*. My family was an unhappy one and I am still trying to figure out why. After experiencing war, I am still trying to comprehend what is within us that makes us kill each other. I was a poor student and thought my teachers could do a better job of teaching so I write books on teaching. Those are the writing territories I have claimed and most of the columns, poems, essay, articles, and books I have written rise from them: the writing and teaching process, sickness and aging, my family and my war.

Listen to what you say inside your brain when you appear silent to others. Look within yourself by writing down what you think about when you are not thinking, what you notice out of the corner of your eye, what interests you, and then start writing about one of those subjects. Writing allows writers to stand back from personal experience, the way an artist stands back from a painting, to see their lives more clearly, and it is a tool for reflection. The great British poet William Wordsworth talked about "emotion recollected in tranquility," the need to reflect on incidents in life and discover their meaning by writing about them. Memory provides us with a perpetual double vision, the past illuminated by the present, the present illuminated by the past. The past adds texture and significance to the moment and the moment puts the past in a new perspective.

I recently had to call 911 for medical help for my wife and that made me go back and explore in writing the first time I had to call for medical help:

> Grandmother has fallen. It is the house on Vassall Street in Wollaston, Massachusetts. She is on the dining room floor. I see the Oriental rug, the sideboard, the china closet in which I saw my face in the house on Grand View Avenue. I help grandmother up into a dining room chair. Her right arm has a huge, round rising lump turning red. She does not cry. She would never cry but her face is fierce, her mouth set. I am six, maybe seven, wearing corduroy knickers. I know grandmother cannot hold the ear piece of the old fashioned telephone with her left hand and dial with her swollen right arm. I go to the phone and ask the operator for Dr. Bartlett and I tell him what happens and he is on his way and I know I have been a good boy.

As I begin, I can only write a small fragment of what I see: the door to the kitchen and the pantry where I spilled the huge crock of hot grape jelly, the window and the branches of the apple tree where I learned to climb, the dining room table whose underside I knew so well because I studied its construction while Grandma, Mother, and Uncle Will forced open my mouth as I lay on the floor and gag at the hated oatmeal, thick skinned, gluey, cold, being forced into my mouth.

Then each memory breeds other memories, long chains of memories that connect and branch off. The British novelist Graham Greene said, "When I construct a scene, I don't describe the hundredth part of what I see; I see the characters scratching their noses, walking about, tilting back in their chairs—even after I've finished writing—so much so that after a while I feel a weariness which does not derive all that much from my effort of imagination but is more like a visual fatigue: My eyes are tired from watching my characters."

And if I write the physical description it will reveal my feelings and my thoughts. My pride at calling the doctor, the terror I felt and the punishment I received from tipping over the hot jelly, the achievement of climbing the tree and what I saw when I spied on the second floor of my home, and the stubborn anger I felt at having the now cold hot oatmeal shoved into my gagging throat.

Of course the remembered experience is textured by all that I have done and felt and thought since. I become again the boy in the back of the classroom who will drop out of high school before the year is out, but now I am not only him, but a teacher who saw himself bored in his classroom. The memory is more complex than the original experience. I am the child who doesn't want to go to bed, the parent who had to make a daughter go to bed, the grandfather who sees himself in his daughter and in his reluctant granddaughter.

Memories also arrive at the most unexpected and often inappropriate times, delivered by each of my senses. My fingers touch a seersucker jacket and I am dressed in a sailor suit I haven't worn since I was five years old. I smell secondhand smoke and become the stupid four-pack-a-day smoker I was as a teenager. I hear a door slam and jump at a bullet from a German sniper. I taste the delightfully bland tastelessness of mashed potatoes and am seated at the kitchen table in my Scots Yankee home.

CHAPTER 7

Take Note

I can't depend on my memory to remember my memories. When I travel back in time and live the life I lead in high school, the Army, as a police reporter on a city newspaper, I find a world rich with details and connections. If I do not have time to write to develop these details and their possible significance, I take notes.

The Daybook

I usually have my daybook nearby in the canvas case I carry with me. I don't know where I first heard the term *daybook*, but a number of years ago I found myself using the term and writing every day—well, almost every day—in a ten-by-eight spiral notebook filled with greenish, narrow-ruled paper, with a margin line down the left. This design works best for me. I write on my lap, in the living room or on the porch, in the car or an airplane, during meetings, in bed, or sitting on a rock wall while resting during a walk. A bound book doesn't work for me. I find a spiral book convenient and easy to handle; and since I write in all sorts of light, indoors and out, I find the greenish paper comfortable. I chose the size because it fits in the outside pocket of the bag I carry everywhere. I tried to keep a journal, imagining I was Gide or Camus. But I wasn't either of those writers or anyone else famous. I was only myself, and what I wrote to imitate others was pompous, full of hot air, hilarious to read, and utterly useless to me as a writer. At other times I tried to keep a diary, but then I found myself recording only trivia—the temperature, or whom I met, or what I ate.

A few years ago, two composition researchers examined my daybooks. They were surprised to find no signs of struggle. I was not. I'm not fighting writing; I'm playing with writing. If it isn't fun, if nothing is happening, I stop and wait until the magic begins. The daybook also keeps my writing muscles in condition; it lets me know what I'm concerned with making into writing; it increases my productivity.

The organization is simply a day-by-day chronology. When I change the subject I write a code word—"novel," "poem," "talk at St. Anselm's," "children's book?"—in the left-hand margin. That way I can look back through the book and collect all the notes I've made on a single project or concern.

How I use my daybook varies from time to time. Since I now do most of my writing using a computer, my daybooks have pages or paragraphs I have printed out and pasted in so I can read, reconsider, and play with the writing during spare moments. All the writing in the daybook is a form of talking to myself, a way of thinking on paper. Much of my "spontaneous" writing can be tracked through years of daybooks in which I have thought and rethought, planned and researched, drafted and redrafted its movement from interesting fragment to possible draft. Here are some of the items you might see in my daybook:

- Questions that need to be answered
- Fragments of writing seeking a voice
- Leads, hundreds of leads, the beginning lines of what I may write
- Titles, hundreds of titles
- Notes from which I have made lectures, talks, or speeches
- Notes I have made at lectures, talks, or speeches of others; also notes I have made at poetry readings, hockey games, and concerts
- Outlines
- Ideas for stories, articles, poems, books, papers
- Diagrams showing how a piece might be organized or, more likely, showing the relationships between parts of an idea
- Drafts
- A running commentary on my writing techniques, habits, problems and solutions
- Observations
- Quotations from writers or artists
- Newspaper clippings

- Titles of books to be read
- Notes on what I have read
- Pictures I want to save
- Writing schedules
- Pasted-in copies of interesting letters I've received or written
- Lists, lots of lists
- Pasted-in handouts I've developed for classes or workshops

I don't use the daybook in any single way. Anything that will stimulate or record my thinking, anything that will move toward writing goes into the daybook. When a notebook is filled—I am on number 116 at this writing—I go through it and harvest a page or two or three of the most interesting material for the beginning of the next daybook. When I'm ready to work seriously on a project, I go back through past daybooks and photocopy pages that relate to the subject I'm working on.

Make your daybook your own. Don't try to follow anyone else's formula. And don't write it for another audience. It's a private place where you can think and where you can be dumb, stupid, sloppy, silly; where you can do all the bad writing and bad thinking essential for those moments of insight that produce good writing.

Your daybook might not—should not—be like mine. It may be a file stored in a computer where I have a folder called DAYBOOK. The poet Mekeel McBride's daybook is a bound sketch pad in which she draws and paints as well as writes. I envy her and have tried to imitate her, but it doesn't work for me. I know other writers who use huge accounting ledgers, scraps of paper stuck in file folders in a drawer, a paper compost heap that flows from desk to floor, a loose-leaf notebook in which the pages become too loose for me. There is no one way and no correct way to write well; there are many ways and it is your job to find what works for you and be ready to switch when it stops helping you write well.

Three-by-Five Cards

My second most effective tool for taking note of my words is a leather case with special three-by-five cards printed by Levenger in a Levenger leather case that fits in my shirt pocket. I am so addicted to this system that I bought another Pocket Briefcase as a backup. Of course I do not need a fancy or expensive system, but I do need a system of note taking that is available when my daybook isn't nearby or when I want to make a note without calling attention to what I am doing.

Since my handwriting is getting worse I have started to also carry a Sony Clie, an electronic calendar/memo with a keyboard. Again, you do not need to buy such an expensive tool but if you are writing, some device for making quick notes is essential.

These shirt pocket notes tend to be even more fragmentary than daybook notes, written in a private code. These words or phrases will open the key to memories, ideas, opinions, thoughts that are stored in my brain, waiting to be explored in writing. For example, today's memo has "invisible." We are selling our house and the woman who is helping us has done a great job of fixing up the yard and the house to be seen by potential buyers. To her surprise, and ours, the real estate agent left her a nice note and a gift certificate. I realized that he had seen one of the "invisible" people who do the essential but menial tasks that keep our society running. I have enough to begin writing.

Another note is "Jeb" for Jeb Bush, the present governor of Florida who has reversed a court ruling that allowed a woman who has been in a vegetative state for 13 years to have her feeding tube removed. Now she will be force-fed. I have given the gift of death to my father, mother, and a 20-year-old daughter. I will explore this issue—her parents want her kept alive, her husband wants her to be allowed to die—not knowing what I will say but knowing that the evolving draft will instruct me—and I hope, my readers.

"Mitt." It is World Series time and I can smell and feel the first baseman's mitt I oiled, tied in just the right position, and slept with for years. This is a nostalgic piece but it will speculate how the sports dreams of young men and women affect their lives.

RECORDING YOUR LIFE

The notes I take fall into one of two categories. The first category is observations, such as the way a father drags his four-year-old son from a restaurant— his rage, embarrassment, and love passing across his face; the report that 50 percent of the households in America are headed by couples that are not married; my efforts to keep walking like an energetic young man although I fool nobody; the "antique" car in a parade that I once owned brand new; the way some voices can be heard by everyone in a restaurant. All are details that may or may not connect in a significant pattern if I start writing.

RECORDING YOUR RESPONSE TO YOUR LIFE

This is the second category. The most important notes record my response to life—my feelings, my thoughts, my reactions. Most of us feel that we have nothing to say, that we have not experienced dramatic adventures worth writing about, that our opinions aren't worth much, that people will not listen to us because we are not famous. All of that is not true, but listening to ourselves is where we begin to understand that our lives are interesting, even significant. If we pay attention to what we do and what the people around us do, we will find that we are all exploring the human condition.

Then we run into another problem. What we see, feel, express is not what other people say they are thinking and feeling. This is good, but it feels uncomfortable. This is why I keep quoting Sandra Cisneros, "Write about what makes you different." Families, employers, clergy, teachers, friends all want us to be like them, but readers want to learn from what makes you different.

My daybook is full of my response to life. My incoherent, agonized notes after the death of our 20-year-old daughter became a book, *The Lively Shadow*, 25 years later. My conflict between pride and shame at what I was able to do in World War II is being explored in poems, essays and a novel I am writing. It was also part of my memoir, *My Twice-Lived Life*. My critical responses to my teachers guided me when I became a teacher at the age of 39 and have resulted in many editions of ten textbooks that often say just the opposite to what my teachers taught. That has been extremely satisfying to my 17-year-old self who disagreed with his teachers and did not graduate from high school.

Pay attention to your life, pay attention to your own reaction to the obvious. My favorite cartoon is framed in my office. George Booth shows a writer sitting paralyzed at a typewriter on a porch. There are dogs on the porch, in the yard, in the house, on the furniture and his wife is saying, "Write about dogs."

CHAPTER 8

I Don't Have Anything To Say

Wrong.

We all feel that way until we learn that writing produces writing. As I have documented in the previous chapters, we begin with a phrase, an image, a doubt, a contradiction, a surprise, a hunch, an obsession, an itch and when we follow it with language we discover what we have to say and as we revise, how to say it.

When teaching I found that the quietist, shyest, least confident students had the most to say—once they didn't look for an idea. We imagine that good writers have focused, well-developed "ideas" before they type a word on their computer screens. Most of the time they don't have a clear, well-developed idea, a "thesis" statement before they sit down to work—and when they do, what they write is not what they expect to write.

The assignment that comes from a teacher, an editor, or yourself may be just "Write!"

Or the assignment may be explicit, "Identify and explain the three major causes of the Civil War," "Explain how Thoreau's essay was developed to stimulate the reader's thinking," "Compare the immigrants who come to America today and those who came between 1900 and the First World War and the difference in their treatment," "Show how 'the melting pot' actually worked." In each of these cases, the writer will feel the same, "I don't have anything to say" but will have to uncover what they do have to say.

Most people believe that the writer thinks, then writes when, in fact, the writer collects, connects, plays with possibility *then* thinks by writing. It is a process of trial, success and failure, with one attempt leading to the next until a draft finds its focus and that focus reveals what the draft needs to clarify the topic to the writer and then the reader.

FIND YOUR OWN WRITING TERRITORIES

When we write we discover we have territories we need to explore. These territories may be interests we want to follow—the new music technology, how Title Nine increased women's sports, how the Internet is affecting marketing, how we might extend medical help to those without it. Most territories we find come from a personal involvement: our knowledge of music expands when a friend from Brazil introduces us to Brazilian music; we watch once-prosperous farmland become housing developments; we watch the journey of a friend who was adopted as she begins the search for her biological mother; we begin to question our family's religion. Our experiences and our obsessions are rich with writing possibilities.

List the subjects that make you itch. What do you think about when you are driving alone in the car, taking a walk, tuning out the people you're with at dinner or a party, doing errands or the laundry, while listening to a boring lecture? What keeps you awake nights? What do you try to avoid thinking about? Donald Barthelme said: "Write about what you're most afraid of."

Of course much of the writing you do in school or at work concerns territories dominated by teachers or employers. It is important to try to make the territory your own, to turn any assignment **into your own**, so you can write with confidence—and to find an abundance of specific information on which you can draw.

FIND YOUR OWN MYSTERY

Our best subjects come from the mysteries in our lives or in the topics we are exploring with language. Many of us know a parent, uncle or aunt, teacher or neighbor whose life was changed by war—World War II, Vietnam, Iraq—but often we do not know the details or the nature of the change. That individual's personal history is a mystery that might help us to understand them—and the nature of war—if we could explore it.

Seek and confront the mysteries in your life to find writing subjects. The mysteries may be personal: What was the influence of my parents' religion on my life? What explains the fact I flunked out of high school in June and led the class in junior college that October? How did winning an Associated Press award in my first year on a newspaper affect me as a writer?

Or they may be impersonal: What makes it possible for a heavy metal plane to fly? Why does one product sell while a similar one sits on the supermarket shelf? What is the impact of sex and violence on TV on our children? The mysteries may be small or large, personal or impersonal, but they engage our minds. They present problems we need to solve and provide us with unexpected answers as we watch our words appear on the page or screen.

Techniques for Discovering Subjects

There are many other ways to discover the mysteries that will produce effective subjects. Play with them to see what works for you.

BRAINSTORMING

One of the best ways to discover what you already know is to brainstorm. When you brainstorm you write down everything that comes into your mind as fast as you can. You don't need to be critical; you do want to be illogical, irrational, even silly. You want to discover what is in your mind. You want to be surprised.

Here I have brainstormed about my childhood to see what topics I may have overlooked that need to be explored in writing. I'll start with the geography of childhood and see where it leads me as I list as fast as I can, not worrying if I am silly or stupid. Brainstorm beside me in the margin of the text. There's plenty of white space. You may discover a subject you want to explore through writing. My list is personal; I'm writing about my childhood. Your list doesn't have to be. Brainstorm any topic, personal or impersonal, with which you have some experience to see if there's something you wish to explore.

Now to brainstorm:

- Geography of childhood
- The block
- The vacant lot
- Empty stores
- Cellar hole
- Under the porch
- Playing doctor
- Sex mis-education
- Behind the garage
- Dogs, Airedale, Chow, scared
- Uncle
- Grandmother collapses
- Alien WASP—white Protestant in Irish Catholic neighborhood
- School
- Nearsighted
- Sat in back row

- Glasses
- "Four-eyes"
- Turn the other cheek—beaten up on playground
- Muddy Ducks
- Fights
- Seriousness of games
- Red Sox, Bruins
- Snow
- Sleighs
- Uncle Will's car up on blocks in winter
- His Buick
- The Sunday drive
- Almost drowning
- Fear of water
- Sickly childhood
- Days in bed—good
- Reading
- Friends who lived in walls
- Fantasy
- Temper—threw hammer at uncle, he fell
- Grandmother's paralysis
- Day I pulled hot jelly over me
- Wood stove
- Mystery of basement
- Mystery of attic
- Den
- Brown, color of my childhood

That took eight minutes. It's possible to brainstorm for a much longer time, but I find short spurts—fifteen minutes, ten minutes, five minutes—are more productive. You can also brainstorm together with another person or a group of people. The important thing is not to censor what you say, not to judge it, not to really understand it—but to let it come.

After you have brainstormed, look at what you've written to see what surprises you or which items connect. These surprises and connections remind you of what you know and make you aware of meanings you hadn't seen before.

It is important not to worry about how the brainstorming list is written. Don't worry about spelling or penmanship or sentences; it is a time to write in a sort of private language of code words that stand for particular meanings in your own mind. When the phrase "turn the other cheek" appeared on my brainstorming list, it reminded me of all the years—from grade one until grade six—when my mother would instruct me not to fight but to "turn the other cheek." If I really believed in Jesus, she said, the fists of the other boys would be held and they would not smite me. Apparently, I was never able to believe enough, because their fists kept hitting me and I lived in fear, humiliation, and guilt at my lack of faith. All that and much, much more would pour out if I wrote about that phrase in a column, novel, or poem; but the simple phrase "turn the other cheek" would be enough to hold it in reserve for another writing session.

I brainstorm before I write important letters or memos. I brainstorm class lectures and novels. I brainstorm articles and poems and textbooks such as this. I also brainstorm before I decide to buy a car or take a job or choose a vacation. Brainstorming shows me what I know, what I need to know, and what the connections are between what I know and don't know.

Look for Surprise

I look at the list to see what surprised me. Whatever you are brainstorming—an academic paper or a job application letter—first go over the list to see what surprises you, to find out what discoveries you have made.

The surprise doesn't need to be enormous. I am surprised by:

- Under the porch
- Playing doctor
- Sex mis-education ←┐
- Behind the garage ←┘

I don't remember what happened behind the garage, and that's enough of a mystery for me to start to explore my childhood world when I first became aware of sex—I thought the facts of life ridiculous when I first learned them—so this topic might be worth exploring.

I also note:

- Seriousness of games
- Red Sox, Bruins

That is all it takes to remind me of the importance of being a sports fan in a town like Boston. It was one of the few subjects that connected me with my father and my uncles—the world of men—and the emphasis on sports and competition probably marked me more than I know. If I write about that subject, I may discover its importance.

An old theme for me but a new twist:

- Sickly childhood
- Days in bed—good

What have we lost because of miracle drugs? Convalescence. I am nostalgic for the long, lonely weeks of recuperating in my bed, and of the fantasy and the reading that helped make me a writer.

Look for Connections

Next I look for connections between the items on my list. I draw lines connecting related entries, creating little bunches that may lead to a subject:

- The vacant lot
- Empty stores
- Cellar hole

Child's delight in playgrounds created by construction and business failures in the Great Depression.

- Alien WASP—White Protestant in Irish Catholic neighborhood
- Turn the other cheek—beaten up on playground
- Fights
- Seriousness of games
- Almost drowning
- Fear of water
- Sickly childhood

Might explore the terrors of childhood.

- School
- Nearsighted
- Glasses
- "Four-eyes"
- Sat in back row

Might reconstruct the school world of a nearsighted kid when you got beaten up for wearing glasses.

MAPPING

Another form of brainstorming that often works is mapping. You put the subject or topic you want to think about in the center of the page and then draw lines radiating out from it when another idea occurs to you. These lines branch off, capturing the fragments of information that you have unknowingly stored in memory.

A map of thoughts I have about my childhood follows.

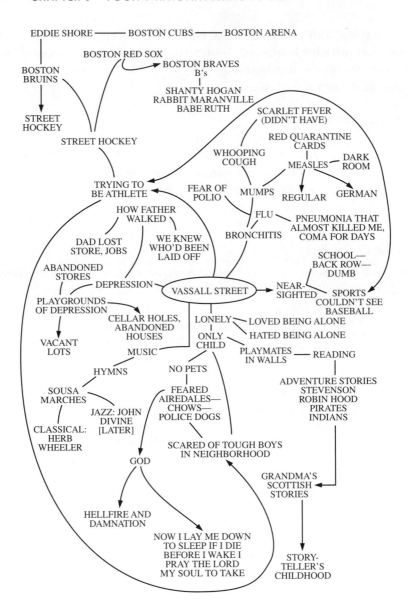

How Mapping Leads to Writing

That map took less than ten minutes to create, about the same time as the brainstorm list, but it produced different information. I rediscovered the red quarantine cards that were placed on the door when anyone had scarlet fever or measles; this memory might lead me into the territory of childhood disease before miracle drugs. The map also made me aware that how much I had learned about the world had come in the form of stories—from the Bible, from

Grandma and the uncles, from the street, from the classroom. Then there was the role of music—my family's hymns and Sousa marches, my jazz and the beginning of my interest in classical music—I could write a musical geography of my childhood.

MAKING A TREE

Another helpful technique to discover what you already know and don't know you know is to draw a tree. The figure below reveals the branches that can grow from a single idea.

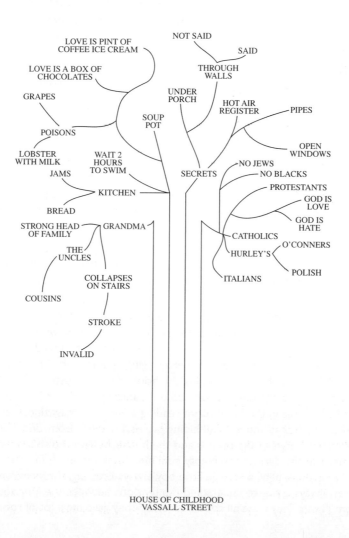

This technique gives you a way of breaking down a subject or letting a subject expand. Some writers who use trees successfully place the central idea at the top of the page and let the tree grow down, whereas others place the central idea at the bottom of the page and let the tree grow up. Both produce excellent results.

This tree took five minutes to create, and it produced some new insights. I discovered the larger complexity of religions with which I grew up and their contradictions, the food myths that were important in my childhood, and the role of secrets in our family.

FREEWRITING

Another technique I have found productive is freewriting. In brainstorming we work with lists. In freewriting we depend on the momentum of narrative flow to force unexpected connections. To free write, sit down and let the writing flow; see if language will start to reveal something that unexpectedly interests you—an event, person, place, idea, feeling. Suspend critical judgment, as you do when brainstorming or mapping, and look for something to happen.

I'm never sure that anything will happen when I free write. But it really doesn't matter. Some days the writing comes, and some days it doesn't. If freewriting doesn't work right away, I try brainstorming or mapping, or staring out the window, or turning to another project, or getting a cup of tea, or taking a walk, or otherwise creating an interruption. It is important in doing creative work to step back from the draft, the canvas, the score, the lab experiment— just far enough to gain perspective, to allow the subconscious to percolate. But in a few minutes I'll return to my desk, and something will work.

Now I'll free write, aware that my freewriting looks more polished than the beginning writer's. It is. I refuse to fake it for the purpose of an example, but don't worry if your freewriting is a lot sloppier than mine. It should be.

> I don't think I was ever alone in that house of childhood. Mother was a woman of the streets, shopping, always shopping, chatting with friends, having lunch with them. She hated housework and cooking; she loved going out. And yet, although Grandma was there singing hymns in the kitchen; and Uncle Will was at his desk, keeping the books for one customer or another; or Father was at the dining room table organizing sales slips from the store and Mother was in the living room reading a woman's magazine; I remember being alone in that house. I had hiding places. My own room, under the dining room table, between the bushes and the house, behind the sofa, at the top of the stairs in the dark, in the empty coal bin.
>
> I must have been a strange little boy, always listening, always making up stories, always trying to understand the tensions between the four adults with whom I lived. They were all so self-centered they gave me a lot of room—space,

we'd call it today. I drove by the house and it is smaller, much smaller, than I remembered. I suppose I was never more than a few feet from anyone, and yet that loneliness is real. And the silence. We did all our hurting with turning away, what was not said, was our favorite weapon.

That few minutes of writing certainly took me where I did not expect to go, giving me a whole new vision of my childhood on Vassall Street.

Velocity in freewriting is important; write fast so that you say what you do not expect to say. Also, note that freewriting isn't really free. It starts to take you somewhere, to tell you what to say and how to say it. After freewriting, look back to see whether you want to follow any of your paths, to explore them so the writing stops being private and can go public to readers. Decide whether you want to share with others what you are discovering. If you do, you'll find that the more personal the writing, the more specific and private, the more it will spark memories and ideas in your readers' minds.

Freewriting is just as valuable a technique to use as a starting point for a term paper, a historical essay, or a review of scientific literature. It's a way of thinking in which you can preserve the flow of thought.

INTERVIEWING YOURSELF

Develop your own "itch list" to help you find a subject. Here are some of the questions I ask myself to discover what I want to "scratch" next:

- What has surprised me recently? What do I need to know?
- What would I like to know?
- How are things different than they used to be? How will things be different in the future?
- What have we lost?
- What have we gained?
- What do I know that others need to know?
- Who would I like to get to know?
- What's not happening that should?
- What's happening that shouldn't?
- Who would I like to see at work?
- What process do I need to know?
- What process would it be fun to observe?
- How can I switch my position so I will see my world differently?
- What have I read, heard, thought that confuses me?

- What connections are being made that surprise me?
- How are people's behavior changing?
- How are beliefs changing?
- What makes me mad?
- Sad?
- Happy?
- Worried?
- Frightened?
- Content?
- What do I expect to see, hear?
- Why?

Most of the writing I did in writing in elementary, junior and senior high school was on tests or projects that seemed designed to reveal how little I knew about the subject. These assignments produced failure, anxiety, boredom, despair. Writing was even used for punishment. But real writing reveals how much you know, not how little. It introduces you to the formally hidden world within your brain that turns out to be rich with information.

■ SHOPTALK ■

Your writing seems awfully personal. Do I have to write about that kind of stuff, take my clothes off in public the way you do?

I hope not. It embarrasses me sometimes. I don't always feel comfortable running around in my birthday suit. And I don't always do it. I do it when it's the best way to help others or to say what I have to say. I never finished my master's degree and I don't have a doctorate. My knowledge about writing comes primarily from personal experience. I'm also a pretty open person. I need to share my life with others and have them share their lives with me. It's my way to live but it doesn't need to be yours. Most writers I know are much more private than I am. You don't have to be an intellectual nudist to be a writer.

What is all this about a process for writing? I don't have a process and I still get A's on my essays.

Everyone has a writing process, but the process is invisible since writers usually write alone. Because writing is a closed-door activity, we have no way of knowing the difficulty an author has with finding a topic or how many times she revises before publication.

We forget too that using a computer has made the process of writing less apparent, since we now can perform multiple tasks at one sitting: drafting, focusing, and drafting again; editing, deleting, and planning; revising, focusing, and drafting once more. When a writer finishes, we usually see only the result: a proofread product, typed, tidy, and ready for the reader's eye.

It's certainly true that some writers (and you may be one of these) can sit down at the computer and hammer out something worthwhile without much effort. But if asked to explain in detail how they compose, even these writers would define some sort of process. They sift through information and focus on an angle for their topic. They revise, insert, delete, and move text around, pausing to read what they have written before moving on. It is the rare, accomplished writer who does not finally read a printed copy of a draft with pencil in hand, looking for ways to make a story or essay even better.

If you are getting straight A's on all your writing, that's great! Your process is working for you. But you might want to ask yourself another question: Is your writing publishable? If the answer is no, it may be time to take your writing to the next plane, to push yourself beyond what is expected of you at school and to think of becoming the best writer you can on your own terms. Concentrate more on planning and revision. Write for yourself instead of for your teachers.

I've already explored my writing process in high school. Don't you think it's a waste of time to do it again in college?

No. Process means fluidity and growth, something that is always evolving, always in flux. While you are probably a more insightful writer from having paid attention early on to your writing process, you will never be finished exploring, changing, and improving the way you write until you draft your final sentence. Since you will be writing in one form or another throughout your life, that final sentence (we hope!) is a long way off.

You may want to think about it this way: You don't finish learning when you finish college. Each new experience becomes part of a longer, continuous process of analyzing and making meaning, of revising the way you view the world and the way you think about older experiences. Likewise, your experiences at college will be different from your high school experiences. You are probably already reprocessing what you know and what you think, even though you may have been at college for only a very short time. Since writing is a way of thinking, learning, and revising, your particular process will change as you change.

Besides, your writing assignments at college will most likely be much different from those in high school, and you will want to adapt your process accordingly. As you explore different disciplines and juggle an increasing number of deadlines, you will have to experiment with different processes. What worked for you in high school may not necessarily work for you now.

> So if process means flexibility, why do I have to follow all the steps of the process in the order that you have them in this book?

You don't. Following a procedure is a good way to get started and move through a draft, and it's a good idea to work through the steps in the order you find them here as a way of beginning and thinking about your process. But it's not the only way. While you will probably complete each step of the process before you are through (and your teacher may insist on this), don't think of these steps as guideposts along a straight and narrow road. Think of them as points along a circle or spiral, sites that you will most likely revisit or pass again on your journey as a writer.

Writing should be an exciting, adventuresome activity. It should be full of surprises, unexpected opportunities, twists in the trail, surprising views, new challenges. You can always vary a method of working and go back to it when you need to. A writing method should never make a writer follow a discipline of writing that ignores the evolving life of a draft.

> How about academic writing, essays I have to do for other classes? How will following a process help me if my teacher assigns a topic?

From a practical perspective, following a process of writing before writing, researching before writing, writing, keep writing, and finish writing will get you from Point A to Point B. It will force you to set a schedule and meet deadlines. Instead of writing your paper the night before class (or not turning it in at all!), you will have a polished product to hand in on the day it is due. This kind of agenda will also be helpful if you get a job that requires reports and other written products.

> But aren't English teachers the only ones who use a writing process?

No. If you ask professors in different fields to talk about essays or books they have written, or if you see all their drafts, you will find that published writing evolves through an extensive process of writing and revision. You will also discover that your professors rely on editors who proofread their work before it is published. None of these professors sits down at the computer and fires off a perfectly polished product the first time around.

> What if my teacher won't let me write from my point of view or use the pronoun *I* when I write? What if she thinks it's too personal?

Even if you do not say *I*, you imply it in all your writing. It is the *I* who is behind every bit of information that goes into your paper and who makes the decisions regarding your writing. While the *I* may receive feedback and suggestions from other readers, that is the person who ultimately sits down to write the piece.

It would be great if you could come right out and say "I think . . ." in all of your papers. But if you can't, try not to distinguish too greatly between personal and academic writing when working through your writing process. All writing is revealing; all writing is personal. While a writer may be distant and detached, his or her choice of words, details, and focus can show what he or she thinks. Even the most "objective" academic writer reveals some sort of relationship with the people and ideas he or she writes about. The long and the short of it is, you don't need to say *I* to write from your own perspective or to make your writing your own.

■ IN THE WRITER'S WORKSHOP ■

ON YOUR OWN

1. Start a writing process log or daybook, picking out a notebook that feels comfortable to you and is the right size so that you can have it with you most all the time. Doodle in it, write in it, paste things in it, record observations and thoughts, ideas and drafts for titles, leads, ends, middles. Create outlines and diagrams. Don't worry about neatness or correctness—this is a place to have fun. Talk to yourself, think to yourself, find out what you are seeing, hearing, feeling, thinking and what it means.

2. Find a brainstorming "room": a cafe, dorm or bedroom, lounge area, or even a spot outside by a river or under a tree. Make it your own. Settle into your space with notebook or personal computer and reserve an hour or so each day just for freewriting or brainstorming. Make a daily appointment with your spot, and commit yourself to keeping it for at least a month.

3. Create the perfect writing area. Splurge on inspirational posters, artwork, a comfortable chair, the right pens and pencils and paper. Go to yard sales or flea markets to buy all the extras that will spiff up your special corner. Make it a place you will want to return to again and again. If you need music while you write, have your stereo and headphones nearby; if you like privacy, enclose the space with a screen. Post pictures of family and friends or of writers whom you admire around your computer or writing desk.

4. Write in your daybook about a project you have completed that made you proud. How about a speech you wrote and delivered in speech class? A car's engine you rebuilt during the summer? A dinner you cooked for your parents' wedding anniversary? The skis you refurbished last winter? When you have finished writing, list the steps you took in planning and carrying out your project. When did you first think of it? Did you have to gather information or do some research in order to complete it? Did you have to revise your plans as you went along? How much time did it take? Was the final product worth it? Was it well

received by others? When you have finished, compare the process of completing your project to the process of writing. How was it similar or different?

5. Make a list of teachers you remember. Next to their names, jot down writing assignments you associate with them. Select two or three names from this list and in your daybook write as quickly as you can about the teachers, what you learned about writing from each one, and how you began, sustained, and completed each writing assignment for that teacher. Be humorous or serious or reflective, but try to trace your writing process through each teacher and each writing assignment.

6. Imagine your writing as a house and draw a blueprint. Don't worry about being highly technical and accurate. Just divide the stages of writing into "rooms" (brainstorming, freewriting, and mapping, for example, might be the doors and entranceways to your house), and furnish the rooms with details about each step. As you write your essay, keep track of where you have to change your blueprint. Which rooms get the most use? Which do you visit the least?

7. Retype a couple of pages from a published author's work. Listen to the rhythm of the sentences as you rewrite them. Think of the words you are putting down and how the author chooses them. Pay attention to punctuation and the stylistic choices the author makes. Then rewrite the passage. Change or add punctuation or leave it out; drop or add details, or go off on a tangent of your own. Move the middle paragraph to the beginning or change the ending. Choose one scene or detail to write about extensively and omit others. Note when and how the focus of the essay shifts as you fiddle with it.

8. Take a piece of your favorite writer's work and imagine the different stages it must have gone through before it was published. Try to step into your author's shoes and imagine how he or she got started. Pretend you're that author and plan the piece from beginning to end.

9. Visit the home or museum of a literary figure where drafts of the author's writing are on display, or check out a biography of an author from the library. Often such displays and biographies track the various stages of a famous work from beginning to end, from idea to publishing. Make a report to your group or class about the writer's composing process.

WITH A WRITING PARTNER

10. Select a writing partner in class and set aside a specific time, fifteen minutes to a half hour each day, to write one another via campus mail or e-mail. Make the main topic of correspondence the craft of writing, but don't be afraid to just talk about life in general; this is where good writing starts. Discuss subjects that you want to write about and ask questions about these subjects. Comment about the actual act of writing, too: where you sit, your ideal

writing environment, when you are most productive, when you are not. Support each other through each stage of writing and help each other "power" through writer's block. Keep copies of your correspondence, and collect them in a binder at the end of the semester. Write a preface about your writing process and your semester as a "pen-pal."

11. Come up with a list of five nouns and ask your writing partner to do the same. Exchange lists and write for five minutes apiece about each word, paying particular attention to sensory details and any memories the words evoke. Choose one of these and brainstorm with your partner about ways to expand it.

12. Write a letter to a class partner about a writing project you have in mind and how you want to approach it. As you take the project through its various stages, write memos to your partner reporting on your progress. Pay special attention to the various phases of your writing process and how you move through, repeat, skip, or merge them. At the end of the semester, join with your partner in "publishing" a small book of your work.

WITH A GROUP

13. Collaborate with a group of classmates on a TV script for a drama or sitcom. Look at the credits of your favorite shows and note how many writers collaborate together on a show. As an alternative, check network Web sites on the Internet, where you can find all kinds of information about popular programs. Decide how you will collaborate on the script, and elect a recorder who will keep a detailed record of the process you used in writing the script.

14. Write a paper quickly the last minute before class. Don't bother to go back and reread, revise, or edit it. Make copies of your paper and pass them out in a small group. Read the paper aloud and then discuss what needs to be done with it. What process will your paper have to go through to make it better?

15. Hold a "bad" writing contest. With a group of classmates, write a short essay that you consider dull, unfocused, and . . . well . . . just generally bad. Exchange your bad essays with another group. Using the stages of the writing process outlined in this book, write up a list of suggestions for the authors of each essay and how you think they could improve it. Don't get stuck on grammatical and spelling errors at this point. Think about the gist of the piece, and read it with an eye toward planning, focusing, and drafting.

16. Choose a passage from a piece of autobiographical writing by a professional author, one that you think conveys a sense of his or her voice. Make copies and pass them around in a small group; ask your groupmates to do the same. Omit any information about the author or the title of the piece. Try to guess from the passage what the narrator is like. What kind of voice does the

writer have? How old do you think the writer is? Is the writer male or female? Write up a profile of the narrator in your daybook.

WITH WRITING MENTORS

17. Invite a local writer—a newspaper columnist, poet, novelist, or essayist—into your classroom. Read selections from the writer's work, and ask the writer to bring in drafts and to talk about his or her writing process. Be prepared with questions about drafting, planning, focusing, and revising. Have on hand copies of publications by the writer, and refer to specific chapters and passages as you talk.

18. If your school has a writing center or lab, ask to sit in on a couple of tutoring sessions and listen to conversations about writing. If you can't actually listen in, then make an appointment with the director of the center or a writing tutor to talk about the various ways people go about writing and how tutors at the center help them through the process. Jot down your observations and then write an entry in your daybook comparing your own writing process with those of others.

19. Talk to professors in your major or area of interest about writing in that discipline. Ask them to tell you about any articles they have written, how they went about planning and drafting them, and how they revised them. Find out what kind of feedback they got from friends, colleagues, and publishers that helped them put together their final drafts.

ON THE INTERNET

20. Find a friend who subscribes to an online mailing list (also called a listserv) or newsgroup, and find out how you can do the same. Explore the hundreds of topics these online discussion groups cover. You can try a World Wide Web site such as CataList, the official catalog of Listserv Lists, at <http://www.lsoft.com/lists/listref.html> or go to Google, <http://www.google.com> and choose the Groups link on the Google homepage to find discussion groups that interest you. (Also see Chapter 11 for more information on finding and subscribing to these.) Make a point to read and respond to the messages posted to the listservs or newsgroups at least once or twice a week. Be attentive to various posts, jotting down what you agree or disagree with, what you learn from them, and what you can add. Then post your own thoughts.

21. Go to a World Wide Web site for and by writers. One way to find such sites is to go to the home page of a search tool such as Yahoo! or Google and work through categories of sites until you find what you are looking for. At Yahoo!, for example, choose the link in the Yahoo! directory for Social Science, then the one for Communications, then the one for Writing. At Google, click

on the Directory tab, then the Arts category link, then Writers' Resources. You'll find lots of useful information on these sites, but you may also be able to take part in forums or chats and "listen" to the conversations among writers about drafting and revising, how they write, when they write, and where they write. Talk with them about your own processes, and choose a mentor from among them. You will find that most writers in these groups will be more than eager to discuss your work.

Research for Writing

If you knew where you were going why would you bother writing? There'd be nothing to discover.

JOHN GUARE

That is the pure pleasure of creation—the not knowing that leads you to the knowing.

BOBBIE ANN MASON

As great architects and others have said, God lies in the details. I would say that Art lies in the details and that the best skill that a writer can develop is an openness, a receptivity to life, at its most basic level, its most intricate details. There's almost nothing that can go wrong in a book that you fix with fascinating, riveting details of one sort or another. That's what life is; life isn't general. Life is texture, process, complexity. The intimate, sometimes terrifying, details of life are to my mind what make life so unexpected and breathtaking. If you can convey a scene in sensory detail, not only can you enter that scene yourself in your imagination or memory, but you can allow readers to walk into that scene also at the level of their senses.

DIANE ACKERMAN

CHAPTER 9

Outline Now or Later

Outline is a nasty word to many students, and I was one of them, because this method is often taught in such a rigid manner that it doesn't work. An outline is not a formal blueprint that has to be followed precisely; it is not a contract, and you can't be sued if you break it. An outline is a sketch, a guess, a scribbled map that may lead to a treasure. Writers may create outlines and then not refer to them during the writing, for what they learned by making the outlines allows them to get on with the writing. Sometimes it is also helpful to make outlines in the middle of the writing to see where you've gone and where you might go, and at the end of the draft to see what you have discovered through the writing and how you have organized your material.

There are many ways to outline. This section shows eleven possible types. None of them is *the* way to outline. Develop your own system of outlining. Outline only if it helps you, and then outline in a way that provides that help.

I will demonstrate each outline on an assignment given by several freshman English instructors at the University of New Hampshire: Describe your hometown.

Outline 1

This one is my favorite form of outline. It is simple, but helps you see how each part of the material you have collected will relate to the other parts.

TITLE
LEAD
TRAIL
END

Demonstration of Outline 1

(TITLE)	My Hometown Was a City
(LEAD)	When other people talk of their hometowns, they mention lawns, trees that arch over streets, and backyard swimming pools. My hometown was a city. I remember alleys, boarded up stores, and vacant lots.
(TRAIL)	• But where I lived was a neighborhood. • Geography of neighborhood. • Who lived there. • Games we played.
(END)	When I visited my roommate's hometown, it was like a movie set. I thought I'd be envious, but the streets were empty, I never saw his neighbors, I wondered how he could stand the quiet that kept me awake half the night.

Outline 2

My next favorite form of outlining is the one I use for my textbooks. It is the one I would most likely use to help me in writing an academic research or term paper.

1. I write the chapter or section titles, playing with them until I get the wording right, until I see a clear line through the material.

2. I write the major headings for each section within the chapter, playing with them until I see a trail through the chapter or section.

3. I write the subheads for each section within the major section, ordering and reordering them.

4. I draft the text for each section, changing heads as the material dictates. Writing is thinking, and the order will change in the writing.

This procedure is a good technique for outlining a research paper, grant proposal, corporate annual report, brochure, any sort of writing that must communicate an abundance of information in an orderly fashion.

Demonstration of Outline 2

1. The title of my sociology paper will be "The Urban Neighborhood as Home Town."

2. The main sections will be:
   • Expanding Horizons
   • Worlds with Worlds [ethnic diversity]
   • Neighborhood Games
   • Neighborhood Ethics
   • Neighborhood Inheritance [Beliefs taken to suburbs]

3. The subsections within the section on Expanding Horizons will be:
   • Apartment
   • Stairway
   • Front stoop
   • Block
   • Back Alley
   • Across the street and away

4. Draft a section within a section at a time. If one doesn't go easily, skip to the next. When you go back, many sections will not be needed, and the rest will be easy to write.

Outline 3

This formal outline style may be appropriate for a formal, very structured subject. It uses Arabic and Roman numerals and capital and small letters to break a subject down into categories and subcategories in a logical sequence. Numerical outlines are also popular in some disciplines, and many computer software programs have a formal outline pattern built in.

The most formal outline style requires a full and complete sentence for each entry, but most writers just use fragments as signals for what will be said. Be careful in using the formal outline, because it may inhibit the search for and discovery of meaning that should come during the writing.

Demonstration of Outline 3

[One section of a sociology paper on urban neighborhoods]

III. Neighborhood games

1. Importance of games

    A. Aldrich study

        a. LePage response

    B. History of games

2. Nature of games

    A. Hiding

        a. Hide and Go Seek
        b. Ring-a-lievo

    B. Sports

        a. Stick ball
        b. Basketball
        c. Street hockey
        d. Soccer

    C. Gender differences

        a. Boys' games
        b. Girls' games
        c. Cross-overs
            1) Boys playing girls' games [rare]
            2) Girls playing boys' games [often]

    D. Ethnic differences

        a. White neighborhoods
        b. African American
        c. Latin American
        d. Asian

Outline 4

My writer friend, Don Graves, uses this outline form. He lists everything that might be included in the piece of writing in the left-hand column; then he moves items to the columns marked Beginning, Middle, End.

Some of the things don't get moved, of course, and others come to mind as the outline is being made and go right into the appropriate columns. Some things in the left-hand column are not used. It's a brainstorming list, and it becomes an inventory of material that may be used. Some items that are not on the list come to mind when the writer is working on the right-hand columns. The items are ordered—by number—within the columns after the writer has finished. Then the writer is ready to write.

Demonstration of Outline 4

Beginning	Middle	End	Brainstorming list
Home town urban	Qualities of neighborhood life:	Home urban attitudes influence	Stick ball
Neighborhood urban unit		How see suburban world through urban values	Latins played soccer
You are defined by your neighborhood	Ethnic comfort/ discomfort		Blacks played basketball
	Diversity comfort/ discomfort		Whites played hockey
	Fears		Don't date X
	Pleasures		Girls' games
	Games		Dress
	Family		Mixed families
	Dating + mating		Loyalty to your own
			Food
			Racial myths
			My values today
			Alleys, loved alleys

Outline 5

A way to use the outline to dramatize the importance of certain parts of the piece of writing to the reader is to make a box outline in which the size of each box represents the importance of each part. The first paragraph, for example, is much more important to the reader than the pages that follow and might be two inches by four. The subject of the next four pages might be indicated in a phrase contained in a box only one-quarter of an inch by two inches. A main turning point might be in a box one inch by three, and then the rest of the piece might appear in another tiny box. Finally the closing might be in a box as large as—or larger than—the first paragraph. This can best be done with boxes, but it can also be done with typefaces.

This outline style really forces me to face up to the importance of the opening and the ending—to the importance of what I'm going to say and how I'm going to say it. It also forces me to see the structure of the piece in stark, efficient terms.

Demonstration of Outline 5

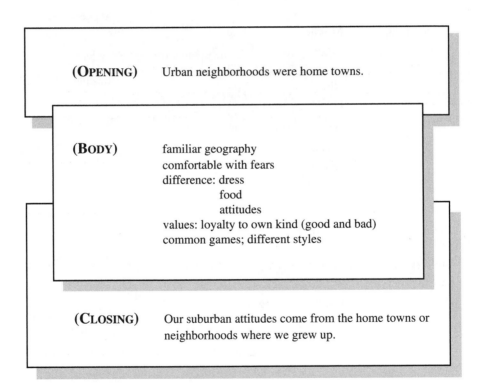

(OPENING) Urban neighborhoods were home towns.

(BODY) familiar geography
comfortable with fears
difference: dress
food
attitudes
values: loyalty to own kind (good and bad)
common games; different styles

(CLOSING) Our suburban attitudes come from the home towns or
neighborhoods where we grew up.

(**OPENING**)	Urban neighborhoods were home towns.

(**BODY**)	familiar geography
	 comfortable with fears
	 difference: dress
	    food
	    attitudes
	 values: loyalty to own kind
	 (good and bad)
	 common games; different styles

(**CLOSING**)	Our suburban attitudes come from the home towns or neighborhoods where we grew up.

Outline 6

A fine way to outline, especially on a complicated subject, is to brainstorm the questions the reader will ask and then put them in the order the reader will ask them.

There will usually be five questions—sometimes three or four, sometimes six or seven, but most likely five. You don't want to use the questions in the draft, but simply give the answers. The questions are in the reader's mind; the writer anticipates and answers them.

Demonstration of Outline 6

The questions are brainstormed, written down as they come to mind:

- Who were your neighbors? Did you get along with them?
- How can you have a home town when you lived in a city?
- How is a neighborhood like a small town?
- How does your home town, your urban neighborhood, influence your life today?

- What attitudes and beliefs did you take away from the neighborhood?
- What was life like in your home town [neighborhood]?

Now the questions are put in the order the reader will ask them and sharpened:

- How is a neighborhood like a small town?
- What was daily life like in your city neighborhood?
- Who were your neighbors?
- How did you get along with them?
- What attitudes and beliefs did you take away from the neighborhood?

Outline 7

The writer can adapt outline forms from other disciplines. I often find it helpful to use a flowchart, similar to those used in systems engineering and business organization study. These charts are designed to show how a factory works, how materials flow from a natural resource to a manufactured product, how power flows in a corporation. Using this device, I can often spot a movement or force that can order my piece.

Demonstration of Outline 7

When we moved to city I discovered neighborhood was home town ⟶

Geography of neighborhood ⟶ Streets and blocks ⟶ Ethnic

boundaries ⟶ Playing and living within boundaries ⟶ Attitudes

and beliefs neighborhood taught me

Outline 8

A related outline form I find useful I've borrowed from computers. Computer users have developed a number of different forms of outlining that break down complicated subjects into their sequential parts. Most of these outlines flow from left to right.

At the left I state an issue: "The home town in the city is the neighborhood." Then I give two extreme responses, one above the question and over to the right—"physical boundaries"—another below and over to the right—"ethical boundaries." I break down every answer this way until I see a pattern of potential meaning emerging.

Demonstration of Outline 8

The home town in the city is the neighborhood

- Physical boundaries
  - Apt. house
  - Street + alleys
  - Block
  - Life on roofs
  - → Live close to people different from you
  - → Have to get along with each other

- Ethnic boundaries
  - Speech
  - Style
  - Dress
  - Humor
  - Courtship
  - Values
  - → Started to become them
  - → Learned lots but lost myself

Outline 9

In many effective pieces of writing, fiction as well as nonfiction, each chunk of writing—a paragraph, a page, a scene—answers a question and asks a new question. For example, will they get married? Yes, but will they be happy? Will the product sell? Yes, but will it bring a profit? You can create an outline by anticipating and listing these questions.

Demonstration of Outline 9

Q. How is a neighborhood like a small town?
A. People know you, you know people.

Q. How well do you know each other?
A. We live on the street.

Q. What is that like?
A. A big stage, everyone watching.

Q. What do they see?
A. In my neighborhood, people of different backgrounds playing/fighting together.

Q. Against each other?
A. No, against other neighborhoods.

Outline 10

Many fine writers, such as John McPhee and John Gregory Dunne, use a card technique to outline. This is the most popular technique for movie script writers.

Each scene or key topic in the writing gets its own card, sometimes using cards of different colors for different characters, or different kinds of material in nonfiction. Then the cards are pinned to a cork board and moved around so the writer can see the pattern of the entire piece—book, movie, or article.

Demonstration of Outline 10

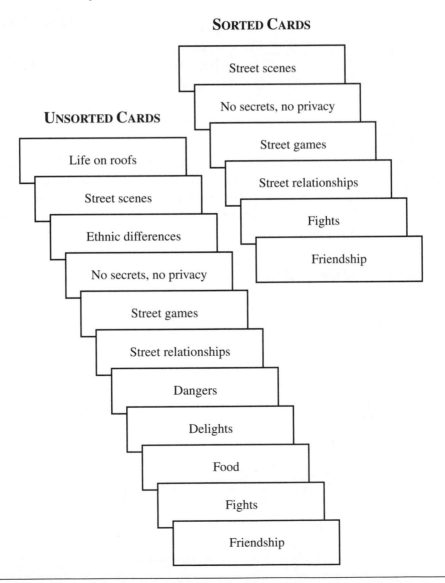

SORTED CARDS

Street scenes

No secrets, no privacy

UNSORTED CARDS

Street games

Life on roofs

Street relationships

Street scenes

Fights

Ethnic differences

Friendship

No secrets, no privacy

Street games

Street relationships

Dangers

Delights

Food

Fights

Friendship

Outline 11

Make a separate file folder for each topic within the piece of writing, a method that is helpful on a large project. You can renumber and move the file folders around, and you can put all your raw material—clips, photocopied articles, notes, photographs—right into a folder. When a folder is full, it may have to be divided. When it has nothing in it, you may have to drop that topic or do more research.

Outline of Chapter 11

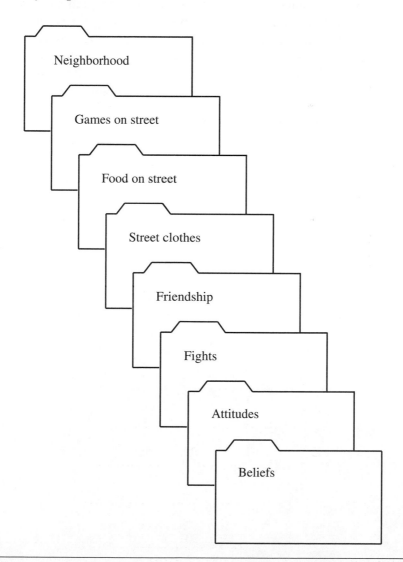

Neighborhood

Games on street

Food on street

Street clothes

Friendship

Fights

Attitudes

Beliefs

Try out these outline forms, and then make up others that fit the way your mind works. There's no one way to outline, and no eleven ways to outline. But you should find some way of pre-seeing what you may write.

Yes, there are writers who say that they do not outline. But if you interview them, as I have, you find that most of them have outlined in their minds, sometimes without being aware they were doing it. That happens to me sometimes; I just know where the writing is going and how it is going to get there. It seems like a feeling, even though it's probably a very organized intellectual act. When this happens to me, I write. I don't outline unless I feel the need to outline. But I do find that most of the time, my drafts collapse unless I have outlines in my mind or on paper.

Of course, when you outline, you may realize that you need more information or that you need a different focus; you may have to go back through one or more of the earlier stages of the writing process. That isn't failure. You haven't made a mistake. That's one of the main reasons to outline, so that you will see the information you need to have before you write the draft. You will see, by outlining, if you have the information to develop the focus.

CHAPTER 10

Plan Your Research

The unexpected discovery is the goal of research, and reaching that goal is the product of an effective plan. The reason we conduct research is to go to the edge of the known—and then beyond. We stand on the shoulders of those who—in the past—have extended that further edge of knowing. We must know and respect their discoveries even if our research eventually disproves them. Their successes and failures may indicate where we should go—or not go. We would not be armed with new knowledge unless we had started on the firm ground of old knowledge. The surprise that is the purpose of all research comes from the unknown. What is *known* is where we launch our expedition into the *unknown.*

Of course our research plan will change as we enter new territory. We find new theories, new facts, even new truths and each affects the research plan. That plan will change during the research process as the explorer's plan changes when there are unexpected rivers to cross, unexpected cliffs to climb.

Limiting your topic breeds specific questions. If the writer has an unlimited territory to explore in writing—the cost of a university education, for example— the writer's questions will be global. How much does it cost to go to college in the United States? Who pays? How do they pay? And the answers will be general, abstract, almost impossible to turn into an interesting, reader-attracting piece of writing. If the writer has a good research plan with limits—how are five single mothers paying for their college education?—the information will be filled with the significant, unexpected details that are essential to lively, convincing writing.

Surprise and instructive failure should be welcomed as we research. It is those elements that refine and redirect our process. The first plan is based on a guess about the unknown, all following plans are based on experience. The writing problems presented by the form in which we write, such as argument, critical review, proposal, personal essay, each provides its own individual need for information that lies within the sources appropriate to the topic.

The Researcher's Attitude

The attitude we bring to a task influences the results we achieve. We all know that attitude wins games, but we should remember that attitude also determines academic accomplishment.

Curiosity

Research begins with the insatiable curiosity of the child: "Why is the sky blue? Where does time come from? Can dogs talk to each other?" The questions continue until our parents shut us up. The good researcher/writer never really shuts up. The why's are not spoken out loud and they are not just addressed to parents, but the why's are there.

We want to know all—and more—that can be known about a subject that fascinates us. My curiosity about the writing process began in elementary school. I did not only want to know the story, I wanted to know the storytellers. Why did they tell stories? Where did they find their stories? What do you mean they made them up? How? Where did they start? How did they continue? How did they know the end? And on and on. Every answer I discovered brought an explosion of new questions and this fierce burning curiosity will continue as long as I can listen, read, watch, and make up stories.

Respect for Specifics

The writer has respect for concrete, accurate information and the sources of such information. The writer values the revealing detail. I remember when I learned as a soldier that the rifleman did not yank on the trigger but had to squeeze it, gently, softly, caressingly, so the weapon remained steady as I aimed. From that single detail I discovered that the soldier in the heat and confusion of battle had to be calm, quiet, detached, the opposite of what I had thought a good soldier would be.

The writer respects good sources: libraries, books, documents, Web sites, authorities that, in turn, seek and respect truth, or the information that will bring them as close to truth as they can get.

Respect for Connections

As the child has an instinct for connecting blocks so that they make walls and towers, writers have an instinct for connection. They take the details they discover and connect them into meaning. Driving near my home in New Hampshire yesterday I felt a new respect for the rolling, empty fields that were left—so far—from the reach of the expanding suburbs. But then I connected those fields with the fact that American Indians who had lived on this land when it was forest must have resented the fields settlers carved out of the woods as I resent the developers who fill the fields with houses. And then I connect that resentment with the irony that I live in a developer-built house. I want to save New Hampshire from me. I am the enemy, the city dweller who moved to the country. I am always connecting what I discover and observe into meanings that seem new, at least to me.

Skepticism

The great novelist and short story writer Ernest Hemingway said, "The most important essential gift for a good writer is a built-in, shock-proof shit detector."

The effective writer/researcher is not cynical, saying that there is no truth, that all people and institutions lie, but the effective writer/researcher develops a healthy skepticism, questioning, doubting, checking and rechecking, applying common sense to each piece of information.

If the writer's mission is to deliver truthful information to the reader, then each piece of information and every pattern of meaning must be subjected to ruthless scrutiny. And those beliefs and ideas and facts the writer has always held demand the greatest disloyalty.

Creating the Research Plan

Remember that we do not write with words, we write with information. The words represent information, the way writing a check represents the money we have in the bank. No money in the bank and the check is worthless; no information on hand and the most skillful writing is worthless.

The reader demands information that is specific, clear, and accurate. The writer has to plan on how to get the information the reader demands.

Research plans will change with the personality, work habits, experience, and abilities of the writer; with the nature of the information that needs to be collected; with the writing form which is going to deliver the information to the reader.

My plans start on my shirt-pocket lined cards, on the pages of my daybook, on my computer screen. At first they are sketchy but they become clear and ordered as I work on them.

The stages I go through to create an effective research plan include:

Overview

First I step back mentally and think about the territory I am going to explore in writing. I am looking for the furthest horizons, seeing what lies within the greatest limitations and what comes to mind or eye from this distance.

I make mental and then written notes, sketches for a map of the territory that will reveal a way to approach and limit the subject. Many times I make important discoveries at this stage.

I might, for example, decide to discover why local control of schools, which is a basic tenet in our political system, advocated by all candidates of all parties in every election, so rarely works. I would think about my local school board and its jumping-bean response to immediate issues that appear and disappear in a year but block long-term professional curriculum planning.

Then I would make notes about other school systems and the way in which school systems are established in other countries, especially in Denmark, Canada, and Great Britain, with which I am most familiar. I would list the advantages and disadvantages of both local and national or regional systems.

Anticipation

I try to anticipate the ways the reader will challenge what I have to say, what questions I must answer to persuade the reader. These are not the questions I want the reader to ask but the questions I *don't* want the reader to ask, that the reader will inevitably ask.

I might make a list in my daybook as a reminder to keep during my research and writing:

- What's wrong with the present local-school-control system?
- What system are you suggesting?
- How will it work?
- What problems will it solve? Produce?
- How much will it cost?

Strategy

I usually decide on the genre or form of writing, such as narrative, exposition, report, critical essay, that will help me explore the subject most effectively We do not often think of the form of writing we pick as a research tool, but it is. Of course the genre may change as what we learn changes, but genre is a lens that reveals what we know and what we need to know.

In this case, poetry, fiction, and drama are not appropriate to the territory—local control of schools—that I intend to map. I am going to write nonfiction.

Now that I know that, it is clear that I must identify the sources of specific, authoritative, and accurate information. I list the categories of sources:

- Federal and state boards of education
- Organizations of superintendents and school board members
- Teachers' organizations
- Faculties of colleges of education
- Local school boards and school-district superintendents

Tactics

I continually narrow my focus. Now that I have decided I should use nonfiction, I consider a few of the alternatives: argumentative essay, analytical article, survey, the profile of a school board, the narrative history of a school board.

Now I have to find a school board that has been subject to radical changes because of political pressures that have influenced school board elections. I will have to:

- Read back issues of the local newspapers that have covered the school board.
- Read the official minutes of the school board.
- List past and present school board members and their public positions.
- Interview school board members—past, present, and announced candidates for the next election.
- Talk to school administrators and teachers, past and present.
- Interview students, parents, and spokespersons for groups interested in education.

Tools

We have an increasing number of tools for research: libraries and the Internet, official records and newspaper files, interviews in person, by telephone, and e-mail, scanners and photo copy machines which can copy documents, fax and mail, and observation of school board meetings.

In researching my narrative history I will depend largely on local written records and interviews.

Achievability

I must always ask myself if I can fulfill the research plan. The biggest mistake I see graduate students make in designing their research projects relates to the question of achievability. Can I get the information I need within the practical limitations of time and support?

I cannot, for example, afford to visit school boards in California, Arizona, Florida, Minnesota, New York, North Carolina. I must focus on a school board I can reach within, say, an hour's drive of my home.

I cannot cover the history of the school board from eighteenth century to the twenty-first. I must limit my territory to the last thirty years, twenty, ten. It has to be long enough to document many changes, short enough so that I can finish the task.

And I can't cover every school board issue: school construction, curriculum, school superintendent hiring, sports. I decide to focus on the continual concern about sex education and limit it again to middle school.

Flexibility

The good plan is flexible. Once the researcher begins, the subject may change, or the sources, or the strategy, or the tactics. Nothing in research is stable.

I may find that the school system I chose will not cooperate but a neighboring system will; that the problem there is not in middle school but elementary school; that the strongest political pressure did not come from those who opposed sex education as I imagined, but those in favor of it.

We must always, as effective researchers, be aware of our prejudices, or assumptions, our beliefs, our own vision of the world. Research is learning and learning causes change.

The joy of research comes from the discovery of information that surprises, challenges, questions, makes us reconsider, reflect, revise. The novelist E. L. Doctorow has said, "Every time you compose a book your composition of yourself is at risk. You put yourself further away from whatever is comfortable to you or you feel at home with. Writing is a lifetime act of self-displacement."

We write to learn and discover new worlds, many of them previously ordinary and interesting. The worlds we discover are not just outside us but inside. The research plan explores and reveals what is in our mind that we did not know we knew.

CHAPTER 11

Using the Internet

When I was a 25-year-old police reporter in Boston, one of my competitors was Theo Finn, a well-stomached, blondish man with a red face and a friendly voice. He was old enough to be my grandfather, and late at night when there were no murders, fires, or other calamities, he would doze or talk about his years as a young police reporter at the turn of the century.

There was only one phone in the city room of the *Boston Post* then, so instead of calling each police station to see what was going on, he'd travel the city on the trolley and the subway, then go back to the city room where he had no typewriter but had to write his stories by hand, standing at a long, high table.

Now it's hard to imagine such primitive days. No computers—just typewriters and copies made by carbon paper. We gathered information by interviewing experts in person or on the phone, looking up clippings of previous stories in the morgue or newspaper library, even mailing letters to get information.

Now the Internet is a major tool of the reporter, allowing the journalist—and anyone else—access to sources wide world. Not just journalists, but those in business, law, medicine, science, and every other occupation that requires research.

I have invited Lisa C. Miller to write this chapter. She used the Internet as a newspaper editor, as a reporter and writer, and as a faculty member doing research. She is a professor at the University of New Hampshire where she teaches Internet research to journalism students and to English teachers who want to use the Internet in their classrooms. She has also published a basic text on using the Internet: *Power Journalism: Computer-Assisted Reporting.*

• • •

We live in an amazing, baffling information age. All the "old" information resources still exist: newspapers and magazines, books and journals, movies, radio and TV. But we also have the Internet, a vast, constantly changing collection of data that we must learn to use and make sense of. This chapter will help you do that, suggesting when you want to use the Internet and when you don't, ways to find what you need, guidelines for determining what is useful information out in cyberspace, and suggestions on using what you find.

WHY USE THE INTERNET?

Because more and more useful information is available online, and it's a great resource for up-to-date information about the world around you. Because your friends, family and peers will be using it and you need to know how to be a savvy Internet information consumer. Because much of the information you find is free and easy to transport or take with you. Because if you don't, you're missing out on some interesting stuff.

WHY NOT USE ONLY THE INTERNET?

There's nothing wrong with looking for information online as well as checking your library for useful books or journals, and maybe setting up interviews with people on campus who can help you with your research. BUT—remember, first, that everything is not online. So if you look for information about a certain topic and can't find it, don't assume there's no information anywhere. It just may not be in cyberspace (or you may need to refine your search which we'll discuss later).

Second, while there's good information on the World Wide Web and through other Internet resources, not all of it is reliable, mistake-free or bias-free. Anyone with a computer and some basic software can create Web pages that look professional; you've got to do much more than glance at a page to decide if you can and want to use the information on it. You need to know how to evaluate the data you find.

Finally, sometimes the best resource for your information is going to be a person—and a firsthand interview with that person. Or a book or journal or report you can take out of the library and read and take notes about and refer to when seeking other resources for your research.

WHAT'S ON THE INTERNET?

On the Internet, you can find people—experts, writers, students like you. There are political discussions and documents, great speeches, government agencies of all shapes and sizes, books and magazines and newspapers and journals and 'zines, music, movies, great art, literature, scientific experiments and breakthroughs, museums, virtual field trips and so much more—information on just about any subject you can think of, and probably some you couldn't imagine. You can use Internet resources to find people to interview, mentors, people to commiserate with; to get ideas to write about; to figure out what questions to ask yourself and others about your topic; to gather useful information and supporting data such as maps or graphs or photos; you might even use it to share your writing with others. It won't necessarily make your research go more quickly; it may even complicate it some. But it will give you current information about lots of topics, let you in on what people are saying and arguing about and taking action on, and broaden your horizons.

The World Wide Web

Let's start with the World Wide Web, the part of the Internet where information is stored not just as text but as hypertext—text with links embedded into it. (Links appear in Web documents, or on Web pages, as words or graphics or photographs that you click on with your computer mouse. The links connect one Web document or page with another.)

The World Wide Web is one of the most fantastic technological creations of our time, as far as I'm concerned. I think this because I can remember when we didn't have the Web, and so I couldn't sit in my office in New Hampshire and, with just a click of a computer mouse, check the headlines of a newspaper from California, watch a video of the U.S. president giving a speech in Texas, check on the weather in the Bahamas, follow the adventures of scientists working at McMurdo Station in Antartica, tour Shakespeare's Globe Theater, and download a recipe for cheesecake—all in a few minutes. So I'm always amazed at the Web.

There are millions of Web sites available to you, and therein lies a problem. It isn't always easy to find just the information you need, or to be sure that the information you find is reliable. But there are some strategies that should help.

FINDING INFORMATION ON THE WEB

There are three basic ways to find information you need on the Web: go to a specific Web site you know about that deals with your subject and browse or search that site for information on your topic; go to a site where librarians or researchers have put together collections of good Web sites and search through these; use a search engine or directory to search a database of many different World Wide Web pages for ones that connect with your topic. (We'll talk more about search engines and directories later.)

Firsthand or Secondhand?

You might want to think first about just what sort of information you want—from primary or from secondary sources? When we use primary sources in research, we're using the raw material—the firsthand accounts of something that happened, results of a scientific experiment or poll, photographs of an event, diaries, speeches, memoirs, autobiographies, records collected by government agencies of births, deaths and other demographic information, even published accounts of events written at the time the events were taking place—materials that let you get as close as possible to what happened.

More and more firsthand, primary source material is available online. One great resource for such information is the Library of Congress web site, <marvel.loc.gov>. You'll find all sorts of information here: collections of old baseball cards, one of Walt Whitman's journals, the papers of Orville and Wilbur Wright, the Civil War photographs taken by Matthew Brady, and firsthand narratives by Americans and foreign visitors recounting their travels in the colonies and the United States from about 1750 to 1920.

If you're looking for demographic information, try the U.S. Census Bureau at <www.census.gov>, where you can learn all about how many computers or cars the average family owns, how many families live in poverty, and much more about how life in this country is changing over time.

One list of primary online sources can be found at <http://www.lib.berkeley.edu/TeachingLib/Guides/PrimarySourcesOnTheWeb.html>, a library research Web page put up by the University of California at Berkeley Library. And the research guide Berkeley has is helpful for finding all sorts of sources, online and not, at <http://www.lib.berkeley.edu/TeachingLib/Guides/>.

People are, of course, great primary sources. We'll talk about reaching people through e-mail a little later in this chapter.

Secondary sources analyze or interpret or comment on original events or primary sources. There are many secondary sources online, from newspapers, magazines and scholarly journals to scientific publications, encyclopedias and textbooks. There are millions of these out on the Web, covering every topic imaginable.

Starting Your Online Research

When you've got a topic, it's tempting to start your research by choosing a search tool such as Yahoo! or Google, typing in a word or words, and diving in. World Wide Web search tools look through collections or databases of Web pages to find ones that offer information on a certain topic. You go to the Web page of a search tool, type into a search box keywords related to your topic and the search tool compiles a list of links to Web sites that might be useful to you. I might go to

Google (www.google.com), type in the words "cancer treatment," and see what comes up. A lot—6,770,000 hits or listings of Web sites. Way too much information. Or maybe I need to find out about global warming: 3,210,000 hits. And I have no way of knowing, just by scrolling through the list of sites I've got on my screen, what might be useful or reliable.

Instead, I'm going to find a Web site put together by an expert or group of experts, or by an organization or museum or university or government agency that specializes in my subject. For cancer treatment information, I might start with the American Cancer Society (www.cancer.org). Global warming? I'll try the Environmental Protection Agency (www.epa.gov). If I need to know what the U.S. Congress is doing about health insurance, I'll start at Thomas, Legislative Information on the Internet (thomas.loc.gov). The National Civil Rights Museum, the Rock 'n' Roll Hall of Fame, the Boston Aquarium, the National Oceanic and Atmospheric Administration, the Smithsonian Institution, The Gettysburg National Military Park, the Art Institute of Chicago—there are plenty of places with plenty of sites you can check out for information on everything A to Z.

I'm not saying there's a guarantee that you'll find exactly what you are looking for on these Web pages. But these sites should have reliable information, explain where the information came from, and often have useful links to other good sites related to theirs.

These sites generally let you search the sites using keywords, so if you don't see what you want right off, don't despair. Check out all the links on the page to see if any might lead where you are going; if not, do a keyword search.

If you're not sure of the Web address of a specific site related to your subject, go to Google or another search tool, type in the name of the organization, and, voila! Or go to Yahoo! (www.yahoo.com) or Google or another search tool site where you can browse through categories, and see what you can find.

Let the Experts Help You

Another place to start your research on the Web is a site set up by librarians or educators. For such sites, these experts compile a database of useful Web sites, and you can do a keyword search, or browse through categories of sites. Try the Librarians' Index to the Internet (www.lii.org), a site sponsored by the Library of California, or the University of Michigan's School of Information research site, The Internet Public Library (www.ipl.org). Other good sites for academic research include these:

- Infomine, Scholarly Internet Research Collections, developed by the Library of the University of California, Riverside (infomine.ucr.edu)
- Best Information on the Net, O'Keefe Library, St. Ambrose University (http://library.sau.edu/bestinfo/Default.htm)

- Academic Info Educational Subject Directory—Online Degree Programs—Test Preparation Resources, University of Phoenix Online (www.academicinfo.net/)
- Voice of the Shuttle, out of the University of California, Santa Barbara (http://vos.ucsb.edu/)

Searching, Searching

If you haven't found anything yet, or haven't found sites that are helpful, it's probably time to use a search tool. But to do this quickly and well, you need to consider a few things.

Not all search tools are created equal. We use the phrase "search engine" for most any search tool on the Web these days. But some are actually subject directories.

When you do a search of the Web with a search engine or directory, you aren't doing a real, live search. You're actually searching through a collection of Web pages, or a database, created for that particular search tool. One important difference between directories and search engines is this: When you conduct a keyword search with a directory, the directory tries to match your keywords with words in written descriptions of the Web sites in its databases, and perhaps with words in titles or subject headings on the Web pages. Search engines, on the other hand, search for matches throughout the entire text of Web pages in their databases.

If you've got a pretty general topic to research, or you're just trying to find a topic or narrow down one you've chosen, a directory such as Yahoo! might be your best bet. If you're searching for information on a very specific or obscure topic, you might need a search engine such as AltaVista (www.altavista.org) or Google.

How do you figure out whether you're dealing with a directory or a search engine? When you go to the Web site of a search tool, look for information about what and how it searches. You can usually find a link labeled *About, Tips, Help, Info* or *Advanced Searching*. Read about the search tool and how it works. This information will help you conduct a more useful search.

You'll also find tools called metasearchers, such as Dogpile (www.dogpile.com). These don't maintain their own databases of Web pages; they search several databases, at the same time, from several other search tools. You can get good results with these, but they do not search 100 percent of the databases they look at. So you could get more (since they search several databases at once) or less than you wanted.

Here is a list of some other search tools on the World Wide Web:

LYCOS: http://www.lycos.com
WEBCRAWLER: http://www.webcrawler.com

METACRAWLER: http://www.metacrawler.com
ASK JEEVES: http://www.askjeeves.com

It's All Boolean to Me

Typing a couple of words into a search box and hitting *enter* isn't always the best way to do your search. Truly. Search tools use Boolean logic–words called *operators* that tell it how to search for the keywords you put in. The operators, named after a nineteenth-century mathematician named George Boole, tell the computer about the relationship between the words you are using in your search. The operator **and** tells the computer to search for all the words you type in—and for many search tools, this is the default—the way the search tool automatically does the search (unless you tell it to do something else); if you just type two or three words into the search box, the search tool assumes you mean to put **and** in between them. If you tell the search engine to search for *campus* **and** *crime*, it searches for pages with both of those words in it. If you ask for a search for *campus* **or** *crime*, it will find documents with either word or both, a much broader search in this case. Or you can use the Boolean operator **not** to exclude some things in the search. You might search for *campus crime* **not** *city* if you are interested only in campuses in rural areas.

Quotation Marks, Plus or Minus Symbols

Many search engines also allow you to use symbols, such as " ", + or -, rather than or in addition to Boolean operators. That's another reason you must read information about the search tool you are using if you want to get the most out of your searches.

Let's try a search with Google as an example. I decide to do a search for animal rights. I type in these keywords, hit Google Search, and come up with 7,150,000 hits. Now Google has assumed I want **and** between these two words, but it hasn't necessarily only found Web pages that include that phrase. The word **animal** might be somewhere, **rights** somewhere else. I'd like to narrow the search a bit, so I'm going to put the phrase in quotation marks: "animal rights." And now I'm down to 666,000 hits, still too many, but better! I might do the same if I were searching for information on musician Miles Davis or architect Frank Lloyd Wright. So when you know the exact name or phrase you're looking for, use the quotation marks.

Use a plus sign to tell Google a certain word is important to your search. Just put the plus sign right in front of the word in the search box. For example, if I want to know about laws dealing with animal rights, I might search for "animal rights" + law—hey, 217,000 hits, so we're getting there.

Use a minus sign if you want to exclude a certain word from your search. I see in the results of my original search that some of the sites are booksellers advertising books about animal rights. I want to exclude those from my search, so I'll use "animal rights" − book as my terms. That gets me 464,000 hits, down from the original 666,000. And you can use more than one of these symbols at the same time.

And be sure to leave a space before the plus or minus sign, but not after.

Not every search tool works the way Google does. But many do, and again, if you read the information about the one you're using, you'll figure it out. A link for *Advanced Search* or *Search Tips* will generally tell you about Boolean operators or other options like the plus or minus sign with Google.

Finding Nothing?

If your search doesn't yield what you're looking for, rethink your search. You might need to use broader or narrower search terms. Think about terms likely to be used by experts putting information up on the Web.

Or try a different search tool—with a different database of Web pages.

You can also check to see if you might have spelled your keywords incorrectly. I like Google because if I type in *Arnold Schwarzenger* it asks me, "**Did you mean: Arnold Schwarzenegger?**" and allows me instantly to do my search again. With the name spelled correctly.

And again, remember: Everything is not on the Web.

Finding Too Much?

If you get 3,000,000 hits on a topic, do not search through all of them. If the first couple of pages of search results don't bring up what you want, try another search. Most search tools sort the pages they find by relevance, so if No. 45 isn't relevant, No. 295,000 definitely won't be.

Evaluating Web Pages

Not all information on the World Wide Web is reliable or useful. You don't need to be any more suspicious of what you find online than you are of other information; just treat it as carefully as you would a magazine article or other resources you might use for research. Review the Web site thoroughly, and look for the following clues about the site's content:

1. *What does the address tell you about the origin of the information on the site?* Look at the Web page address, or the Universal Resource Locator (URL). With the Web site address, www.unh.edu, the "edu" at the end indicates that this Web page is part of an educational institution's Web site, in this case the University of New Hampshire. The suffix "com" means a commercial organization; "gov," a government agency; "org," a nonprofit organization. The address offers one clue

as to whether a page offers reliable or unbiased information. Do realize, though, that the university or nonprofit group might not necessarily control the content of pages people put on their sites. So you really have to read what's there. If you see a Web page address that includes a section starting with a tilde like this, **~miller**, this can indicate the page is that of one individual and is not necessarily sanctioned by some organization.

2. *Who is the author of the information on the page? What are his/her credentials? Can you figure out from what's on the page if the author is affiliated with a school or government agency or well-known organization? Is there a way (e-mail address, probably) to contact a person or organization connected with the site?* If there's no e-mail address, and no clear indication of author or authors, or no way to tell where information on the site comes from, you probably don't want to use what's on that site. You'll have no way to know if it's accurate. If an author or organization is named, but no other information is given, do a Google search and see if you can find out anything more.

3. *What is the purpose of this Web page or site? Is a specific point of view represented? Is the site presenting just facts, or trying to persuade you to agree or disagree with a certain point of view?* If the information on a Web site seems biased or to be presenting only one side of a two- or many-sided argument, you want to take that into consideration. For example, if the information on the site supports only the view that Congress should repeal all gun control laws because people should not have to be licensed to own guns, you are probably reading someone's opinion on the subject. That may be what you're looking for. But if you want plain facts or want to explore varied opinions on the subject, you may need to look elsewhere.

4. *Does the Web page cover its subject in detail? Does it provide any supporting evidence? Does the author explain where the information came from and identify authorities cited on the page? Is there a list of works cited or a bibliography?* Look at the assertions made on the Web site. Are examples or other evidence given to back these up? Suppose the document you're reading includes this statement: "Binge drinking is becoming a huge problem on college campuses." Are there statistics or examples or statements from experts to prove that? If not, how do you know the statement is true? And if you can't tell where information on the site came from, you won't know if it's reliable, and you'll have trouble citing it in your work.

5. *Is the information presented accurate? Is the document free of grammatical and spelling errors?* Look closely. Check the information you find on one site with the information you find on others. If there are errors of fact or many errors in grammar or spelling on the site, it's probably not a reliable source of information.

6. *How old is the information on the site? When was the site last updated?* Often this information is posted on the site; if you can't find it high up on the

page, scroll to the very bottom of the page and look for a date. If the page hasn't been updated recently, or isn't being regularly maintained, or you can't find any information about this on the page, this might not be a page you want to rely on. You might be looking at old information or a page with links that are outdated and don't work any more.

E-mail for Research

Let's look at another Internet resource you probably use all the time—e-mail. Certainly one thing you can do with e-mail is brainstorm with friends or classmates about an assignment, bouncing ideas off of one another till something clicks. But you can also use e-mail to find subjects to write about, to find people who know something about your subject, and to interview those people.

To find people on the Web to interview, you can begin by investigating your chosen topic by searching for that subject on a bookstore site to see if someone has written about it, or try some college or university sites—including your own—to see if any scholars are publishing research or teaching about the subject. You might find Web pages about these people, and/or their e-mail addresses. And there are Web sites devoted to finding experts—you can do a search for "finding experts" with one of the search tools.

One e-mail resource researchers use is the online mailing list or listserv. A listserv—this name comes from the name of a software program used to create a mailing list—is an online discussion group, and there are hundreds of them on all sorts of topics serious and not so serious. For example, there's a list that discusses solar cooking; another discusses the care and feeding of ferrets; another for Red Sox fans. But there are also lists for cancer survivors, for folks who want to discuss politics or environmental issues or human rights. You can "lurk" on a list, just reading all the messages that come through, and get ideas for subjects you might want to write about; you can contact individuals who send messages to the list to interview them; or you can post a message to the whole list asking for information about a subject. Some listservs archive messages on the Web so you can read though those, too.

To take part in an online mailing list, you subscribe to the list using your e-mail program; once you've subscribed, copies of all the messages anyone sends to the list are also sent to you, via your e-mail. You can reply to an individual who posts a message or to the whole list, or save or delete or print out a message. And you can unsubscribe, if you decide you don't want to keep getting messages posted to the list. You subscribe and unsubscribe, or send a message to a mailing list, simply by sending an e-mail message. **But the e-mail address you use to**

subscribe and unsubscribe is DIFFERENT from the one you use to send a message to the mailing list. You need to carefully check the information you get about the mailing list and make sure you're using the right one.

For example, to subscribe to the BOSOX list—Boston Red Sox Baseball Mailing List—I sent an e-mail message saying SUB BOSOX to the e-mail address <LISTSERV@APPLE.EASE.LSOFT.COM>. But to post a message to the discussion group, I'd have to send my e-mail to <BOSOX@APLLE.EASE.LSOFT.COM>.

There are sites on the Web where you can search for listservs dealing with subjects you are interested in; the information you get will include the addresses you can use to subscribe or unsubscribe to the list and to send messages to the list. Check out the following:

> **Topica: http://www.topica.com/**
>
> **Catalist, The Official Catalog of Listserv Lists: http://www.lsoft.com/lists/listref.html**
>
> **Tile.Net: http://www.Tile.net/**

When you get ready to post a message to a listserv, stop and consider—do you really want to post a message to the whole group, or only to the person who recently said something interesting that piqued your interest? Maybe it makes sense to send an e-mail only to that individual.

In that same vein, don't post a general question and expect listers to do your homework for you. You will get FLAMED, meaning someone will send you a nasty e-mail. Be specific with your requests for information, and make them when you've narrowed your topic down. Don't write this: I'm doing research into censorship of information on the Internet. What can you tell me? Instead ask this: Can anyone suggest good Web sites that discuss court cases that deal with censorship of information on the Internet?

People have busy lives; you want responses—and the more easily someone can help you out, the more likely it is that he or she will do so.

Listserv Netiquette

- When you are e-mailing, to the group or to an individual, put something in the subject line that will grab their attention. Don't just put the word "question."

- Don't write all in caps—it seems like you're screaming at the person. Do use correct grammar and punctuation. We tend to be more informal in e-mails than we are with other written communication, but if you are a serious researcher and writer and want to be treated like one, pay attention to how you write your e-mail.

- If you decide to unsubscribe to a listserv, do it the right way—and look it up again if you must. If you start sending unsubscribe messages to the wrong address, you're going to get flamed again, and nobody on that list is going to want to help you out again should you need them.

- Be clear about who you are and what you're doing. When you interview someone in person or over the phone, you explain who you are and why you want the interview. Do the same with online interviews. Tell people how you're going to use the information they give you.

- Should you use quotes from old postings? It's OK—but why do it? You have the poster's e-mail—get a firsthand response from him or her to your question, explaining why you want it, and use that. If you are going to use something old, you should get permission. This is someone else's thinking and writing you're using, remember; you can't just take it.

Newsgroups

Another type of online discussion group you might run into online is the USENET newsgroup. These are similar to listservs in that there are many of them and they are organized by subject. You don't use e-mail to participate in newsgroups: you use a newsreader program. (Your browser, the software program you use to look at World Wide Web pages, may have a newsreader program. With Netscape, for example, you choose the *Newsgroups* option from the *Communicator* menu; with Internet Explorer, you choose *Mail* and *News* from the *Tools* menu, then Read News. Or you can work on the Web: go to Google and click on the *Groups* link to get a page where you can search for groups by subject.

These groups tend to be somewhat less formal than listservs and so perhaps not quite as useful for research. But they're worth checking out.

If It's On the Internet, It's Free for the Taking—Right?

Wrong. One problem with the ease of gathering information you find on the Internet is that people have started to forget that taking someone else's ideas (or writing) and passing them off as your own, without attributing them to the other person, is plagiarism, and it's wrong. You don't lift paragraphs out of a book, put them into your paper, and not tell where they came from. You can't do that with Web pages either, or e-mail messages sent to a listserv, or postings to a newsgroup. You have to cite everything you find online, just as you do magazine articles or books.

There are many Web pages that offer information about citing Internet resources. The Purdue Online Writing Lab is one place to check, <owl.english. purdue.edu>. There's all sorts of great information for writers here. Or go to the Writing Center at Colorado State University Web page, www.writing. colostate.edu/index.cfm, and try the Interactive Demonstrations link. Purdue also offers a Web page listing online writing labs at <http://owl.english. purdue.edu/internet/owls/writing-labs.html>.

Another good resource is the list of online writing labs put together for the International Writing Centers Association: <http://iwca.syr.edu/IWCA/ IWCAOWLS.html>.

Some OWLS allow you to submit papers and get feedback from writing center staff, so do some exploring if that's something you'd like to try.

CHAPTER 12

Ask the Research Question

Groan. The research paper *again*. By sixth grade most of you have been as-signed a research paper and that assignment is repeated through high school, college, graduate school and at work where a marketing report, a lawyer's brief, a sports reporter's profile of a quarterback are all forms of the research paper. As a teacher, a writing consultant, and a writer myself, I see us all responding to these assignments by snorting and grubbing around like wild hogs in libraries and on the Internet, starting one way, going off another way, circling back, dis-tracted by every sniff and sound that might be interesting.

There is a secret to writing effective, readable research: It is the research ques-tion. It is not a topic that lies flat on the page: "the poor and immigration." It is not an idea: "the poor may have had difficulty paying their way to America." It is a question the researcher has to ask—and answer with information that may interest a reader.

During the thinking before writing, the reading, and the interviewing, the experienced writer/researcher keeps honing the question, sharpening it, limit-ing it so it can be answered.

Here is a family story I would like to research. My grandparents came to work in the woolen mills of Fall River, Massachusetts. They were indentured, a form of economic slavery where they had to work to pay out the expense of their travel. My grandparents met and decided to get married, but my great-grandmother became ill in Scotland. My grandmother took the savings they were going to use to get married, went back to Scotland and nursed her mother until death, then re-indentured herself to join my grandfather and, at last, get married.

This family anecdote could start me down many research trails:

- How did immigrants pay their way to America?
- How did immigrants in the late 1800s pay their way to America?
- How did immigrants in the late 1800s pay their way to work in the woolen mills in America?
- How did Scottish immigrants in the late 1800s pay their way to work in the woolen mills in America?
- How did Scottish immigrants in the late 1800s pay their way to work in the woolen mills in Fall River, Massachusetts?
- How did my father's parents pay their way to work in the woolen mills in Fall River, Massachusetts?

Each question breeds more questions but the researcher has to be realistic:

- Can I find adequate sources?
- Can I finish the research and have time to write to the deadline?

Answer the Research Question

Once the research question is asked, most us respond in the same way. We delay. We avoid. We put off. And we feel guilty. But as the great essayist E. B. White said, "Delay is natural to a writer. He is like a surfer—he bides his time, waits for the perfect wave on which to ride in. Delay is instinctive with him. He waits for the surge (of emotion? of strength? of courage?) that will carry him along." I no longer feel guilty about delay. I have learned that there are two forms of research:

First I perform *internal research* in which I discover what I knew that I didn't know I knew.

Then I carry out *external research* in which I discover what others know.

Of course they often interact. A specific detail or theory or experience or idea discovered through external research, reminds you of a memory, a half-thought, an idea, a feeling. An idea that unexpectedly rises up from your subconscious needs to be developed and documented by external research.

INTERNAL RESEARCH

It is always a mistake for me to plunge into external research without exploring the caves within my skull where experience, thoughts, feelings, questions, answers without questions have been stored for future use. What I know illuminates the research question, points me in directions I should go, and connects my life with the topic that had been distant and insignificant.

We best begin the adventure into the unknown by looking into ourselves. What do we already know about the topic? What have we experienced? What do we remember? What have others told us in conversation? What connections are there between the research question and what we already know?

School teaches us to look in the library, on a CD-ROM, on the Internet, in the laboratory, but the writer first looks inside at what is stored in memory. By writing, we make use of all that we have lived, felt, thought, know, if we respect and make use of what we have unconsciously stored in memory.

Memory

The first place from which to collect information is memory. You have recorded far more than you may realize on most subjects. When I remember my Grand-mother Murray, thin, stern, who had to work hard to smile, I think of the mills she worked in and the trips she made across the Atlantic. I make notes on how she spoke, how she related to her sons and daughters, the apartments in which she lived. She did not tell me stories of Scotland or working in the mills, so I would make notes on what her children told me. And I would recreate the last time I saw her. She was 89 and sick for the first time in her life, made ill, it turned out, by the tuberculosis that she picked up in the mill and which had laid dormant for 70 years. I held her hand as she died, at last a broad smile of relief on her grim face.

EXTERNAL RESEARCH

The research question tells you what you want to know. It is the beginning point for your adventure into the unknown. It is important to remember that it is only the beginning point. As part of the unknown becomes known, you will probably have to revise the research question. As you begin to learn about in-dentured immigrants, you may discover the terms were different for workers with different skills or that one ethnic group was paid more or less than an-other. You face a fork in the trail. You may have to take one or the other, nar-rowing and limiting your research question. Research is an adventure into the unknown and as part of the unknown becomes clear—farmers who knew how to repair tools were desired the most, Scots and Irish immigrants were paid differently—you realize you can't go in both direction at once. You have to revise the research question.

The external search extends the internal one, reaching out to library and com-puter online sources, authorities that can be reached in person, by mail, e-mail, by phone, on the Internet. It combines all the normal techniques of the scholar with on-the-scene research and interview techniques of the journalist, sociologist, anthropologist.

Reading

There are as many ways to read as there are to write, yet most people—prisoners of habit—usually read in the same way, at the same pace, no matter what the reading task. Never let school give you the impression that reading always has to be work, a purposeful job of collecting information. Reading can often be play: It is one of the best ways to leave the real world and escape to others.

Many people say that they read slowly but they remember what they read. The research I have read—and my own experience—denies this assertion. Of course, there are times when you have to—or want to—read slowly to savor or decode a text, but speed itself can be a benefit to reading. When you read fast, your effort concentrates the mind. You pay attention; your mind doesn't wander; you enter into the text and are carried along by the logic, the emotion, the music of language. Many times you have to read fast to allow the threads of the text to weave themselves into meaning. Read too slowly and you see only an individual thread or two, not the pattern evolving. Try it. Many schools teach speed-reading, but you can do it yourself by forcing yourself to read fast at the point of discomfort.

Stop here if you are a slow reader. Don't read each word individually but make yourself read in groups of words or lines, not single words. Move right ahead. See what happens afterward. You may have to go back and read a selection again or study one passage carefully, but then your attention will be concentrated on what you know you need to understand—and I suspect you will remember more than you expected to remember.

Fast reading can also produce immersion in the text where you lose yourself in the mood, the poetry, the sweep of the account that puts you on a street in a strange city, in the hospital waiting room, in combat. By reading fast, you get the feel of a subject and the sense of the writing itself.

Fast reading reveals connections that are central to a good piece of writing. Information that connects with other information in the text, in other texts, in your notes and drafts, in your mind. Remember that you are writing to discover meaning, to allow specific pieces of information—represented by words—to arrange themselves in many patterns until one reveals significance.

Skimming

Skimming the surface of sources you have to read is necessary. A fishing expert can scan the surface of a brook or inlet and sense where the fish are. The reader has to be able to skim the surface the same way. To collect information efficiently, the reader has to get through many books, articles, and reports to discover what needs close attention. Here's a checklist that may help you organize your reading by skimming:

- The title should suggest just what the book or article covers.
- A book's table of contents and an article's abstract may reveal their subjects.

- An author's biography may help you discover the relationship of the writer to your topic, as well as the author's authority to write on the subject.
- The index will lead you to discover specific references.
- The bibliography will send you to other sources to explore.
- Scan the text itself to find revealing section headings or key words.

The reading writer needs to develop these techniques, which, of course, may be applied to scanning newspapers or microfilm or files the writer finds through computer online research.

Interpreting

Once your eye has caught a key word or a specific revealing detail, interpret its meaning by putting it in the context of the piece you are reading or writing, or both. A college's brochure may boast, for example, that 60 percent of its student athletes actually graduate. One reader may be impressed by the statistic, while another may be appalled at the high percentage who fail to earn degrees.

Meaning never lies in isolated facts, but in context. It is the job of the reader to try to determine the information within the writer's context and then to use that information in a context that is appropriate and accurate.

INTERVIEW

The interview, in which you ask questions of an authority on your subject, is one of the basic tools for collecting significant information. Most people are shy about interviewing others. It helps to remember that the person who is being interviewed is being put in the position of an authority, and most people like to be authorities, to tell others what they know.

An interview can be informal—just a casual conversation—or formal—for which you make an appointment, prepare carefully, and probe deeply into the subject.

Prepare yourself for an interview by finding out as much as you can about the person you are going to interview. Prepare at least four or five principal questions you must ask in order to get the information you need. (Those are usually the questions the reader would like to ask if he or she were there.) Think of the reader; ask the reader's questions.

It's important to listen to what your interview subject has to say; don't go on asking the banker about interest rates after she has said the bank is closing. The interviewee may surprise you by what he or she says, and you have to decide on the spot which lead to follow.

Some interviewers take notes by hand, but it is more common to use a tape recorder. You should always ask permission to use a tape recorder on a telephone interview when the subject can't see the recorder. Face to face, when the recorder is visible, it is a courtesy, not a necessity, to ask permission to record. Most people prefer taped records to an interviewer's notes. Some even insist on the interviewer using a tape recorder—or make their own taped records of the interviews. You should, however, practice taking notes by hand, capturing the essence of what people say, even if you use a tape recorder. Sometimes the tape doesn't work, and if you're not taking notes yourself, you may become lazy and miss what's being said.

It's always best to interview a subject in person, so that you can see the expression on the face, the body language that emphasizes or contradicts what is being said, the environment in which the person lives or works, the way the person interacts with others. If you can't interview someone in person, then you may have to do so by telephone, mail, or even by e-mail.

How the Interview Can Lead to Writing

When you are researching any topic, from criminal justice to urban blight to environmental hazards, don't forget to use live sources. Talk to the people who are involved. They will not tell you the truth; they will tell you their own truths, and then you will have the challenge of weaving all the contradictions together into a meaning.

USE THE TELEPHONE AND THE MAIL

Organizations are also good sources of information. The library has directories of organizations that will help you find groups whose main function is distributing information on one side of a public issue—they are for or against abortion, distributing condoms to fight AIDS, allowing individuals to own handguns, saving wilderness areas from development. They will send pamphlets, brochures, or reports and answer your questions.

Governments—local, county, state, federal, and even international organizations such as NATO and the United Nations—have many groups that will provide you with reports, speeches, laws, regulations, proposals. Your local members of Congress can help you find the right agency and the office within the agency to contact.

USE THE LIBRARY

One of the greatest sources of material is the "attics" in almost every town, city, and state in the country, as well as in schools, universities, and the nation's capital itself. These attics collect books, magazines, newspapers, pamphlets, phonograph records, films, TV and audio tapes, photographs, maps, letters, journals—all the kinds of documents that record our past.

Every library has a card catalog and/or computer file that identifies resources available there and gives their locations. Frequent more than one library, if you can. When I was freelancing, I found it a good investment to pay for cards in four library systems. Libraries are elemental sources for a writer, as important as wind is to a sailor.

If you are not yet familiar with your library, most have tours that will show you how they work. Take the tour. Most libraries also have pamphlets that help you find what you need to know. Study such materials. Most of all, use the library.

Browse. Wander. Let the library reveal its resources to you. If you need help, ask for it. Cultivate a good working relationship with your librarian. Librarians are trained to be of service, and all of us who write are indebted to their patience and skills in finding information for us.

It's important when you find a reference in the library to make a note of all the essential information about it so that you can use the library easily the next time, and so that you can list the source in footnotes or a bibliography. Even if you write something that doesn't have footnotes or a bibliography, you should know exactly where you got the material so that you can respond to questions from teachers, editors, or readers.

Usually you should record the author's last name first, then first name, then the middle initial, the title of the work (underlined if it is a book, or within quotation marks if it is an article), the publisher, the place of publication, the date, the page numbers, and, for your own use, the library reference number together with the name of the library. Such notes tell you where the information is. It's important to keep a record of the books and other sources you found worthless, so you won't go over them again, as well as the ones that are particularly valuable. Most research doesn't result in big breakthroughs, but a slowly growing understanding of the subject.

USE THE INTERNET

As Lisa Miller in Chapter 11 has described, the personal computer and the Internet have radically changed how we search for information for writing, but we shouldn't forget the important skills human beings developed long before the computer that are still valuable today.

OBSERVE

Don't overlook one of the writer's primary sources of information: first-hand observation. See how many of your five senses you can use to capture information—and to communicate that information to your reader.

Go to a place that is important to your topic. It may not be the place where you write. You may be writing about the Continental Congress in which our nation was born; you can't visit it, but you will understand that process better if you visit a legislature, a city council session, a town meeting.

AWARENESS INCREASES AWARENESS

As you train your eye, you will discover how much you notice: the way an old lady dresses for her weekly trip out to the supermarket, how the candy and gum is placed so it can be grabbed by children riding high in their seats in supermarket carts, the look of boredom on the face of the cashier as she enthusiastically greets you. I am never bored because my eye makes the world interesting, exposes the extraordinary in the ordinary, the significant in the trivial.

Remember that although you may be writing out of your curiosity, the research report is written to serve others who will explore the same topic. We all stand on the shoulders of those who have gone before. The research paper should be written in a clear, direct, objective, and professional voice. You are adding to humankind's accumulated knowledge.

Some disciplines, corporations, and agencies have special forms that those in that particular world expect. Check to see if there is such a form and if so, use it. Each item should have attribution within the text or in a footnote. Why? Because future researchers may need to visit your sources. The same thing is true of the bibliography. Our research articles and books are designed to serve the reader by delivering specific information that can be used by readers in their searches into their own unknowns.

DESCRIBE THE TERRITORY TO BE EXPLORED

As I have said, my father's father and mother came to this country by a system of indenture in which they had to pay off the cost of the trip by working in a mill.

How did the indenture system work? I have heard that they not only had to pay the mill owners back for their passage, but for their living quarters in factory housing that was required as was the fact they had to buy groceries and clothes at a factory store.

State the Question

What was the system of indenturing immigrant mill workers?

Focus the Question

Was the system of indenturing immigrant workers as "profitable" for the workers as it was for the mill owners?

Demand a Specific Answer

How long did it take Scottish mill workers who were indentured to New England Mills to pay off their indentured debt?

Limit the Question

Were the indentured Scottish mill workers in Fall River, MA, between 1880 and 1900 treated fairly?

Is It Significant?

Yes. We know about racial slavery but few of us know that our ancestors came here through a system of economic slavery.

What Are Your Sources?

U.S. census data on immigration; books of the subject; Fall River birth, voting, citizenship, and death records; historical groups and libraries in Fall River and the surrounding area. Each source will lead to more sources.

Do You Have Access to Your Sources?

Not yet, but I am contacting the sources and asking them if the records I need are available and open to me.

What Method Will You Use?

I will try to depend on primary sources such as actual indenture contracts, town and mill records. I hope to find first-hand accounts of indentured workers.

The research question will keep changing as you research, but to be effective you must keep limiting the question so you can complete the research and have time to write before deadline. To do this you should start writing drafts on what you are finding. These early fragmented drafts will tell you what you know, what you need to know, and start you learning what the information you have found means.

■ SHOPTALK ■

I'm okay with exploring my own life. That's no problem. But what about someone else's life? What right do I have to barge into their world asking questions?

Just thinking about this issue means that you have all your writer's senses attuned to the people around you, that you are being sensitive in the truest sense of the word! You are also feeling the full ethical weight of what it means to be a writer.

It's true. You certainly don't want to trample on someone else's privacy in search of material. But you don't want to look at people as completely isolated beings either. Lives bump up against one another. We make sense of our own lives by comparing them with others—by watching people live, solve problems, celebrate successes, and survive tragedies. Just because we observe, interview, and write about people doesn't mean that we are voyeurs or have a sadistic urge to see others exposed or in tears. It only means that we seek a common ground between our world and theirs, that we tread the terrain between one life and the next in search of what's similar and what's different.

Besides, writing is thinking, and thinking means asking questions. That's why good writing requires barging around a bit. Be sensitive. But also be inquisitive.

What if I don't get other people's lives right when I write about them?

There are no right or wrong ways to portray people; there are only different perspectives. Certainly, you don't want to be vicious or uncaring in the way you gather information or write about others. As long as you are not consciously harming people, you shouldn't worry about asking questions or examining how other people live and what they think.

What if people won't give me information?

Give them a reason to give you the information. Flattery is a good reason. If that doesn't work, then you have to find another good reason: Do they want to help educate you? Do they want to persuade? Do they want revenge? Do they want to raise money for their cause? Do they want to defend themselves?

Some people simply want to talk. Many people go through their lives unheard. This is often true of the elderly or people whose jobs or positions in society don't generally put them in the limelight. People like this are often thrilled that you consider their input significant, and they are usually happy to help you out.

There are many reasons why people will give out information; you just have to find the one that will unlock the information you need.

How do you know who's an authority and that what they tell you is true?

If you are interviewing people face to face, it's a good idea to find at least three sources for any important data. It's not so much that people lie as that they're uninformed; they believe what they're telling you, but it may not be true. As a researcher, you have to keep your common sense in good working order. When you are suspicious about a statement or a detail, pay attention to that hunch and check it out.

If you are getting your data from the Internet, checking sources may not be so easy. Web pages, chat rooms, bulletin boards—all of these sources may contain interesting information, but there is usually no single way of judging its accuracy.

Always question what you read over the Internet (or for that matter in any printed text!). If you can, find information about the same issue from several different sources. You may also need to qualify your sources as you write up your data; let your reader know which you think are accurate and which you question.

> So I should stick with only official sources, right? I should always go straight to the top for information?

If you want an expert on a particular subject, the best way to find the authority is to ask the people in that business who's the best. Ask nurses in the hospital, police officers on the force, teachers in the school, scientists in the lab with whom you should talk to to find out about your subject. They work with all the authorities.

They are also authorities themselves, and this is an important point. Never underestimate the value of information you can get from those who are not "top dogs." These people have perspectives that may very well differ from those of official sources, and if you want to get a complete picture of an organization or site, you shouldn't forget these "everyday" people. They keep things running, and they also operate in the thick of activity instead of shutting themselves away in offices. While they may not be able to give you official documentation about your topic, they will certainly have an abundance of personal experiences to add to your information. Combined with other sources, interviews with these people will help you round out your research.

> What if there are no books written on my topic?

That doesn't mean that your topic is not worth writing about or exploring. It may mean that you have a unique perspective on your topic.

Writers who are just beginning to explore often become discouraged when they find that no single "authority" has written about what interests them. They forget that exploring means searching and synthesizing clues and information. It means going on an adventure of discovery rather than a package tour of a well-known land. It means being a detective rather than a collector of facts and figures.

Rather than finding a single book that will cover your topic, find many different sources that refer to the subject you want to write about. You might check out data in magazines or newspapers, on the Internet, or in government documents, for example. You might interview people and send away for information from certain organizations.

> Okay. I've gathered different sources and interviewed lots of people, but none of them agrees with any other on anything! Now what?

Don't be discouraged if all your sources don't say the same thing. Gather as many different perspectives as you can on your topic, and arrive at your own conclusions. That's the whole purpose of exploring. It's also one of the main reasons we write.

But first you will want to organize all your data so you can be clear about the issues and points of disagreement. To do this, draw a line down the middle of a page in your daybook. On the left, sum up very briefly all of the arguments of your various sources. Next to each argument on the right-hand side of the page, sum up in one word or sentence the main issue it addresses.

Now go back and organize your sources according to issues, making sure to note just how each agrees or disagrees with other sources. When it comes time to write your paper, you will have a clearer idea about the issues and the points of disagreement, and you will probably have formulated your own opinion from reviewing the issues and arguments.

I can't write using an outline. Never could and never will. I freeze when I see one.

If you can organize your paper without an outline, don't make one. Some people never use outlines, and others only do when they're faced with an unfamiliar writing task. Many writers let their pieces shape themselves and then impose structures on them. Do what you feel is best for you, but don't be afraid to experiment either.

What if I have a teacher who wants me to stick to an outline when I want to change it after I begin writing?

You may want to talk to your teacher about your new ideas. Have your new outline on hand for him or her to look at. If your teacher still insists that you stick to your original outline, then you will have to explore your topic within certain perimeters; these perimeters may not be what you would like, but they will still allow you to think and write critically about your topic.

Some teachers fear that if their students deviate from outlines, they will write papers that are disorganized and hard to read. These instructors are concerned that their students will not learn enough about their topics by writing this way. Another teacher might want you to discover very specific information about a topic and so ask you to adhere to a specific outline.

Whatever reasons your teacher has for requiring a strict outline, you can still explore within those restrictions. You can draw information from a variety of sources, experiment with point of view and angle, and choose a focus within the perimeters of the outline.

So much information is available on the World Wide Web—why do I need to go to the library, or to anywhere else? I can even take virtual tours of places online!

The Internet is a great research tool, and you need to learn to use it well. But you can't find everything online. For now, at least, you still have to visit libraries or museums or other archives to get some information, especially from primary sources. And there's a serendipity to research at an actual site that you can't quite recreate online—finding the book you looked up in the library records and then seeing, on the shelf, another two or three books down that looks more interesting, or wandering through a museum exhibit for one object and finding another you didn't know existed that really grabs you. When you're browsing a Web site, you're often looking only at a collection of links concerned with one narrow subject; when you do a search on the Web, you get a list of names of Web pages but not much else that will lead you off your already chosen path.

And while you've got video and audio on the Web, you've got to really go places to smell, taste, or touch. Also, you're getting someone else's interpretation of what a place or event is like. Use the Internet—but get out and see the world for yourself too.

How do I know the people at the other end of my e-mails are who they say they are?

Try doing a Google search for their names and see what comes up. Also, remember that if an e-mail address ends in "edu," that person's e-mail account comes through an educational institution; "gov," a government agency. If someone says he or she works for a certain university, company, research institution, government agency or whatever, or the address you see on the e-mail indicates this, do a Web search to find a site for that organization or business, then search for that person's name on the site. Finally, if you are really concerned about who you're e-mailing, go low-tech—ask for a phone number and give him or her a call.

I've found tons of information on the Web. Now what do I do with all of it?

Evaluate what you've found, using the criteria mentioned earlier in Chapter 11, and weed out anything you can't really use. Then go through what you've got, carefully, noting quotes or facts you think you might definitely want to use in your own piece. Become a mini-expert by doing this; be able to talk to a friend about the subject, giving your own opinion about it. Write out what you think; then go back through the stuff you gathered to find information to back up what you have to say. Essentially, you're telling the reader what makes you believe what you believe.

■ IN THE WRITER'S WORKSHOP ■

ON YOUR OWN

1. Take your daybook to a public space, such as a restaurant or cafe. Write down as accurately as possible the conversations of people who pass by or converse at tables in your vicinity. Pay attention to the sound and rhythm of speech and record as many comments and dialogues as you can. Don't worry about following any one conversation from beginning to end. Just try to catch the gist of what people are saying.

2. Go to yard sales and list interesting or unusual items you see for sale. Find out as much as you can about the histories of the objects, who they have belonged to and the people who are selling them. Observe the people who buy the objects, and listen in on the comments they make about them. Between sales, sit down somewhere and write about the most interesting items, people and conversations you've observed and listened to. Be on the lookout for humorous remarks, surprise purchases, and odd or interesting characters. List or write about as many of them as you can.

3. Draft a family history. Interview relatives and family friends. Use the Internet to look up genealogies and Web pages of relatives, or go to the library's genealogy section. Make a family tree or start a family newsletter that focuses on a different aspect or branch of the family every month.

4. Explore a topic through different genres of writing. If you are interested in football, for example, find novels, poems, movies, plays, essays, songs, newspaper columns, editorials, television shows, or public records that pertain to the game. Select three pieces written in three different genres, and report to the class about how they are different from or similar to each other.

5. Walk through a cemetery and observe and record as many details as possible: names and dates, sizes and conditions of headstones, genders of the deceased, relationships, years lived, the vaults, statues and tombstones, the cemetery landscape itself. Write a history of the cemetery just from what you observe. Do you think some "residents" were richer than others? Later, go to the church or public office that keeps the cemetery's records and read them for more information. Visit your local library, and check out newspaper stories and other printed sources about the cemetery and the deceased. Then revise your history according to the new details you gather.

6. Think of a famous or historical local figure you want to find out more about. Begin at the library with biographies about the person, and look in the online database or card catalog for general information about your subject. Ask reference librarians what related materials are available. Then contact your local historical society and ask them where the personal papers and diaries of the person you have chosen are located and whether you can gain access to them. Such papers, called primary sources, are often housed in university or local town libraries or special museum archives. Sometimes you need official permission to read them but most institutions will cooperate with you if you are doing research.

7. Go to the library and use Infotrac or a similar computerized database to track a story in newspapers and magazines. Use other databases to see what has been written about the story in literary and academic journals. Listen to various news broadcasts on the radio. Watch national news programs to see how they report the story. Gather as much information from as many different sources as

possible and keep track of which sources yield the most and which the least. Pay particular attention to the different angles and perspectives each source takes.

8. Pick up a local newspaper and focus on an issue being debated in your town. Research the issue by visiting government offices, Web sites, and local libraries. You might also want to check with the office of deeds, wills, and other records. Town libraries often keep extensive records on civic debates. Call the town or city hall and get a list of public offices, check a Web site for your city or town, or look in the phone book under the listings for your local government. These sources will give you a better idea of where to start.

9. Explore your local or school government. Attend city council or student senate meetings, and keep up on the issues by looking in newspapers and listening to reports on local radio and television. Tune in to the local talk shows and interview officials and citizens. Keep a log of issues that interest you and details that pertain to them. Use your writer's eye and other senses to take in the whole scene and analyze the people and debates involved.

10. Browse through bibliographies. These are lists of books and magazines by other authors whom writers consult when exploring and gathering information about their topics. Go to the library and select a book about your topic; copy the bibliography (usually located in the back of the book or at the end of each chapter). Exchange bibliographies with a classmate and discuss the different angles and perspectives that writers listed in the bibliographies have taken on your topic. Circle on the bibliographies a few of the books or periodicals you want to look at. Locate these materials and consult their bibliographies.

11. Visit the special collections departments, rare book rooms, or archives or your school or town library. These departments often house books and other materials pertaining to local or university history. Some include first editions of local authors' works or the letters and diaries of local literary and historical figures. Explore these collections by listing in your daybook as many of the resources as they offer and as you can and the possible topics for writing and research they suggest.

WITH A WRITING PARTNER

12. Paste interesting newspaper articles or personal artifacts in your daybook. Share your daybook with a writing partner and ask him or her to choose at least three items from it and to interview you about their significance and what prompted you to choose them. Ask your partner to take notes while you talk and get a copy of these notes for your daybook.

WITH A GROUP

13. With a group of classmates, take a sensory tour of a site—a favorite eating spot on campus, a freshman dorm, a local bookstore, a neighborhood, or

perhaps a place of historical significance. Ask each person in the group to be responsible for one sense—seeing, hearing, tasting, smelling, or touching—and to record as many sensory details as possible. Reconvene as a group and write up a portrait of the site.

14. Choose three of the most helpful or unusual sources you have found and write them on the board in class. When your classmates have done the same, go around the room and describe your sources and how you have used them. Choose six sources from the board that you have not yet used but would like to try.

15. Write an exploratory draft on your topic and pass out copies in a small group. Ask your classmates to comment on the quality of the information they find in your piece and where they want to see more. Have them suggest sources that might be useful to you.

INTERVIEWING OTHERS

16. If you have older students in your class, explore an event or events that happened during their lives (such as the Civil Rights movement, the Challenger explosion, the first music videos on MTV). First write down in your daybook everything you think you know about the event, and then come up with a list of questions to ask your older classmates. Pay special attention to the language they use, listening for the slang or jargon of the period you are studying. Ask questions about things you don't understand, but also let your interviewees focus on whatever they want.

17. Visit a nursing home or senior citizen's apartment and ask to meet residents who want company. Meet them individually or invite them to gather as a group. Tell them that you are interested in hearing about their lives and the eras in which they lived. As you listen to their stories, jot down all the facts and details you can, asking questions as you go along. When your interviewees are comfortable with you, ask them if they would mind allowing you to see personal snapshots, letters, or diaries. Make a commitment to visit them once a week over a semester and offer them services in exchange for their time and stories, such as rides to church or the hairdresser, or a steady arm for a walk around the block.

18. Treat "invisible" people as significant sources of information. Such folks include custodians, food-service workers, clerical help in university offices, homeless people on the street—people we often tend to dismiss as insignificant. Ask them questions about their lives, and invite them to tell stories about what they see, hear, and experience around them every day.

ON THE INTERNET

19. Using a Web search tool, do a keyword search for information on your topic. Use some of the techniques outlined in Chapter 11 to narrow your

search, if necessary, or try more than one search tool to see if you get the same results from each. Browse through some of the Web sites, and print out, bookmark, or write up a list of information and Web sites that interest you. Share these with your classmates.

20. Choose three or four Web sites you find after doing a Web search for your topic. On your own or with classmates, browse these sites, making note of what you like about the sites and what you don't like. For instance, is it easy to find exactly what you want on the site, or do you have to spend a lot of time trying different links before you get to the information you need? Are the graphics interesting and useful, or just decoration? Is it easy to figure out where the information on the site comes from? Work with classmates to list criteria for "good" sites and problems you find with "bad" sites.

21. Evaluate Web sites you and your classmates find using the criteria described earlier in Chapter 11. Make a master list for the class of useful, interesting, and reliable sites you've all found.

22. Check out an online writing lab, or OWL—many universities have great ones on the Web, featuring advice about researching and writing. Tell your classmates about any sites you find helpful.

Begin Writing

If writing a book is impossible, write a chapter.
If writing a chapter is impossible, write a page.
If writing a page is impossible, write a paragraph.
If writing a paragraph is impossible, write a sentence.
If writing a sentence is impossible, write a word and
teach yourself everything there is to know about that
word and then write another, connected word and see
where the connection leads.

RICHARD RHODES

It's like being on a high board, looking down to a cold,
chilly pool. Then I give myself a little push. The water
isn't as cold as I thought.

NEIL SIMON

CHAPTER 13

Take Your Eye Off the Ball

When anyone praises a researcher, I never see in my mind a happy person in the library stacks laughing, smiling, giggling, turning to a colleague to share a ridiculous fact or quotation. I imagine research is always serious business. The researcher's face is grim, brows furrowed, eyes squinting along a trail to wherever the assignment is expected to go. No surprises. No happy accidents. No unexpected connections.

The biggest failure of most researchers is that they do keep their eyes on the ball, never allowing thought, curiosity, imagination to roam off course where the most important fact may lay waiting to be found. Finding expected facts and predicted meaning satisfies. Teachers and administrators are comfortable with predictability. "Don't you ever surprise me, " says the insecure boss.

Writers, however, are self-recruited from the bored kids in the back of the classroom, hungry for surprise. They take pleasure in accident, instructive failure, what is disloyal and contradictory, what is not supposed to be true, what changes, what confuses.

But you said the carefully planned research question is the secret of effective research.

You have to aim, to have a plan, a sense of direction you return to when you stray off course but if you don't stray off course you will only write what you—and your readers—already know. The researchers that attract our attention and hold it have taken advantage of what they—and you the reader—did not expect. Surprise waits in ambition along the road of intent. As the novelist Ernest J. Gaines explained, "A novel is like getting on a train to Louisiana. All you know at the moment is that you're getting on the train, and you're going to Louisiana. But you don't know who you're going to sit behind, or in front of, or beside; you don't know what the weather is going to be when you pass through certain areas of the country; you don't know what's going to happen South; you don't know all these things, but you know you're going to Louisiana."

That's the contradiction: You have to have a research question to move forward with traditional methods but you also have to see what is off track, behind the bushes, in the shack, around the corner, reflected in a window pane, what is right in front of your eyes unseen until the moment of recognition you did not expect.

Writers work on the side streets, trading in the obvious that is not obvious until they call attention to it, in the commonplace which becomes uncommon when it appears in an essay, poem, novel, screen play.

As a searcher for meaning through language, I keep in training for the unexpected connection. This book and others of mine develop the idea of the writing process, that effective writing is usually the result of a sequential series of activities and attitudes. I was not, for example, studying composition when I had the idea of process; I was doing a story of the early intercontinental missiles and discovered system engineering. When I started teaching I saw that my students needed to learn to pre-write, write, and rewrite, a systems engineering concept of making writing. This research technique is called *serendipity* from a story by Horace Walpole years ago who made up a story of what travelers to Serendip discovered on their journey.

If you are researching a story about the young people who are condemned to a life of crime and prison, you may see that few read. That seems normal, unimportant. These kids hang out in alleys not libraries. But someone tells you that they have an unusually high number of reading problems, so you may want to research this to find out when these problems appeared, but were not treated. They were excluded from the system of education. A new research question: "What role do reading problems play in the development of young criminals?"

A specific detail—common, ordinary, obvious—may change the direction of the whole research project. As you draft the bibliography on your research project telling how a corporation has avoided contaminating the rivers and lakes of northern Maine you realize that all your sources come from books of the same publisher. A bit more research and you see that the publishing company is owned by the corporation that owns the polluting plants. Now the research paper is not on how a corporation protects nature but how they have subsidized research to document their defense against environmental charges.

Surprise brings its own problems for the writer that have to be answered in the practical conditions in which the researcher/writer works. The new material has to be fitted into the original or revised research question or put aside for the next project. The research supervisor has to be kept informed so they are not surprised by a result they do not expect.

Most of all you have to create new connections between the contradictory materials you have discovered. Researching and writing above all are thinking, revealing to yourself and your reader the significance of what your research has produced. So be brave and take your eye off the ball.

CHAPTER 14

The Writer's Eye

We all have a writer's eye. We see with that eye—the well-dressed woman who shoves her way to the head of the express lane with twice the limit of groceries, the driver who apparently cannot see over the dashboard, the grandmother, mother, and child in the supermarket who are all tattooed with snakes, the teacher who reads lecture notes head down, never looking a student in the eye. Most of the time we do not know how we will use those mental snapshots when we write, but the images are filed in memory ready for us when we need them to develop or document a draft.

What we learn when we write is that our mental camera was taking pictures of what we did NOT see at the time, were not aware of seeing. The professional basketball player does not know he has been recording the moves of a teammate until he needs to pass to him and he is there, moving toward where the pass will go. We do not think we saw anything before the car went off the road, but then realize we saw the trees rushing by, the first tipping of the car before it turned over, the terrified Labrador trying to escape the station wagon's back end. In fact, the mental camera has taken many more pictures that we did not see than the few we saw.

I have a poor quiz show memory, but when I start writing, the pictures I did not know my brain had taken in come to mind. Don't believe me? Try it. Pick an event that was important to you—your first crush, your first class on the first day of college, your first trip in an airplane, your first trip to the emergency room for stitches. Write a few lines on a three-by-five card or small piece of paper. Don't think before writing; think by writing. When you finish that card in three to four minutes, take another card and without looking at the first one, write again, repeat it at least another time. Then look at the cards and see how much more you "see" on each card.

I am going back to first grade at the Massachusetts Fields School in Wollaston, MA, in 1930. Since these are quick drafts, I have not corrected any of my typos.

1. I see a large woman with a grim, determined look, striding down Vassal Street. Her right hand is locked around the left wrist of a young boy who has to hop every once in awhile to keep up. The school is red brick. His mother takes him to edge of the asphalt playground and then shoves him away into a seas of children whose mothers had not taken them to school.

> *I should not be surprised that Mother took me to school, but I am. Her grip on my hand is so tight it hurts. I could write to explore the relationship between my mother and school, but I want to see what another quick write will bring.*

2. I find my classroom and see my teacher. Miss Kelly. One of the Irish Catholics Mother warned me about. She is as big woman like my mother, the same attack bosom, the same red splotched cheeks, the same tight, angry mouth. I had never seem a classroom, There were row upon row of desks and chairs nailed to the floor. She gave a seat in the front row where she could "keep an eye on me." I climbed up to the chair. My feet dangled, did not reach the floor.

> *When we write about our childhood it is difficult to place ourselves at an early age, eliminating all we have learned since that time. Usually we write about our childhood, not only creating it and putting the reader in the moment, but also seeing our actions then from an adult perspective.*

3. When I go back in memory to my elementary school playgrounds, one hard, skin scrapping asphalt, one hard, skin scrapping grassless earth. I see circles of boys crowded togethet, shouting, jumping with sxctement moving closer but allowing a hollow circle in the middle thyat I can not see. No matter, I know what is happenijng. One boy has bene shoved into the circle, then another. They have bneen told to fight and they push each other and then one talkes a swinbg and another. When recess is over there will be at least one bloody nose.

> *I have not been on a playground for seventy years, but the writer's eye returns me to those dreaded tests of manliness. And we are told that only this generation is violent. I realize I have a potential essay there in which I compare the violence of those days with today. As I describe I will discover what I think and feel about those not-always good old days.*

4. I scan the playground and see tall, austere Mr. Sampson the principal, striding by the fighting circle. He does not stoop. Then I see the teachers assisgned to recess duty, all woman but ion man, all standing with their arms crossed across their chests. They just watch. Once I hidden in the school during recess.

But was found and dragged out to the "playground" I so feared We had fighting before school in the morning, during morning recess, at lunch when we headed back, after lunch there were more fights and still more when school let out. This was normal behavioorsr, not onlpy allowed but encoiuraged by the teachers as a part of the information curriculum.

> *My writer's eye has made me see what I had forgotten or thought I had forgotten and the more I write about these fights, the more the details will come back. I just saw a boy pull a stocking cap down over his opponent's eyes and then when he was blinded, hitting him again. I would not have known I knew that had I not done this quick write.*

What the Writer Sees

Central to exploration is the writer's eye. The writer's eye sees what is, what isn't, what was, what may be. An athlete's eye is inherited. For years I went to an eye doctor who treated many players on the Boston Celtics basketball team. I asked him if their eyes, not just their height and jumping ability, differ from those of the rest of us. He held up a finger far out of my peripheral vision and explained that all the Celtics could see the finger that I could not.

The athlete's eye is genetic, but the writer's eye can be developed. You can train yourself to see revealing specifics. A revealing specific is a detail, fact, quotation, word, phrase that gives off extra meaning. The male politician on the platform may pay close attention to a series of speakers, then look away, paying no attention, when the next speaker is a woman. It is an accurate detail that gives a clue to his attitude toward women. The screaming of the basketball coach that confuses his own players, the students who sit together at lunch and the ones who want to sit with them but don't, the trustees' decision to spend money for a hockey rink but not for faculty salaries are all revealing specifics.

The writer's eye collects the concrete information that readers like: a statistic, a fact, a direct quote, a specific act. Concrete details give a draft liveliness and authority. Writing seems to ring with authority when it is specific, but specific details need to be backed up by concrete information.

The writer's eye gathers information, using all the senses—the way the overhead light glints off the surgeon's scalpel, the eyes that reveal so much—and so little—above the surgical masks, the smell of medicine and sterilizing steam, the brass taste of fear, the feeling of helplessness a patient experiences when lashed down on a surgical table, the comfort of the nurse's touch.

Lying there, with part of your body asleep but your brain wide awake, you hear what isn't said, see what doctors don't do as well as what they do, the looks that pass from doctor to nurse to technician. You feel something of what it must have been like to have surgery before modern anesthesia, what surgery may be like with the further development of the laser. You see what is, what is not, what was, what may be.

The writer's eye sees patterns. Specifics have to add up, to lead the reader toward a conclusion, to answer the tough question, "So what?" You see the way the police stop the driver of a Lexus that goes through a red light but treat her with courtesy. Then you see the police stop a battered Chevy for the same offense, make the driver get out of the car and slam him up against the hood, while another officer calls in to see if the car is stolen or if the driver has a record. You are aware of the skin color of the second driver and begin to remember a relative's prejudiced comments at a family dinner when you were a child, how the teacher commented when an African American student showed up in an elective math class—"No special treatment here, Darius,"—what the history textbook said about the Holocaust. You connect all such specifics into a pattern of prejudice.

I always keep in mind E. M. Forster's advice, "Only connect," wise instruction for the writer who deals with context and implication. Specific details are not enough by themselves. The way the police handle a suspect must be connected with a pattern of police brutality, training, prejudice, whether or not the treatment is appropriate or excessive.

The writer sees past and future. My mind turned backward in a recent "Now and Then" column, when I wrote of looking out at snowy woods and seeing snowball fights when I was a boy, and firefights during the Battle of the Bulge in World War II when I was a young paratrooper; I recalled my first sled rides with Uncle Will and a snow hut I built as a boy. I walk by a new building on campus and see within it the memory of the old building on the same spot that was torn down. Cows turn into parked cars, and I see the future shopping mall destroying the farm. The writer is always looking backward and forward, studying the present to discover the causes of events and to imagine their effects. The writer lives in a changing world, seeing what is, what was, what may be. As Robert Cormier says,

> What if? What if? My mind raced, and my emotions kept pace at the sidelines, the way it always happens when a story idea arrives, like a small explosion of thought and feeling. What if? What if an incident like that in the park had been crucial to a relationship between father and daughter? What would make it crucial?
>
> Well, what if the father, say, was divorced from the child's mother and the incident happened during one of his visiting days? And what if . . .

The writer's eye instructs; it sees meaning where the writer did not see meaning. Writers write from what they don't know as much as from what they do know.

As I write about my war experience—how much distance there had to be between us when we dug in along the front line, how we kept from getting to know replacement soldiers because most of them would be wounded or dead soon, how we could not admit our terror to those around us—I begin to remember how lonely infantry combat was, how little comradeship there was at the front lines. Language defines, develops, and changes my world.

The writer's eye provides the abundance the writer needs during writing. When you write about a person, place, or event important to you, you begin to remember details you didn't know you had stored in memory years before. I start to describe my first car and remember the high, crooked gearshift, the feel of the accelerator pedal; I hear the rasp when I apply the hand break; I smell the oil and gas and exhaust and the city smell in the wind that strikes my face. The more details I write, the more I have to write. This marvelous eye gives the writer a resource of revealing detail. What is most magical to me is that my writer's eye saw all sorts of specifics of which I was not aware until I wrote.

Stop reading, and take a piece of paper. Return in your mind to an important experience in your life, and using all your senses list the details you remember. Soon your writer's eye will reveal what you didn't know you saw at the accident scene, in the locker room, on the first day of school in a new town, last Saturday night.

CHAPTER 15

The Focusing Line

I always feel I have not written enough, but others tell me I am a productive writer. About six years ago I began keeping a daily count of how many words I wrote, and in those six years I have produced a million and a half words. But we're not talking quality here—just quantity. Quality is always the product of quantity, and generally comes later in the process.

My secret is that even before I practice the writer's essential rule—ass in chair—I come to the desk with an igniting line or image in my head. All the time I have been away from the desk, my mind has circled the next day's writing task. This is not the hard, disciplined thinking that some writing tasks that many academic disciplines demand, but a drifty, wandery, dreamy kind of thinking in which language and images pass through my brain like shooting stars seen and gone.

Not to worry. If they are important they will return again and again as you prepare to write and as you produce a first draft. The line may be a fragment of language, rarely a sentence, sometimes a word, or an image or statistic or fact, something that produces an itch that you want to explore. And if this line is caught and pursued, it will provide the focus that will guide you during the writing.

When we snap a picture, we focus on the spot where the most interesting or revealing detail may be captured in a photograph. It is the same with writing. The writer may focus on an event, a moment in a person's life, a decision, an act, a discovery, a cause or an effect, a problem or a solution, but it always defines a place where the writer expects to find significance by writing.

My primary focusing technique is the *focusing line*. The focusing line is the words the writer uses to capture the focus, the starting point of the drafting process. It is more often a phrase—"an ordinary war"—than a sentence— "I write in my daybook that I had an ordinary war and think of the horrors that war makes ordinary." The sentence prematurely closes in on the subject, limiting what I may say; the phrase opens up the subject, stimulating me to think about unexpected connections and territories to explore.

The focusing line is often written in rather ordinary language, but it captures some tension, conflict, problem, irony, contradiction in the subject. This element gives the writer the energy to pursue the potential meaning that lies within the as-yet-unwritten draft.

The focusing line is often confused with a thesis statement; a lead (the first lines of a piece of writing); or an introduction. A thesis statement implies the final meaning of the writing to be written. A thesis statement may be helpful if the writer—and the instructor or editor—are willing to change it radically or abandon it when the draft contradicts it. Too often, a thesis statement implies that the thinking is done and the writer has agreed to a contract to deliver on the thesis statement. Writing is thinking; writing is discovery of new meaning. Therefore, I prefer the focusing line, which implies thinking during writing.

A *lead*, a journalistic term for the beginning or opening of a piece, often evolves from the focusing line but it doesn't need to. The focusing line inspires the piece of writing; the lead is designed to draw the reader into the text.

An introduction tells the reader what the text is going to say or why the writer has written the text or what methods the writer has used to research the subject. It places the cart before the horse for most readers, though. They will be put off by being given information they often do not know they need to know. The skillful writer weaves in the introductory information the reader needs to know at the moment in the draft where the reader needs to know it.

IGNITION

The spark that starts my writing engine occurs when I translate the images and the specific information I observe, read, or remember—as well as my feelings and thoughts in reaction to them—into words in my head or in my daybook. I walk around, as we all do, talking to myself.

> Those kids are teasing the golden retriever tied to a long chain. The chain yanks him back. That must hurt. His tail is wagging and he seems to be barking happily but I wonder. They run into his territory, then dash away, offer him a stick, then pull it out of reach, never let him get the stick. What did that ancient Greek, Bion, say, let's see, "Though boys throw stones at frogs in sport; the frogs do not die in sport, but in earnest." I'd like to give that to the dog. He could put it up on the wall of his doghouse. I remember the uncles teasing me at family dinners, tickling me while every body else laughed.

Maybe that last sentence is a focusing line. No, not for me. Not this time. It doesn't itch enough. I don't need to pursue it. I allow my mind to run its strange course, as erratic as a dog following this scent and then another and another.

Those kids teasing the dog are the same age as the kids I saw on the TV news last night. Was it the Middle East? No matter. Their play is real. But childhood is tough. Learning about falling and the monsters in the closet at night and parents divorcing and pets dying and trying to figure out why people laugh at you when it isn't funny. Childhood—serious business.

There's a focusing line: Childhood—serious business.

Surprise is what tells us we have a focusing line. We think of something that is different from what we expect: Childhood is not all play for the child. The focusing line—childhood is serious business—has tension, conflict, surprise imbedded in it. We think—or try to think—of childhood as a happy time, but often it is not. When we smile at children at play, they may not be playing but tasting real terror, rejection, fear. It is hard work being a kid. I do not know what I have to say about this subject. I will only discover what I have to say if I write a draft. But I have the focusing line: Childhood is serious business.

That focusing line may not appear in the final draft, but it is the starting point. It is something I need to think about, something that may produce more thought, more surprise, first for me, then for the reader.

The focusing line often appears as ordinary language, as this one did, at first. It is the writing of the draft that reveals the extraordinary in the ordinary, but the line provides the energy that moves the writer and the writing toward meaning.

I write my newspaper column every week, work on a chapter of a nonfiction book or a novel, write poems, and they all start with a focusing line, an image, a mental picture that intrigues and haunts me, or a written line, a fragment of language that I know contains a piece of writing. Once I have the focusing line, I can start writing immediately or wait until I have time. The spark will be there.

Most of the time, the focusing line is a response to life, but if I have a specific assignment, I still seek a line of my own. I continue to live my life in a state of passive awareness, a receptive alertness in which I absorb the life I am living and pay close attention to my reactions to that life. Certain signals within a line compel me to pay attention and to write.

Consider some of the elements in an effective focusing line that reveal the energy necessary to drive a draft forward.

CONFLICT

The most common beginning point is a conflict revealed by the line. Guilford College in North Carolina is a Quaker school, dedicated to nonviolence, but its football team is called the Fighting Quakers. I wrote in my daybook, "I had an ordinary war" and started writing a book about the extraordinary that becomes ordinary in war.

TENSION

A focusing line contains a conflict or problem that needs to be explored in writing. The quick note in my daybook reads "add/steele." Translation: "I must go back and read Addison and Steele to see how these eighteenth-century writers I once studied so carefully influenced me as a journalist." This might be a critical essay on how Addison and Steele relate to op-ed page pieces in papers like the *New York Times, Washington Post, St. Petersburg Times, Boston Globe.*

MYSTERY

Usually there is a mystery in a focusing line, something I didn't understand and that I want—better yet, need—to understand. Line: "grdma tuff, kids weak." Translation: "My grandmothers lost their husbands early. They were immigrants with small children, and they had to be strong, but somehow their necessary strength made their children weak."

SURPRISE

I read what I do not expect. I write "they should stay in the graves" and report on a true and disturbing human feeling: my anger at those who I have loved and lost that will not be forgotten.

INFORMATION

Specific information reveals an issue or situation that demands attention and is full of implication. Line: "Est Ger Secpol." Translation: "The East German secret police 'consisted of a force of 85,000 regular employees, . . . 109,000 secret informers: that is, almost 1 of every 80 persons in the country. . . . The surveillance involved 1,052 full-time specialists who tapped telephones, 2,100 who steamed open letters, and 5,000 who followed suspects.'"

WORRY

I noted "My young daughters were proud" when I got out of the car and attacked a driver who had tried to run me off the road. Apparently, the girls saw a powerful man who could protect them. The police saw my attack and did not stop it. They even thought I was right to attack the other driver, but I felt within myself the paratrooper-trained ability to kill. Yes, I was proud that

I could attack him, proud that I could win the male confrontation, but I knew that my hands—experienced in combat—could easily, almost casually, have killed him, and I wrote about my fear of what is within us.

JOY

I wake in the morning and take delight in "the coming of light." My writing celebrates the moment of waking—carpe diem, seize the day.

CONNECTION

I observe my grandson's "war games" and connect his play at war to my playing in war, when those who fell down dead did not jump up laughing. One of the most important things the writer does is to connect what is not usually connected so it reveals meaning.

PERSONAL TERRITORIES

Each of us has territories that we are compelled to explore, places where we find meaning. As I mentioned previously, my personal territories are a childhood that was strange and full of questions I have not yet answered, a fascination with the creative process and language, the war, school where I did so badly and later returned as a teacher, my experience in combat and what I discovered about the enemy: myself.

POINT OF VIEW

I write "skinny, bespectacled kid" and see myself as others saw me. As a grandfather, I also see myself when I was a boy or a young father. I see my daughters when they were the ages of their children, hear them saying now what we said to them—and I have a piece to write.

VOICE

The experienced writer hears the music that reveals the emotional content, or even the meaning of a piece, in just a fragment of language. You will too after you become used to listening to your language as you write. "I meet my cousin's son and am startled to see how much he looks like my father does in the snapshot of him taken before I was born. I feel I am meeting my father when he was young." I hear a reflective music in that line, a thinking back and musing music that makes me think of the childhood my father never had and how that experience shaped him—and perhaps me.

NEWS

I read in the newspaper about a new school testing program and that makes me think about what we can actually test. It is always the most superficial element: spelling not ideas, grammar not voice, correctness not creativity. Testing programs drive everyone to the common center, trying to bring up the bottom half of the class, while bringing down the top half.

SIGNIFICANCE

A focusing line has to reveal a subject that is potentially important. Line: "artists teach writers." Translation: "I'm going to write a scholarly essay [or book?] on what artists have to teach writers. I go to the art museum to learn to write. [Another essay on music? Interview my son-in-law, Michael Starobin, composer?]"

Other focusing lines might reveal a potential genre—a research paper, a memo, a short story—I should write. I might discover a need I have that others might need to know as well. I might see a pattern of behavior that should be exposed, an answer without a question or a question without an answer—until I write it.

Find the Focusing Line

A focusing line is the product of all the observation and thinking that comes before writing: listing, brainstorming, mapping, freewriting. If I plunge ahead and write before finding the focusing line, it is usually a waste of time; if I have the line, however, the process of focusing, researching, drafting, revising, and editing usually goes well.

Of course, the focus of a piece changes as the writer gathers information and discovers its significance through writing. But without a draft focus, the writer wanders. I think the focusing line is one of the most important writing techniques I practice, and I learned it late in my life-long apprenticeship.

Here are some focusing lines from my daybook that have produced pieces of writing. These lines are similar to brief artist's sketches, notes in a private language that will spark my imagination at my writing desk. Note that without explanation, they may not mean much to an outside reader. Each one is not the end—a thesis statement—but a beginning—an ignition statement.

I always listened from the other room, learned the language of walls.

This line gave me a poem about the importance of stories in my childhood, how I lived by stories, trying to make sense of my world.

Saw old movie with Clark Gable. He yells, "Get me Rewrite" so he could dictate his story.

> *I was the rewrite man who was got when I first worked for a newspaper. This line could ignite an essay for college English on how dictation might help students to improve the effectiveness of their writing.*

As I look back on my life, I visit the geographies that contained my world.

> *I haven't written a piece based on this line. It may be a poem, an essay, a short story. I visited a neighborhood where I had lived when I was in elementary school and became fascinated with the shrunken horizons of my world.*

Editor tells me, "Cut it in half." Piece better.

> *Study the manuscripts of famous writers and see what they cut. Is there a pattern that would help apprentice writers? Article for* **The Writer?**

Waking in the morning.

> *This private phrase inspired a proposal for my book* **My Twice-Lived Life— A Memoir of Aging** *that explored the world of my aging, where waking in the morning is an exciting event.*

My father called in the middle of the night to ask, "How you doin'?"

> *I expected more from this first call from the dead, but all he wanted to know was the ordinary. Someday this thought will ripen into a poem.*

Looks—was I somebody?

> *This note scribbled on a piece of paper in a Washington, D.C., restaurant led to an essay about the whole business of celebrity and personal identity.*

What the Focusing Line Gives the Writer

We are all terrified when we begin a first draft and step off into the unknown, but the focusing line makes this step less terrifying. The focusing line solves a great many of my writing problems in advance. Let's look at one of the lines above and see how it helps as I begin a draft:

As I look back on my life, I visit the geographies that contained my world.

POSSIBLE DIRECTION

I have a strong indication of where my mind might travel in writing a draft.

RESEARCH

I could choose to research my childhood neighborhood and examine the political, economic, and sociological changes in that area.

REFLECTION

I could think back upon my childhood and how that geography affected my life.

DESCRIPTION

I could map my childhood world in words and see how our vision of an area changes as we grow old: My first trip around the block was more exciting than my first trip to Norway.

LIMITATION

What I write will not be about my high school neighborhood, the battlefields on which I fought, the neighborhoods in which my children spent their childhoods. The line helpfully excludes.

POINT OF VIEW

This can be thought of in two ways.

Angle of Vision

The point of view determines the place from which the writer and the reader observe the subject. The angle of vision includes everything that can be seen or known from that point. I may, for example, write from the point of view of an eight-year-old who has not yet questioned the prejudices of his parents, or I may write from the point of view of an adult critical of those prejudices. Sometimes point of view refers to first, second, and third person: I, you, he/she.

Opinion

Point of view also describes the opinion the writer has of the subject. It is important for the writer to have an opinion of the subject—my parents made the new neighborhood a fearful place because of their prejudices, an attitude that I as a child found unjustified.

VOICE

Voice is the word music that reveals and supports the meaning of the piece. We all respond to what is said to us and, especially, how it is said. Voice is the *how*.

In the focusing line, the writer's trained ear often hears the music of the piece: "The first lesson of my childhood was, 'Stay on your own side of the fence.'" This statement has a different music than: "My parents talked about a God of love, but the God they described disliked more than loved, never reaching across the backyard fence to our neighbors."

FORM

Form is the type of writing: fiction, nonfiction, poetry, screenplay, argument, memo, lab report, book review. It includes the tradition of the type of writing; the reader knows what to expect from a story, a poem, an argument. The line "The Good Book was, in my home, a Bad Book—full of what not to do" may ignite an autobiographical essay or a memo to a textbook publisher arguing for more positive approaches in textbooks.

STRUCTURE

Structure is the way I anticipate getting from the first line to the last; it is the trail of meaning I will follow as I produce a draft. Structure may take many forms. In a narrative, the actions and reactions between the characters create a chronological structure that pulls the reader forward; in an argument, the logic of one point leading to another may drag the reader toward the writer's conclusion. The line "I read Hazlet before Orwell or E. B. White" implies a chronological survey of essay writing, going back to the nineteenth, and perhaps the seventeenth, century.

OPENING

The focusing line often becomes the first sentence or paragraph of what I write. This lead leads—draws, entices—the reader into the writing. A focusing line like "my neighborhood had fences to keep out those who were different" might develop into the following lead: "Recently I visited the Land of Prejudice, the geography of my childhood where good fences did not make good neighbors." Do I consciously march through all those elements when I develop a focusing line? Not always. But sometimes it helps to take apart what the cabinetmaker put together, to discover how she knew those pieces of burled wood could become a corner cabinet.

Techniques to Find a Focus

Here are some other techniques I use to find a focus.

THE STEINBECK STATEMENT

The great novelist John Steinbeck used to write down what a book was about on a single three-by-five card. He might write a five-hundred-page draft, but his focus would be on that sentence or two on the card. I have found it a valuable technique to do this when I have trouble with focus. That statement includes and excludes. It keeps my eye on target.

BUT—and don't forget this *but*—the statement will have to be revised as you write. You may know what you hope to write about when you start, but all writing is a voyage of discovery. You have to make course adjustments, refining and revising your initial statement as you discover what you have to say.

BEGIN BY ENDING

Many writers, including Truman Capote, Raymond Carver, John Gregory Dunne, William Gibson, Joseph Heller, John Irving, Eudora Welty, Toni Morrison, claim to know the end of a draft before they begin. They all have a destination that may be changed once they begin writing, but destination gives their first draft focus.

It may be helpful to write a dozen or two dozen last sentences. Once you choose one and know where you are headed, you may know where—and how—to begin.

A CONTROLLING IMAGE

When you started to write as a child, you sometimes drew a picture first, sometimes wrote the caption first. You worked back and forth calling both drawing and writing writing. I think writers still work that way. I see what I write, and many times the focus of my writing is an image: My mother and I are lifting my paralyzed grandmother in her bed and someone says something that makes us stop and laugh until we literally weep with humor; I see myself making a thick baloney and strawberry jam sandwich that I once thought tasty; I see myself driving along the road beside Wollaston Beach in the car five of us bought when we were in high school—for five bucks each—looking for girls.

Pay attention to what you see with your mind's eye—or with your real eye—as you research or think about what you are going to write. The focus may lie in that vision. You may have a controlling image that will give a landmark to guide you through the writing.

ANTICIPATE THE READER'S NEED

The focus of a piece of writing may come from the reader. In writing memos to a dean when I was English department chairperson, I knew what the dean wanted to hear and how he wanted to hear it—documented with statistics. My job was to focus a wandering discussion of our department needs in a way that would lead the dean to "buy" our argument and give us the fiscal support we needed.

Put yourself in the reader's place to see if you can understand what a particular reader needs to learn from the text. That may be your focus.

MOVE THE ANGLE OF VISION

When writing, the writer invites the reader to stand at the writer's side so the writer can point out the view and comment upon it. The place where the writer stands gives focus to the draft. In writing for teachers, I often ask them to stand beside me when I was a high school dropout. Many teachers were honor students and viewed school differently than I did, but if they want to reach all students, they need to see school as the less academically interested view it.

Often the writer moves the point of view or angle of vision, taking readers along as the view changes and their understanding of what they're seeing increases. It is where the writer and reader stop and what they pass by that keeps the writing in focus.

ADJUST THE DISTANCE

Distance is a key element in writing. Distance is how far the writer places the reader from the subject. Many writers always write close up; others always stand back at the same distance. Movies and television have made us all aware that the camera can put us on the mountain ridge watching the far-off cattle rustler and then move us in close to see one steer rolling its eyes in terror.

Move in close up, and you'll see in detail. The lens frames the revealing action, response, or object. You'll gain immediacy and intensity, but you can lose context, what the detail means. Stand way back and each detail is in context. Pun intended, you see the big picture. The frame extends so that you have a broad view, but you lose intensity.

The trick is to stand at a variety of distances, each appropriate to what is being said. The writer moves in close to increase intensity, then moves back to put what has been seen into context; the writer stands back to establish context, then moves in close to make the reader see, feel, think, care.

There is no ideal distance apart from subject. The craft is to always be at that distance that most effectively helps the reader see, feel, and understand. The skilled writer uses a zoom lens, adjusting the distance so that the reader experiences intensity without losing context, has enough detachment so that the reader has room to respond, is close enough so that the reader is forced to respond.

Play with distance as you focus and draft—describe your grandmother's hand as you held it in the nursing home, describe her in the group picture of the family arriving in America when she was the little girl in front—to see how it will help you explore your subject and communicate it.

ASK THE RESEARCH QUESTION

In the academic world, the focusing line becomes the research question. The sociologist, historian, physicist, economist, literary critic, health ethicist, philosopher, biochemist, or member of any other intellectual discipline needs to learn how to ask a good research question. The research question is central to the term paper, the master's thesis, the doctoral dissertation, the grant proposal, the paper at an academic meeting, the scholarly article and book.

MAKE A THESIS STATEMENT

The thesis statement is a fully developed focusing line: "Toni Morrison reveals the tensions of small-city, Midwestern life for everyone, not just African Americans."

The advantage is that the thesis statement provides focus for the research and the writing. Academic writing in many disciplines has historically favored argument, and the thesis statement in such a piece provides the writer and reader with a clear debating point. It encourages, for example, the reader to say, "Whoa! I'm not so sure Toni Morrison does that. Let's see your evidence."

Many teachers demand, for these reasons, that writers articulate thesis statements before researching or writing papers. The great danger is that the scholars will only look to document those statements when, in fact, they might discover different critical views.

In that case, a writer should submit the revised thesis statement to the instructor: "Toni Morrison's novels document how different the small-city, Midwestern experience of African Americans is from that of their white neighbors."

START A NEW WRITING TASK

The writing process you are learning can be adapted to any writing task and to changing conditions. As you proceed through school and beyond, new classes and new jobs will demand new forms of writing: memos, reports, fund-raising letters, poems, case histories, theses or dissertations, sermons, police reports, book or literature reviews, grant applications, letters of sympathy, job or graduate school applications, screenplays, scientific or laboratory reports, legal briefs or judicial decisions, marketing plans.

A particular type of task will require a long piece or a short one, only text or text coordinated with a complex graphic design, writing alone or with a partner or a committee, completed in a day or less or a month or more.

In every case you will be able to adapt your experience with the focusing line.

CHAPTER 16

Read the Reader

When I hear students or professional writers blaming the reader—a teacher or editor—for not understanding what the author has attempted to say, I hear the echo of my own voice. It took me a long time to realize it isn't a question of the reader or writer being wrong.

The challenge is communication. If one person doesn't understand, others will not understand. The reader is not an enemy. I like to think of my readers as companions who join me as we explore and clarify meaning. The reader is not the enemy, but a companion who you are inviting along on an expedition toward meaning. I am having a conversation with an interesting friend.

WRITING AS A CONVERSATION

You may not have much experience writing, but you have years of daily experience in conversation. Listen to yourself as you have a conversation with a friend, listen to the friend's response, stand back and watch others as they hold a conversation. Writing is not a mystery. It is a form of communication you have practiced before you were out of diapers. Draw on your experience with conversation as you write.

ANTICIPATE THE READER'S RESPONSE

Before we speak, we anticipate the friend's interest in what we plan to say. The friend may or may not follow the Red Sox, may even find baseball boring; have political opinions opposite or the same as yours; delight in gossip or be uncomfortable talking about the behavior of people you know; have a sense of humor or not; have prejudices similar to yours or just the opposite; like to talk about personal feelings or not.

SAY SOMETHING INTERESTING

The conversation begins when you say something that will interest your friend. Most of us would deny it, but we rehearse what we have to say, knowing what will interest or bore a friend. We deliver information that will speak to the friend's interest.

DOCUMENT IT

Usually we back up the information by mentioning our source or delivering more details that will support what you have said. We speak—and write—with specific, revealing, interesting, significant information.

LISTEN TO THE RESPONSE

Listening is not thought of as a writing skill but it is—and one of the most important. It took me years to learn that no matter how clear I thought I had written, it was not worth publishing unless I role-play the reader, reading the draft for what it may say to a reader, not what I intended it to say.

The solution was easy once my ego realized it didn't matter how well I had written unless readers got the message. My students often would blame the reader for not understanding, saying they were dumb, lazy, distracted, prejudiced, whatever, but that didn't matter. They may be right or wrong. So what I had to learn to do was stand back from the easel as the artist frequently does and see the painting with the viewer's eyes. If I am going to have a successful conversation with readers, I have to hear what they are asking and respond to it.

As I write each draft, I hear the reader more and more clearly as I get to the final draft. You know the questions and comments because they are the ones you ask yourself when you are reading:

SO WHAT?
WHO SAYS?
WHAT DOES THIS MEAN?
WHO NEEDS THIS?
SLOW DOWN. YOU ARE GOING TOO FAST.
ENOUGH ALREADY.
I NEED TO KNOW MORE.

The more you don't like the response of the teacher, editor, reader, yourself, the more you should pay attention. And that is easy if you just listen to the reader and respond.

CHAPTER 17

Unblocking Writer's Block

"My father never had truck driver's block" is what the writer Roger Simon said in a seminar on writing I attended. It is the quotation that has most helped me practice what the mystery writer Robert Parker preaches:

> There is no one right way. Each of us finds a way that works for him. But there is a wrong way. The wrong way is to finish your writing day with no more words on paper than when you began. Writers write.

Writing is what I most like to do. It is my hobby and my vocation and yet there are days when I do not get to the writing desk. It is not that it gets harder to write; it sometimes gets harder to get to the writing. Interruptions are my biggest problem. Because of my wife's illness, I am on duty 24-hours a day. And I should be. She has been my companion and my support for 53 years. I was taught by my family to always put the needs of others ahead of my own and I find it hard to escape phone calls, e-mails, visitors, and invitations to lunch.

But all writers are masters of avoidance. If interruptions don't occur, writers create them. They make phone calls, travel far on unnecessary errands, cut wood in July, buy snow shovels in August, play computer games, read and send e-mail, babble in a chat room, surf on the Internet. When it is time to write, writers read, attack the correspondence and the filing, sharpen pencils, buy new pens, change the cartridge in their printer, shop for a new computer, make coffee, make tea, rearrange the furniture in the office. When writers get together, they share, often shamefaced, new ways to avoid writing.

Some of that avoidance is good. This waiting is purposeful since most writers discover that starting a draft prematurely causes a total collapse three, five, or seven pages along, and it's harder to repair a train wreck of a draft than to start one along the right track.

Writers, of course, being writers, are never sure whether they are allowing their subjects to ripen properly or are just being lazy. This waiting is often the worst part of writing. It is filled with guilt and doubt, yet it is essential.

Then comes the time—often commanded by the deadline—when there can be no more delay, when the writing must be done. Here are some ways to overcome inertia and start writing:

1. *Nulla dies sine linea.* "Never a day without a line." Make writing a habit. Sit in the same place with the same tools every day and write until it becomes uncomfortable not to write. Then writing will come as a matter of course.

2. *Make believe you are writing a letter to a friend.* Put "Dear" at the top of the page and start writing. Tom Wolfe did this on one of his first *New Journalism* pieces. He wrote the editor a letter saying why he couldn't write the piece he'd been assigned. The letter flowed along in such a wonderful, easy fashion that the editor took the salutation off and ran it. It established a new style for contemporary journalism.

3. *Switch your writing tools.* If you normally type, write by hand. If you write by hand, type. Switch from pen to pencil or pencil to pen. Switch from unlined paper to lined paper, or vice versa. Try larger paper or smaller, colored paper or white paper. Use a bound notebook or spiral notebook, a legal pad or a clipboard. Tools are a writer's toys, and effective, easy writing is the product of play. Sometimes I will change the font, the type size, the shape of the text on the page, allowing the computer to show me what I have said in a different form.

4. *Talk about the piece of writing with another writer, and pay close attention to what you say.* You may be telling yourself how to write the piece. You may even want to make notes as you talk on the telephone or in person. Pay attention to words or combinations of words that may become a voice and spark a piece of writing.

5. *Write down the reasons you are not writing.* Often when you see the problem you will be able to avoid it. You may realize that your standards are too high, or that you're thinking excessively of how one person will respond to your piece, or that you're trying to include too much. Once you have defined the problem, you may be able to dispose of it.

6. *Describe the process you went through when a piece of writing went well.* You may be able to read such an account in your journal. We need to reinforce the writing procedures that produce good writing. A description of what worked before may tell you that you need to delay at this

moment, or it may reveal a trick that got you going another time. Keep a careful record of your work habits and the tricks of your trade, so that you have a positive resource to fall back on.

7. *Interview other writers to find out how they get started.* Try your classmates' tricks and see if they work for you.

8. *Switch the time of day.* Sometimes writing at night when you are tired lowers your critical sense in a positive way, and other times you can jump out of bed in the morning and get a start on the writing before your internal critic catches up with you.

9. *Call the draft an experiment or an exercise.* Good writing is always an experiment. Make a run at it. See if it will work. The poet Mekeel McBride is always writing "exercises" in her journals. Since they are just exercises and not poems, she doesn't get uptight about them, but of course if an exercise turns into a poem, she accepts it.

10. *Dictate a draft.* Use a tape recorder, and then transcribe the draft from it. You may want to transcribe it carefully, or just catch the gist of what you had to say. No matter how experienced you are as a writer, you are a million times more experienced as a speaker, and it's often easier to get started writing by talking than by simply writing.

11. *Quit.* Come back later and try again. You can't force writing. You have to keep making runs at it. Come back ten minutes later, or later that day, or the next day. Keep trying until the writing flows so fast you have to run along behind it trying to keep up.

12. *Read.* Some writers read over what they've written, and they may even edit it or recopy it as a way of sliding into the day's writing. I can't do that; I despair too much, and when I read my own writing I feel I have to start over again; it's worthless, hopeless. If you don't feel that way, however, it may be a good device to go over the previous day's work and then push on to the new writing, the way a house painter paints back into the last brush stroke and then draws the new paint forward.

13. *Write directly to a specific reader.* The too-critical reader can keep you from writing, but you can also get writing by imagining an especially appreciative reader, or a reader who needs the information you have to convey. If you can feel that reader's hunger for what you have to say, it will draw you into the text. Sometimes when I write, I imagine the enjoyment I expect my friends Don Graves, Chip Scanlan, or Nancie Atwell to feel at an unexpected turn of phrase, a new insight, or a different approach. I read their faces as I write, the way you read a friend's face during a conversation.

14. *Take a walk, lift weights, jog, run, dance, swim.* Many writers have found that the best way to get started writing is by getting the blood coursing through the body and the brain. As they get the physical body tuned up, the brain moves into high gear. Exercise is also the kind of private activity that allows the mind to free itself of stress and interruption and rehearse what may be written when the exercise is done. Running, walking, bicycling, or swimming are great ways to let the mind wander while the body is working.

15. *Change the place where you write.* I write in my office at home, but I also write on a lap desk in the living room or on the porch. I like to take the car and drive down by Great Bay, where I can look up from my lap desk and watch a heron stalk fish or a seagull soar—the way I would like to write, without effort. Some writers cover their windows and write to a wall. I like to write to a different scene. In the 1920s writers thought the cafes of Paris were the best places to write. I don't think I could work on those silly little tables, but my ideal writing place would be in a booth in a busy lunchroom where nobody knows me. When my writing doesn't go well, I move around. I imagine that the muse is looking for me, and if she can't find me at home I'll go out somewhere where I may be more visible.

16. *Draw a picture, in your mind or on paper.* Take a photograph. Cut a picture from a magazine and put it on your bulletin board. When small children start writing, they usually first draw pictures. They do on paper what writers usually do in their minds—they visualize their subjects. Last summer I started my writing sessions by making a sketch of a rubber tree that stands on our porch. I wasn't writing about the rubber tree, but the activity of drawing seemed to help me get started and stimulate the flow of writing.

17. *Freewrite.* Write as hard and as fast and as free as you can. See if language will lead you toward a meaning. Freewriting isn't very free, for the draft starts to develop its own form and direction. But the act of writing freely is one of the techniques that can unleash your mind.

18. *Stop in the middle of a sentence.* This is a good trick when the writing is going well and you are interrupted or come to the end of the day's writing during a long project. Many well-known writers have done this, and I've found that it really helps me at times. If I can pick up the draft and finish an ordinary sentence, then I am immediately back into the writing. If I've stopped at the end of a sentence or a paragraph, it's much harder to get going. If I've stopped at the end of a chapter, it may take days or weeks to get the next one started.

19. *Write the easy parts first.* If you're stuck on a section or a beginning, skip over it and write the parts of the draft that you are ready to write. Once you've got those easy, strong pieces of writing done, then you'll be able to build a complete draft by connecting those parts. A variation on this technique is to write the end first, or to plunge in and grab the beast wherever you can get hold of it. Once you have a working draft, you can extend it backward or forward as it requires.

20. *Be silly.* You're not writing anyway, so you might as well make a fool of yourself. I've numbered the day's quota of pages and then filled them in. One of my writer neighbors loves cigars, but he won't let himself have a cigar until he has finished his daily quota. Reward yourself with a cup of coffee or a dish of ice cream or a handful of nuts. It is no accident that some writers are fat; they keep rewarding themselves with food. Do whatever you have to do to keep yourself writing. Jessamyn West writes in bed the first thing in the morning. If the doorbell rings she can't answer it; she isn't up and dressed. Use timers, count pages, count words. (You may not be able to say the writing went well, but you'll be able to say "I did 512 words," or "I completed two pages.") Play music or write standing up. (Thomas Wolfe wrote on top of an icebox, and Ernest Hemingway put his typewriter on a bureau.) Start the day writing in the bathtub as Nabokov did. Nothing is too silly if it gets you started writing.

21. *Start the writing day by reading writing that inspires you.* This is dangerous for me, because I may get so interested in the reading I'll never write, or I'll pick up the voice of another writer. I can't, for example, read William Faulkner when I'm writing fiction: a poor, New Hampshire imitation of that famous Mississippian is not a good way to go. The other day, however, when I couldn't get started writing, I read a short story by Mary Gordon, one of my favorite authors. Reading a really good writer's work should make you pack up your pen and quit the field, but most of us find reading other writers inspiring. I put down Mary Gordon's short story and was inspired to write.

22. *Read what other writers have written about writing.* I may not write as well as they do, but we work at the same trade, and it helps me to sit around and chat with them. As I mentioned in Chapter 4, you may want to start your own "Commonplace Book," the eighteenth-century journal in which people kept their personal collections of wise or witty sayings. I find it comforting to hear that the best writers have many of the same problems I do, and I often browse through my collection of quotes as a way of getting started.

23. *Break down the writing task into reasonable goals.* A few years ago I watched on TV as the first woman to climb a spectacular rock face in California made it to the top. It had taken her days, and as soon as she got over the edge, a TV reporter stuck a microphone in her face and asked her what she'd thought of as she kept working her way up the cliff. She said she kept reminding herself that you eat an elephant one bite at a time. You also write a long piece of writing one page, or one paragraph, at a time. John Steinbeck said, "When I face the desolate impossibility of writing 500 pages a sick sense of failure falls on me and I know I can never do it. Then I gradually write one page and then another. One day's work is all I can permit myself to contemplate." If you contemplate a book, you'll never write it, but if you write just a page a day you'll have a 365-page draft at the end of a year. If you're stuck, you may be trying to eat an entire elephant at one gulp. It may be wiser to tell yourself that you'll just get the first page, or perhaps just the lead done that day. That may seem possible, and you'll start writing.

24. *Put someone else's name on it.* I've been hired as a ghostwriter to write for politicians and industrialists. I've had little trouble writing when the work will carry someone else's name. Most of the time when I can't write I'm excessively self-conscious. Sometimes I've put a pseudonym on a piece of work, and the writing has taken off.

25. *Delegate the writing to your subconscious.* Often I will tell my subconscious what I'm working on, and then I'll do something that doesn't take intense concentration and allows my subconscious mind to work. I walk around bookstores or a library, watch a dull baseball game or movie on TV, take a nap, go for a walk or a drive. Some people putter around the house or work in the garden. Whatever you do, you're allowing your mind to work on the problem. Every once in a while a thought, an approach, a lead, a phrase, a line, or a structure will float up to the conscious mind. If it looks workable, then go to your writing desk; if it doesn't, shove it back down underwater and continue whatever you're doing until something new surfaces.

26. *Listen. Alice Walker says, "If you're silent for a long time, people just arrive in your mind."* As Americans we are afraid of silence, and I'm guilty too. I tend to turn on the car radio if I'm moving the car twenty feet from the end of the driveway into the garage. One of the best ways to get started writing is to do nothing. Waste time. Stare out the window. Try to let your mind go blank. This isn't easy, as those who have tried meditation know. But many times your mind, distracted by trivia, is too busy to write. Good writing comes out of silence, as Charles Simic says. "In the end, I'm always at the beginning. Silence—an endless mythical condition. I think of explorers setting out over an unknown ocean . . . ." Cultivate a quietness, resist the panic that the writing won't come, and allow yourself to sink back into the emptiness. If you don't fight the silence, but accept it, then usually, without being aware of it, the writing will start to come.

These are some ways to get writing. All have been tested at my writing desk. You will come up with others if you make a list of techniques from other parts of your life that may apply here. A theater major may know all sorts of exercises and theater games that could work to spark writing. A scientist may be able to apply experimental techniques to writing. Art majors know how to attack a white canvas, and ski team members know how to shove off at the top of a steep slope. Keep a record of methods of starting writing that work for you.

■ SHOPTALK ■

I went to a great concert this weekend, and I want to write about it from beginning to end so I can remember all of it. I do not want to leave anything out. Do I really need to find a focus?

One of the best things about writing is that it is something you can do by yourself and for yourself. That's why many of us keep diaries that list sequences of events and activities we don't want to forget. We want to look back on these entries years from now to remember an incident that seemed significant to us at the time of writing. And that's okay.

But writing for a class or group is always a negotiating process between making personal meaning and making meaning purposeful; while you will want to be true to your own experiences when you write, you will also want to convey those experiences in a way that will entice your reader, make him or her want to dive into your essay and follow it through to the end.

Just because your reader may not have been present at the event you describe doesn't mean that he or she craves a blow-by-blow account of the entire day. What your reader is looking for is something that makes your experience at the concert different from the experiences of the thousands of others who also attended.

Getting down every detail in your first draft is a great first step; you can always keep this draft as your own personal record of the event. But your next step should be to find a focusing line, something that will label the experience as your own and give your reader something to think through. You may, for example, choose to focus on a chance meeting with an old friend at the concert, or the interactions between particular groups of people, or even the outrageous clothing that many of them wore. Whatever your focus, it should convey a sense of your unique perspective and experience, the ingredients that make you different from other people and other writers.

> What if I don't have a unique perspective? How can my focus possibly be interesting to other people?

New writers often think they have nothing different or important to say to an audience. They are afraid that their experiences are so insignificant that they will never fill up the number of pages required for any one writing assignment. So instead of narrowing their focus and going for depth, they broaden their focus and skip across the surface, filling up as many pages as they can.

Finding a focus doesn't mean writing about experiences no one else has had or ever will have; it doesn't mean being a genius or clever or breaking new ground. If you think in these terms, you will be afraid to write at all! What finding a focus means is locating a significant or provocative corner of your larger experience, then making yourself at home in it, furnishing it with vivid details, and inviting your readers to occupy that corner with you.

If a television or movie director were to film a single event in your life, he or she would certainly not film every single person you met, every meal you ate, your entire drive to or from the event, or every conversation you had. A good director would highlight only particular moments, scenes that convey a sense of who you are and how you relate to your world.

Let's take MTV's *The Real World* program as an example. A documentary about young adults living together, the show gives viewers glimpses into—not a panoramic view of—its characters' lives. While we see the young stars engaging in everyday activities, we view those activities through a very selective lens. The camera crews may very well film hours and hours of interactions and conversations among these people, but the directors edit the film so that we see only bits and pieces of it.

Include all the details you want about a day or an event when you write in your diary or when you draft an essay. Then go back and choose a handful of interesting images and try condensing them into one focusing image. If you want, arrange particular images, lines, or sentences from your draft into a poem that will help you focus. Use this focusing poem as a kind of outline for your draft.

> What if what I want to focus on isn't what my readers think is most important?

Getting feedback from readers while you are drafting is an important step in writing. Reader feedback helps you see around corners and uncover blind spots in your essay; it lets you know when your writing is engaging and when it is just plain boring—when you could say more and when you've simply said enough!

But sometimes you can reach an impasse in your relationship with your readers. When you find yourself being tugged and pulled between your own ideas and theirs, you may have to clarify your focus so that your readers can understand it better, or you may need to gather more information and develop your own ideas.

At times like this, don't automatically dismiss the reactions of other readers. At the same time, feel free to take a risk and try out the focus you want. You may find that the tension between your readers' wishes and your own will forces you into a deeper exploration of your ideas.

> What if my readers want me to focus on one thing only and I want to focus on several?

Don't be surprised if the more you explore, the more complicated your focus becomes; what may seem like a single focal point at the start of your draft may quickly turn into several. It's okay to write about two or three things that are equally important. But then you have to find a way of making the combination of them most important. For example, "Most law school professors agree that there are three qualities an effective courtroom lawyer needs," or "There are four equal forces that came together and led us into the conflict with Iraq."

> Some of the greatest books were written by writers who hardly left their rooms! Everything they wanted to write about they already had in their heads. So why make such a big deal out of seeing, touching, and experiencing the world?

Because the image of the solitary writer in the garret, oblivious to life, is largely a myth. Sure, some writers like to cultivate this image—it makes the rest of us think they are geniuses, and it puts a romantic spin on the actual hard work of planning, drafting, revising, and editing. These writers would like us to believe that composing is purely a matter of inspiration, of becoming attuned to the world, through the mind's eye alone rather than through all seven of the writer's senses—seeing, hearing, touching, tasting, smelling, imagining, and remembering.

But even these writers usually keep some sort of journal or notebook in which they record their observations and jot down the details of everyday life. If they do not, you can bet that they have perfected their writers' senses through years of using them, of honing them through the experience of writing itself.

Don't be fooled by the myth. If you decide to isolate yourself and write from the mind alone, you will cut yourself off from the richness of living, not to mention writing. When you experience your environment through your senses, you are fully embodied; when you write through your senses, you embody the world.

> If I want to write a poem or story, I can see where the craft of vision is useful, but if I want to write scholarly essays, how will "seeing" help?

Whether you are writing an analytical essay or a personal narrative, as you engage in the process of composing, you will find yourself using terms that refer repeatedly to seeing: Point of view, perspective, angle, focus, and revision are just a few of these terms. If you think of these words, they do not always literally mean using the eyes to see; they also mean envisioning or revising, seeing the world afresh through concepts and theories. Most of all, seeing through imagining.

Most of the world's greatest contributors to science, religion, and history were revolutionary "see-ERs." When talking about people such as Albert Einstein, Marie Curie, Mahatma Ghandi, Martin Luther King, Jr., Susan B. Anthony, or Rosa Parks, we often use the term *visionaries.* We praise these figures for their "foresight" or their "fresh outlooks" on life. We discuss the ways in which they "opened our eyes" to new ideas and "revised" our ways of thinking. We refer to them as "farseeing" people who refused to turn "a blind eye" on the world's injustices. We recognize them as people who argued ideas, took stances, and persuaded others through speaking and writing.

When you look deeply into concepts and theories, you become a visionary of a sort, an *insightful* writer who brings new perspectives to old ideas and issues—a thinker who sees in order that others may see.

But how can research involve new ways of seeing? Doesn't research, by its very name, mean that someone else has already searched my topic and found all the answers?

That's one way to look at it, especially if you are writing a research paper that involves only gathering specific facts and figures about your topic. But if you want to write a paper that allows you to think through data and come up with your own opinions and ideas, you will understand research as a way of bringing new perspectives and insights to a particular issue or problem.

Think of the term *research* itself, a word that suggests re-seeing. When thinking innovatively about your subject, you will find yourself using words and terms that reinforce this idea of seeing. You'll want to *re-view* your topic and what has already been written about it. You'll begin to see the issues involved from different *perspectives* and perhaps develop a whole new *outlook* on the problem. As you discuss your topic with classmates or your teacher, you'll probably respond in terms implying sight: "Now I see . . ." "This author opened my eyes to the fact that . . ." "This writer overlooked an important idea." Research in this sense doesn't mean reporting. It means re-visioning through writing.

I'm visually impaired. I literally cannot see very well. Does this mean that my writing will lack a particular richness?

No. It means that your writing will be enriched, because you have learned to "see" through your other senses. Fully sighted people who are inexperienced writers often rely too much on their eyes at the expense of hearing, touching, and tasting. You, however, have probably learned to use all your senses: You hear the rise and fall of conversation, smell the fragrances of seasons, taste the nuances in flavors of food, and test surfaces with your hands. This too is seeing. This also is writing.

In fact, your "limited" or "distorted" sight may give you a personal and artistic vision of our world. I have a book by a famous British ophthalmologist, *The World through Blunted Sight*, by Patrick Trevor-Roper and Allan Lame (London: Penguin Press, 1970, 1988) that documents how nearsightedness, farsightedness, astigmatism, color blindness, cataracts, glaucoma, muscular dystrophy, and degrees of blindness have affected great artists and, in effect, contributed to production of great art. These artists, because of "defects" in vision, have made it possible for us to see the world anew in their work.

■ IN THE WRITER'S WORKSHOP ■

ON YOUR OWN

1. Brainstorm a list of relatives and freewrite about each. Choose one or two whom you want to learn more about and focus on them, or choose a couple of relatives you know well and want to write about.

2. List songs that you love and that evoke a certain moment in your life. What memories do these songs bring back to you? Think of all the sensory details you associate with these songs and the events they represent—the taste of fruit punch at the junior prom, the fragrance of your crumpled corsage, the smooth wooden pew at your friend's memorial service, the grief-stricken look on her mother's face, the feeling of cold water cascading over your body at the shore, the odor of hot dogs steaming on the vendors' carts. Come up with all the memories and sensory details you can for each song.

3. Make an authority inventory, listing all the things you're an expert on, that you have focused on: the jobs you can do, the things you can repair, the places where you've lived or visited, the problems you can solve, the hobbies you enjoy, the people you know, your family background. Each of us is an authority on many things, and our best writing usually comes from what we know and care about.

4. Wander out into the hallway or situate yourself at the busy entrance of a building. Record the conversations of passersby. Freewrite about these conversations, imagining what they mean to the participants, or write about similar conversations you have had with friends.

5. Pause at intervals and at different times of the day or night along your daily route home to your dorm, apartment, or house. Look and listen for what

you have overlooked or never heard before. Note details in your daybook and describe how they change or remain the same.

6. Draw a line down the middle of a page in your daybook. While watching a suspenseful movie or television show, sum up on the left-hand side what happens in each scene. Record on the right-hand side all that you think is left out of the filming. What don't you see during the show? What does the director include or omit? When you finish, go back over your list and in a few sentences describe the focus of the show, trying to sum up the main point.

7. Choose a favorite sitcom or drama on television and videotape at least one scene. Returning to that scene as often as you need, jot down all the details of setting, dialog, and acting. Rethink the scene from the perspective of a writer and reader rather than as a viewer. Write it up in your daybook not as a script, but as a passage in an essay or story. Since your assumed reader cannot see the scene as it was shown on television, adjust your focus and flesh out the details.

8. Visit an isolated or quiet spot, such as a church or wildlife sanctuary. Sit still and listen for at least fifteen minutes. Write down in your notebook everything you hear. Then add a layer of details by describing what you see and then what you smell. Finally, note everything you feel—cold, wind, snow, rain, sun, or heat on your skin. Then write a short descriptive essay about the spot using these details.

9. Visit a room or place you go to everyday and see it anew. List as many details as you can, from the unusual to the ordinary. Then circle the details that you noticed for the first time. Return the next day and notice what you didn't notice the last time.

10. Go to a newsstand and examine the covers of one kind of magazine—news magazines, for example, or beauty, men's fitness, or home decorating magazines. List the various story titles and kinds of images the magazines feature on the front. What patterns do you see? What do they say about the particular genre of magazine? What do they say about our culture?

11. Look in a mirror and sketch a portrait of yourself. Then in your daybook describe your portrait and the process of drawing it. Did sketching your likeness help you see yourself differently? What details did you notice that you may not have noticed before?

WITH A WRITING PARTNER

12. Draw a map of a place you like or dislike. Be as creative as you wish, but don't worry if your map isn't artistically beautiful. When you have finished drawing, freewrite about your place, what it means to you, why you drew it the way you did, what memories you have of it. Then trade maps with a writing partner and freewrite about each other's maps. What do you think the space

you see represents for your partner? What does it say about him or her? Brainstorm a list of questions about the maps and when you have finished, read your questions to one another. Using these questions, freewrite about your own place again, and read your freewrites to one another.

13. Take a writing partner on a personalized "tour" of your hometown, city, or neighborhood. Begin by quickly listing in your notebook all of the "hot spots" or places that have meaning for you. Skip over the spots you consider dull and move from one hot spot to another. Jot down stories about each spot, and then read your list and stories to your partner. Ask your partner to draw a map of your hometown based on what you have read and then have your partner choose a spot on the map he or she would like to return to. Freewrite about that spot.

14. Visit the library reference room with a partner and split up. Browse through the many specialized encyclopedias, dictionaries, and bibliographies. Select those that interest you and record their titles in your daybook. Look through these books and select three entries or topics that you want to know more about, or that you already know something about, and write them down. When you get back to class, compare lists. Choose four of the topics—two from your list and two from your partner's—and freewrite about each.

15. Go to a particular site with a writing partner and write about it separately, each from your own viewpoint. Compare notes and discuss the differences and similarities in the way each of you viewed the same space.

WITH A GROUP

16. Brainstorm a list of subjects that entice you, confuse you, anger you, please you. When you finish your list, jot down one word next to each item that you feel sums it up. Choose three words from this list and write them on the board. After all your classmates have done the same, choose six words from the entire list. There may be no rhyme or reason why you choose the words: They may remind you of something, or you may simply like the way they sound. Beginning with the first word, freewrite on each. Then choose one freewrite you'd like to expand and, with the help of a writing partner, list three more words about that topic. Repeat the process until you have narrowed your focus and gathered plenty of details.

17. Solve a mystery. Join a group of classmates in ferreting out information about a local issue or problem. Focus solely on that issue. Interview people and read up on the problem in newspapers and other media. How did the labor dispute at the local factory begin? Why do coaches earn more than faculty at some schools? Who painted the classrooms in your buildings institutional green? Collaborate on a draft, and in your daybook keep track of who does what in your collective writing process.

18. Freewrite on any topic you want and read it aloud to the class. Ask your classmates to go to the board and write down one word, sentence, or fragment that they remember from the freewrite. Have them explain their choices and how these pieces of your essay can help you focus. Then write about your topic again, choosing a focusing point from their suggestions.

19. Join a group of classmates in choosing a campus issue to research. Conduct interviews and gather information, and then exchange topics and notes with another group. Research your new topic using the information you have been given. Find out at least three new things about your topic that the previous group missed. Practice seeing beyond the data for what is missing instead of what is there.

20. See an argument from different cultural perspectives. With a group of classmates, choose a topic, such as affirmative action or immigration, and find one article each about the subject, making sure to include all perspectives, especially those of minority groups whose opinions may not be represented in mainstream publications. Be as objective as you can in your search, and when you have finished, list and compare the main points of each argument. Don't debate these points; discuss what they say about different cultural viewpoints and modes of seeing.

INTERVIEWING OTHERS

21. Try some intergenerational seeing. If you are a young student, think of an issue or topic that an older relative or friend might view differently from you; if you are older, choose a young friend or relative. Write your viewpoint in your daybook and then interview your friend to get his or her perspective. Describe how your ways of seeing are similar or different and why.

ON THE INTERNET

22. Find two Web sites, created by different people or organizations, dealing with one subject you're interested in. Do both sites include the same information, and the same kind of information—opinions, surveys or polls, photographs, charts, what? On your own or with classmates, list the most interesting and effective pieces of information you find on the sites and explain why these are the most effective.

23. Working with a subject you choose or one that's been assigned to you, do a Web search to find a site dealing with that subject. After browsing through the site, sit down with your daybook and draw or write up a plan for the home page for a Web site you would create about the same subject. What information would you put on that page—what would you want your readers to see

first? What would you put on other pages that you would link the home page to? What other Web pages—ones you've found in your cyberspace travels—would you link to from your page, and why?

24. E-mail a good friend about a writing project you're facing. Tell him or her about the project and what you already know about the subject. Ask your friend what he or she would like to read about the subject, but also see if writing about this project gives you some idea of what you want to focus on.

Keep Writing

There is no pleasure in the world like writing well and going fast. It's like nothing else. It's like a love affair, it goes on and on and doesn't end in marriage. It's all courtship.

TENNESSEE WILLIAMS

Sometimes if things are going badly, I will force myself to write a page in half an hour. I find that can be done, I find that what I write when I force myself is generally just as good as when I'm feeling inspired.

TOM WOLFE

Once you start writing, keep going. Resist the temptation to get up and verify a fact. Leave it blank. The same holds true for the word or phrase that refuses to come to mind. It will arise much more easily on revision and the economy in time and momentum is incalculable.

JACQUES BARZUN

CHAPTER 18

Begin a Discovery Draft

Miss Leavitt was my high school English teacher in the eleventh grade and then the following September I was surprised to be assigned to Miss Leavitt again. She made it clear her dismay matched mine. She was a severe, sincere maiden lady—no married women teachers were allowed in those days—who taught by rules that were repeated over and over and over again.

I had wanted to be a writer since fourth grade, but her rules hung on me like diving weights and heaviest of all was: "KNOW WHAT YOU WANT TO SAY BEFORE YOU SAY IT." I had started a secret craft book full of what writers said about how they wrote. None of them said that, but neither did they deny it.

Miss Leavitt praised my writing, was appalled by my grammar and sick to her stomach at my misspellings, but I had not known what I wanted to say when I was writing the essays she liked. I was attracted to writing because of the stories that surprised me on the page when I wrote without knowing what came next, and where it all was heading. But apparently the good students actually knew what they wanted to say in advance of the first—and only— draft. I must be dumb I thought and feared I could never be a writer and might have to sell ladies underwear like my father.

It took me years before I stopped knowing and wrote to know. I get the best results when I just plunge in and start writing what I call a *discovery draft*—a draft that will reveal what you know and what you need to know. Sixty-one years later I still don't know what I will write. I just run to the pool edge and leap. No matter how familiar you are with the subject, no matter how well you have thought about and researched the topic, no matter how well you have planned solutions to the problems in the draft, you will be surprised by what appears on the screen or the page.

The first draft—the rough draft—does not say what you expected. Be thankful. The writing is instructing you, telling you what to say and how to say it. The first draft makes your argument stronger or weaker; it reveals a different problem or solution than you had intended to write about; it contradicts or deepens your previous beliefs; it reveals a new meaning or changes an old one; it speaks in an unexpected voice or grows into an unintended form. In these ways and others, the draft betrays the writer's intentions, and the inexperienced writer often believes that these surprises are failures.

Just the opposite. Writing is not what has been thunk—thought completed before the draft and transcribed to the page—writing is thinking. As we think, our thoughts change. We use language to discover what we know, what it means, and how we feel about it.

A writer writes to see what the blank page reveals. Writers welcome—encourage, cultivate, even force—surprise, contradiction, the unexpected. Wallace Stevens said, "The tongue is an eye." We speak, and we see what we did not see before. Words hold meaning still, sentences clarify and connect, paragraphs develop and place in context, all revealing an evolving meaning that is more than we planned.

But as long as I have been writing I still often freeze before plunging in and starting the discovery draft. I want to know what I am going to say and how I am going to say it. I want neatness, order, correctness. We should be scared of the unknown. We will discover that we think or feel differently than we want. We will reveal ourselves to ourselves and others. We will write stupidly, clumsily, without apparent meaning. All this is essential to creativity but still we stand back and leave the page blank.

I treat this paralysis by listening to the counsel of writers I have collected to encourage and even to kick me off the edge of the pool.

> I do a kind of pre-draft—what I call a "vomit-out." I don't even look at my notes to write it. It says, for example, "U.S. Journal, Chicago," followed by the title, and starts out, at least, in the form of a story. But it degenerates fairly quickly, and by page four or five sometimes the sentences aren't complete. I write almost the length of the story in this way. The whole operation takes no more than an hour at the typewriter, but it sometimes takes me all day to do it because I'm tired and I've put it off a bit. Sometimes I don't even look at the vomit-out for the rest of the week and I have an absolute terror of anybody seeing it. It's a very embarrassing document. I tear it up at the end of the week.
>
> I don't write a pre-draft for fiction or for humor, but I can't seem to do without one for nonfiction. I've tried to figure out why I need it, what purpose it serves. I think it gives me an inventory of what I want to say and an opportunity to see which way the tone of the story is going to go, which is very important. Also, this is about the time that I begin to see technical problems that will come up—for example, that one part of the story doesn't lead into the

next, or that I should write the story in the first person, or start it in a different way. And obviously, the most important and difficult parts of writing a piece of nonfiction are building the structure and setting the tone and point of view. In any case, almost always, I think, the first paragraph of the pre-draft has something to do with the story that I end up with. *Calvin Trillin*

If writing a book is impossible, write a chapter. If writing a chapter is impossible, write a page. If writing a page is impossible, write a paragraph. If writing a paragraph is impossible, write a sentence. If writing a sentence is impossible, write a word and teach yourself everything there is to know about that word and then write another, connected word and see where the connection leads. *Richard Rhodes*

I believe that fiction feeds on itself, grows like a pregnancy. The more you write, the more there is to draw from; the more you say, the more there is to say. The deeper you go into your imagination, the richer that reservoir becomes. You do not run out of material by using all that's in you; rather, when you take everything that is available one day, it only makes room for new things to appear the next . . . You don't need to know a whole book in order to write the first page. You don't even need to know the end of the first page. You need only the desire to create something that will say what you feel needs to be said, however vague its form at the beginning. You need a willingness to discover the wealth and wisdom of your own subconscious, and to trust that it will tell you what to do and how to do it—not all at once, but as needed, step by step. You have to take a deep breath, let go of your usual control, and then begin walking in the dark. *Elizabeth Berg*

Too often I wait for the sentence to finish taking shape in my mind before setting it down. It is better to seize it by the end that first offers itself, head and foot, though not knowing the rest, then pull: the rest will follow along. *Andre Gide*

These writers console and instruct me as I leap into another discovery draft.

I write as fast as I can as long as I can. It is almost an unconscious act as I am carried along by the flow of language. I listen to what I am saying as I say it. I do not worry about typing, spelling, even getting the right word. I don't worry about sentence or paragraph structure, punctuation, or documentation.

All those are matters for later. They must be dealt with in their time. They are important to make my meaning clear to others but now I am trying to discover my meaning. The draft will reveal my subject and my reaction to that subject to myself. If I am lucky I will surprise myself by how much I know, think, and feel—and I will discover what I have to do to clarify and document that meaning so others can stand beside me and see my vision.

CHAPTER 19

Write Out Loud

Turn off your computer monitor.

Begin writing a first draft. Choose an event that was important in your life and tell its story—with a blank monitor.

Most of you will discover that you do not see what you are drafting, but hear it. You are writing out loud. No matter how bookish you are, you hear speech far more often than reading and you speak far more often than you write. Your ear tells you how to say what you need to say, even how you think and feel about your topic.

If you didn't find it easy to write without the screen on, then you should work to hear what you are saying as you say it. Fluency, grace, believability, feeling, meaning all come from the music of the writing. When we read a good writer, we hear an individual voice. Although a draft is written down, I think voice is the most important element in effective writing.

Of course there is no point in writing without a monitor turned on most of the time. The more we draft and redraft and edit, the more we need to see the evolving text. We check our ear with our eye but the ear comes first. To be an effective writer in most situations, we have to create the illusion of speech so the reader can hear the beat, the pace, the melody, the music of our writing—as it is being written.

Voice is style and tone and more. It is the human sound that arises from a written page. Voice is rhythm and beat, inflection and emphasis, volume and pause; it is the manner in which the author speaks; it is the flow of what is spoken; it is the emotional content of writing; it is energy and force; it is the presence of an individual writer speaking to an individual reader. Voice is the most important, the most magical and powerful element of writing. During writing and revising, the writer hears the voice of the draft and tunes it to the meaning being developed and made clear.

One way to hear the voice of the draft is to speak aloud while writing. Then you will hear the tone of what you are saying, the background music that communicates mood and emotion. You can do this by "silently" speaking what you write, as I am doing now. Then you will be able to hear what you are writing—and tune the voice of the draft to what is being said.

Voice is magic but not mysterious. From another room, you can recognize the voices of those with whom you live; you know if they're mad, sad, having a good time, asking, rejecting, commanding, pleading. You can accomplish the same effect through your writing. You establish a voice that arises from the page.

We each have a personal voice but within it are many voices: familiar, academic, explaining, arguing, persuading, professional. We have known this all our lives. We have playground voices, church voices, kitchen table voices, street voices, grandmother voices, sibling voices. We speak in many voices long before we write.

I write in my daybook "*the melancholy of a sunny day.*" By writing in a voice that connects two words we think are never combined—"*melancholy*" and "*sunny*"—I hear a fragment of a voice describing something I feel that is different from normal expectation.

Now I try other voices:

- When the sun Is out, the world bright and clean, I fear something bad may happen.
- Rainy days give me energy.
- I like the challenge of bad weather, slush and sleet, snow and ice, puddle and skid.
- I was always glad, no matter how bad it got that I was fighting a winter war in Northern Europe, not a jungle war of heat, sweat, and creepy crawlies.

I keep playing with the music of my writing, feeling like a jazz musician, doodling around, waiting for a line to follow.

Read aloud—and I mean right out loud—the first sentences of the following passages to hear the voices of each of these writers:

• THE JOY LUCK CLUB •
Amy Tan

My father has asked me to be the fourth corner at the Joy Luck Club. I am to replace my mother, whose seat at the mah jong table has been empty since she died two months ago. My father thinks she was killed by her own thoughts.

Amy Tan's voice takes you right into her world. Her father's command estab-
lishes a new relationship with his daughter, who is "to replace my mother" (his
wife). The next sentence explains why this new relationship and the last sen-
tence creates a mystery; he does not have a conventional, twenty-first century,
American cause of death such as cancer or heart disease. The narrator's voice is
direct, simple, spare of emotion, neither resentful of her father nor sad for the
loss of her mother; it is the voice of a young observer of life who is recounting
an event that has significance to discover its full implications.

• THE REMAINS OF THE DAY •
Kazuo Ishiguro

It seems increasingly likely that I really will undertake the expedition that has
been preoccupying my imagination now for some days. An expedition, I should
say, which I will undertake alone, in the comfort of Mr. Farraday's Ford; an
expedition which, as I foresee it, will take me through much of the finest
countryside of England to the West Country, and may keep me away from
Darlington Hall for as much as five or six days. The idea of such a journey
came about, I should point out, from a most kind suggestion put to me by
Mr. Farraday himself one afternoon almost a fortnight ago, when I had been
dusting the portraits in the library.

Now we hear a radically different voice, the formal voice of a British butler,
created by a young writer recognized as a master stylist.

• THE MERRY ADVENTURES OF ROBIN HOOD •
Howard Pyle

In merry England in the time of old, when good King Henry the Second
ruled the land, there lived within the green glades of Sherwood Forest, near
Nottingham Town, a famous outlaw whose name was Robin Hood. No archer
ever lived that could speed a gray goose shaft with such skill and cunning as
his, nor were there ever such yeomen as the sevenscore merry men that
roamed with him through the greenwood shades.

This is the old-timey voice of one of my childhood's favorite books. It is a tra-
ditional storyteller voice that attempts to imitate a minstrel, preserving oral
history.

• THE THINGS THEY CARRIED •
Tim O'Brien

First Lieutenant Jimmy Cross carried letters from a girl named Martha, a junior at Mount Sebastian College in New Jersey. They were not love letters, but
Lieutenant Cross was hoping, so he kept them folded in plastic at the bottom
of his rucksack. In the late afternoon, after a day's march, he would dig his

foxhole, wash his hands under a canteen, unwrap the letters, hold them with the tips of his fingers, and spend the last hour of light pretending.

O'Brien, perhaps the best of the Vietnam novelists, uses a reportorial voice, somewhat detached, that allows him to reveal the horrors of war—in this case a soldier's loneliness and distance from the woman he loves.

• BELOVED •
Toni Morrison

124 was spiteful. Full of a baby's venom. The women in the house knew it and so did the children. For years each put up with the spite in his own way, but by 1873 Sethe and her daughter Denver were its only victims. The grandmother, Baby Suggs, was dead, and the sons, Howard and Buglar, had run away by the time they were thirteen years old—as soon as merely looking in a mirror shattered it (that was the signal for Buglar); as soon as two tiny handprints appeared in the cake (that was it for Howard). Neither boy waited to see more; another kettleful of chickpeas smoking in a heap on the floor; soda crackers crumbled and strewn in a line next to the doorsill.

Another storyteller's voice that recreates an oral tradition on the page. No reader can escape the power, energy, force of this voice by one of our most respected writers.

• WILDFIRE •
Richard Ford

In the fall of 1960, when I was sixteen and my father was for a time not working, my mother met a man named Warren Miller and fell in love with him.

Richard Ford, another of our most respected writers, has created a sentence of utter simplicity that reveals, in a few words, a very complicated story that would be told—and explored—by a sixteen-year-old narrator.

• THE KNOWN WORLD •
Edward P. Jones

The evening his master died he worked again well after he ended the day for the other adults, his own wife among them, and sent them back with hunger and tiredness to their cabins. The young ones, his son among them, had been sent out of the fields an hour or so before the adults, to prepare the later supper and, if there was time enough, to play in the few minutes of sun that were left. When he, Moses, finally freed himself of the ancient and brittle harness that connected him to the oldest mule his master owned, all that was left of the sun was a five-inch long memory of red orange laid out in still waves across the horizon between two mountains on the left and one on the right. He had been in the fields for all of fourteen hours. He paused before leaving the fields as the evening quiet wrapped itself about him. The mule quivered, wanting home and rest. Moses closed his eyes and took a pinch of the soil and ate it with no more thought than if it were a spot of cornbread. He worked the dirt around in his mouth and swallowed, leaning his head back and opening his eyes in time to see the strip of sun fade to dark blue and then to nothing. He was the only man in the realm, slave or free, who ate dirt, but while the bondage women, particularly the pregnant ones ate it for some incomprehensible need, for that something that ash cakes and apples and fatback did not give their bodies, he ate it not only to discover the strengths and weaknesses of the field, but because the eating of it tied him to the only thing in his small world that meant almost as much as his own life.

The writer has two problems. One is to create a voice that takes us inside a slave's mind and at the same time he uses a second commentary voice that places the slave in the larger context of slaver.

• TAMING THE BEAST WITH TWO BACKS •
Barbara Kingsolver

Reader, hear my confession; I have written an unchaste novel. It's a little shocking, even to me. In my previous books I wrote about sex by means of the spacebreak. One reviewer claimed I had written the shortest sex scene in the English language. I know the scene he meant; the action turns when one character notes a cellophane crackle in the other's shirt pocket and declares that if he has a condom in there, this was her lucky day. The scene then proceeds in its entirety: He did. It was. [Spacebreak]

This excerpt creates a character and a world in great detail, and the writer does it in two two-word sentences.

• THE INVENTION OF CLOUDS •
Richard Hamblyn

At six o'clock one evening in December 1802, in a dark and cavernous laboratory in London, an unknown young amateur meteorologist untied a bundle of handwritten pages, carefully balanced a roll of watercolor drawings beside his chair, and prepared himself to speak on a subject curiously at odds with his subterranean surroundings. It was a cold evening, colder still in the basement of the old building in Plough Court, and as the young man rose to address his audience, answering the supportive smiles of one or two of his friends, his slight shiver might have been due to the cold as much as to anticipation.

The writer of today creates the voice of a world that existed a long time ago.

• LUCKY JIM •
Elizabeth Gilbert

Jim MacLaren doesn't have any memory of the first accident. He can't tell you what it feels like to be hit by a New York City bus and thrown eighty-nine feet in the air, to have your bones shattered and your legs crushed, to have your organs pulverized and to be pronounced dead on arrival at the hospital, because he can't recall any part of it.

In this journalistic voice, the author writes with information, getting out of the way so that the reader's imagination can re-create the experience of the accident.

• LORI •
Lori Schiller and Amanda Bennett

It was a hot night in August 1976, the summer of my seventeenth birthday year, when, uninvited and unannounced, the Voices took over my life.

The personal "I" voice immediately takes you into her world and what it is like.

• BREADCRUMBS •
Mary Pipher

December 2

Dear Laura,
    Last night I sorted through some old black-and-white photographs. In one of my baby pictures, I am asleep with a magazine on my chest. Even then I "read" myself to sleep. In another, I pose joyfully in a high chair covered with dinner, happily stuffing cake into my mouth. Still today, good food is one of my greatest pleasures. Another photo shows me standing beside my brother Jake in front of a big, red brick building. It is our first day in a new school. We're dressed in ill-fitting, old fashioned coats. We look skinny and scared, our eyes wide with alarm. He's leaning into me and I am holding his hand.

The writer uses the form of a letter to share her examination of her past and its relation to the present.

• FROZEN GRIEF •
Pauline Boss

I grew up in a midwestern immigrant community where everyone I looked up to came from somewhere else. Parents and grandparents had crossed the Atlantic in the early 1900s to find a better life in the fertile valleys of southern Wisconsin. But it wasn't always better, because ties had been severed with beloved family members back in Switzerland. Letters came at least until World War II, but they were bittersweet. They always ended with lines like "Will we ever see each other again?" I remember my father being melancholy for days after he got a letter from his mother or brother. And my maternal grandmother pined ceaselessly for her mother back in her homeland. She knew they would never meet again because of poverty and then World War II prevented travel. Homesickness became a central part of my family's culture. I never really knew who was in or out of our family—or where home really was. Was it in the old country or the new? Were these people I had never seen really my family? I did not know them but I was keenly aware that my father and grandmother did.

> *This writer's voice takes us back to when the author was young and describes the world in which she was brought up.*

Each of these voices is different but each is true to the author and to the story the author is telling. Each one makes me want to listen, to read on. Each writer has an individual voice that comes from such influences as genes; ethnic, religious, and regional heritage; social and economic class; and educational background. The important thing is to take that personal voice and tune it to the meaning of the text. All of these examples of voice serve the meaning of the text. Think of a musical score that tells you when to be scared, when to laugh, when to be sad. The music of written language does the same thing: It tells you what to think and feel.

Hear the music of those with whom you converse, hear your own voice as you talk. Seek the natural, the unaffected, the appropriate music for the message and the appropriate message for the music, writing with your ear.

And turn the monitor off once in a while to remind you of the importance of writing a speaking page.

CHAPTER 20

See Within the Draft

Let me repeat the wise counsel given by the great novelist Joseph Conrad: "My task . . . is by the power of the written word, to make you hear, to make you feel—it is, before all, to make you see." Writing is a visual art. To make readers see, writers have to see. And the draft is the writer's lens.

We know that writers have to be aware of their world, to see what is and what isn't, to capture the revealing specific before they write. What those who do not write do not realize is that the greatest amount of seeing is done while writing the draft.

Stop reading and write with me.

List what itches, what you think about when you are not thinking, what keeps returning to mind, what you need to understand. Pick one of your itches and make the reader see by seeing through the lens of language.

Look at what I do in the exercise AFTER you have written.

- snow
- bodies rising when snow melts
- how tall snow was when I was little.
- Flexible Flyer sled
- winter combat—the Battle of the Bulge in 1944–5
- canned heat—Sterno?

Now I will try to help the reader see by writing a first draft:

After we got off the C-47 that took us from England to Belgium and counted the antiaircraft holes in the plane—more than 150—I walked over to a group of soldiers huddled together in a circle. I tried to see what was in the center but didn't ask. They had come from the front, were hollowed cheeked unshaven with eyes that still seemed to be looking at where they had been, not where they were.

> *I had forgotten their faces until this draft made me see. I am going to write this same paragraph again. You do the same with your paragraph and perhaps you will see more.*

I edged closer to the troops back from the front who we were going to replace. Even in the cold they stank. Sweat and urine and dried shit. Their eyes seemed focused on where they had been not where they were. And they were silent. None of the usual black humor, ribbing, kidding that solders practice.

> *And again.*

What held the attention of these soldiers? What drew them together? I edged my way to the center of the circle and saw a single can of Sterno, what you usually find under warming pans in a buffet line. Twenty or so men trying to warm themselves from one tiny can of Sterno that would soon flicker out. They were cold. I was going to be cold as I went to where they had been.

And again. And again. And again. Each time you will see more and that will make you see even more.

Here are some of the kinds of seeing that occur as I write:

- Zoom in and out. Move in close, then stand back. See the subject near and from afar.
- Read the implications of a specific detail—one can of Sterno.
- An anecdote, a brief story that needs to be developed or makes you "see" another story that needs to be told.
- A typo. In working on a draft, I meant to type "they were so young" but instead typed "they were son young." That reminded me of my family when I was at war and the memory of my mother selling my civilian clothes when I was overseas thinking I would not come home. And then I see the itchy orange tweed suit which was the only one I could afford. And I couldn't afford a better suit because my mother had stolen all my savings.

As I write, I see more and more things to write, more and more information to develop in what I have written. The problem becomes one of focus so that I do not run off in all directions at once like a puppy, discovering this great new world with his nose.

The first gift of writing is an aggressive awareness of the life we have lived and are living. I am rarely bored because I am always harvesting writing topics from the ordinary that is invisible to most other people. I capture the revealing detail, changes and what they mean, behavior that contradicts promise, relationships, connections, answers to questions I haven't yet asked, doubts, insights. Writers explore the commonplace and find it rich with significance; writing stops time and holds the moment up for careful examination.

See With the Seven Senses

Before writing the writer scans the world and that process continues through the writing of each draft. As we learn to use one sense, the writer learns to develop other senses.

The writer needs to exercise the seven senses—sight, hearing, touch, taste, smell, memory, imagination. I'll pick a nearby subject, and while I'm recording it with my senses, you should pick your own subject and do the same. I look out my office window at the woods behind the house, the rock wall, the abandoned woodpile, the great tree stump that has become a banquet table for a huge pileated woodpecker, and then I spot my wife's compost piles just beyond the rock wall where she turns garbage into fertilizer to my disgust. It is such an unlikely subject, and I feel so strongly about it, I must pay attention.

SIGHT

My wife used to make a square of yard-long pieces of wood, stacked alternately so the garbage would be contained and yet receive the air essential to good rotting. Now the wood has rotted as well, and she just builds up circles of garbage—peels and shells and pizza crusts and leftovers, cooked zucchini and green, moldy bread, banana skins and apple cores and spaghetti and a greenspotted custard pie.

HEARING

I heard the "caw-caw" of the crows after a Wednesday dumping as they advertise what we had for Sunday dinner and before. We have no secrets from our gossipy crows.

TOUCH

One of my chores as a boy was to carry out what Uncle Will called "the swill"—the slimy, slithery ick in Mother's leaky sink garbage container. Now we have a garbage disposal unit in our sink, but my gardener wife keeps a plastic box in which she stores compost. When I have to carry it out, I do it at arm's length so I can't see the disgusting waste, what had to be cut away, what was rotting, what we weren't allowed to eat, what we refused to eat. I don't allow my fingers to touch the damp, gooey mess.

TASTE

Taking out the compost, I taste last Saturday's supper—how great it had tasted at 7 P.M. and how it rose in my throat at 3 A.M., burning, sour, rancid. Its memory rises from the compost.

SMELL

My wife lifts the cover off the kitchen compost box, and a stink, thick as pea soup, heavy as a wet tarpaulin, pushes down my throat then rises up inside my nose.

MEMORY

During one trip to the compost bins, a sweetish stench this time, I remember the afternoon in Berlin, at the end of the war, when they opened a subway where hundreds had been buried in an air raid months before—the sweet perfume of death spread across the city, street by street.

IMAGINATION

I hate to garden, but I imagine I am a gardener and see in the death of plants, birth. At the top of the compost pile, a small green shoot, a single leaf, new life rising from what was discarded, tossed away to return to earth.

As I write the landscape of my life, I have learned that it is important not to focus on what doesn't work but what does. Years ago I took a draft and photocopied it on large sheets of paper. As I revised it by looking for failures, I discovered that I was not correcting error but developing what worked. I was seeing what is and what could be in the draft. I find out how much I know that I didn't know I knew and the draft changes me as well as my text.

CHAPTER 21

Your Friend—The Deadline

The secret of artistic productivity is THE DEADLINE. Productive writers write. Some days it goes well, other days badly, but the bad writing often turns out to be a breakthrough to better writing. Failure is instructive. It is your editor, teacher, colleague.

The late playwright Samuel Beckett told us to "Fail. Fail again. Fail better." The basketball great, Michael Jordan said, "I have missed over 5000 shots in my career. I've lost almost 300 games. 26 times I've been trusted to take the game winning shot—and missed. I've failed over and over and over again in my life . . . And that is why I succeed."

It is the deadline that forces you to fail—and succeed. I am told that the term *deadline* comes from military prison camps. A line is drawn on the ground around the prison and if you cross the line—bang.

We all have two choices: to fight deadlines, try to extend them, delay, complain, tell the world how much better you would write if you had more time, deliver at the last moment or to make the deadline serve you.

First I made myself a master of avoidance. In my eleventh grade English class I made delay my pride. Some of us started a competition when we were assigned in-class papers. The last one who started and passed—a 65, precisely between a C and a D—was the winner. I usually won. In college I developed an aesthetic principle: a term paper begun late at night of the day before it was due guaranteed that it was spontaneous. They certainly were spontaneous—and disorganized and sloppy.

When I was graduated from college I went to work on a newspaper where I bored myself—and everyone else—by whimpering, complaining, trying to avoid deadlines which were all unreasonable. Then I was assigned to rewrite where there was no revision. I took notes for stories from reporters over the phone and wrote them. Of course each reporter would delay and then near deadline for the first edition—10 P.M.—the phone would start to ring. Between 8 P.M. and 10 P.M. three of us would each average 325–345 stories.

These deadlines were truly ridiculous. Impossible. But I had no choice if I wanted to eat and pay my room rent. Of course I often wrote with clichés and stereotypes, but when I reread my copy at the end of the night, I discovered that my stories that were written to an impossible deadline were clearer, crisper, more informative than my works of aesthetic delay. I was following George Orwell's "Good writing is like a window pane." I got out of the way of the story, not letting my cleaver, artistic writing getting between the reader and the story.

Now I insist on a deadline if an editor or publisher does not provide one, then I make my own deadlines working back from the publication's deadline. My *Boston Globe* Tuesday column has a Monday deadline, but I set my own deadline a week ahead so there is time for accidents, revision, and failure which causes me to write a new column. With a magazine article, a novel, a poem, a nonfiction book, the final deadline seems a long way off but it isn't and so I make my own personal deadlines.

In this book there were deadlines for reviews of the previous edition, a deadline for the editor and I to respond to those reviews and make our own decision on what would be kept as is, what would be changed, what would be new. I had a deadline for delivering a final draft, a deadline for my editor to decide what needed to be changed, added, cut, clarified, then I had a deadline for making those changes and a deadline for it to be delivered to publisher and printer. Did I meet those deadlines? No. My wife who has Parkinson's took a turn for the worse. We had to sell our house, get rid of 40 years of accumulation and buy a one floor condominium—all unplanned when the project began. The publisher agreed to extend the deadline for delivery of the final draft to my editor a month and I made it, well, just about made it, with the last chapter being delivered the morning after the deadline.

I did it by constantly adjusting my deadlines. In making my working deadlines I follow the practice of most prolific writers as documented by Robert Boice, a psychology professor who studied academic writers. He found that productivity is NOT the product of long, last-minute rushes but "brief daily sessions" at the writing desk. I have found that a maximum of 90 minutes each day is ideal. In fact, few days I manage that, but I am productive morning by morning. Here is how you might set your deadlines:

What is the instructor's deadline for the research paper?	Deadline Dec 5
How much of a cushion do you need if there are interruptions you cannot control? And Thanksgiving. Two weeks.	Deadline Nov 21

How much time to edit the paper? Another week.	Deadline Nov 14
How much time to write a final draft? A week.	Deadline Nov 7
How much time to write a developed draft? A week.	Deadline Oct 31
How much time for a discovery draft? A week	Deadline Oct 24
How much time to outline the paper? A week.	Deadline Oct 17
How much time for research? Five weeks which might be broken down into deadlines for different research tasks.	Deadline Sept 12
How much time to find your topic and principle sources? A week.	Deadline Sept 5

The deadlines will keep changing. Sometimes you will get behind, but there will also be times when you get ahead—it may take you an evening not a week to outline your paper. And within the limits of the deadline you will have the time to do the rewriting that is necessary for a piece of writing that reads as if it were spontaneous.

The Writing Habit

The deadline is easy to establish but delivering to deadline depends on your writing habit. Here are a few ways to help you get the writing done.

The myth: Published writers—screenwriters, playwrights, novelists, poets, nonfiction writers, short-story writers, as well as composers and artists—lead lives of Bohemian excess, smoking stuff, drinking stuff, and chasing stuff all night long.

The reality: Writers write; the artistic life is a life of discipline. Gustave Flaubert said, "Be regular and ordinary in your life like a bourgeois so that you may be violent and original in your work." And remember Flannery O'Connor's strategy? "Every morning between 9 and 12 I go to my room and sit before a piece of paper. Many times I just sit for three hours with no ideas coming to me. But I know one thing: If an idea does come between 9 and 12, I am there ready for it."

Sounds simple, doesn't it? It isn't. Getting the writing done day in and day out, despite interruptions, phone calls, obligations, duties, responsibilities, inertia, exhaustion, poor health, bad weather, invited and uninvited guests, too much drinking, too much eating or too little eating, wars, storms, births, deaths, marriages, divorces, travel, letters that come and letters that don't come, and a million other problems, is what separates the writer from the hope-to-be writer.

TIME

We have two kinds of writing times: fragmentary and insulated.

Fragmentary Time

The few minutes you have before a class begins, sitting in a doctor's office, waiting for a friend to show up for lunch, waiting for a bus, or during the commercials while watching TV.

The writing I do is performed mostly in small fragments of time that can be measured only in minutes, sometimes in seconds. This writing is done in my head and in my daybook. It isn't a question of hours but of minutes.

Try it yourself the next time you have a few extra minutes. See how long it takes to brainstorm five essay titles, write a lead paragraph, draft a description, focus on a definition, sketch an anecdote, or even outline an article. I suspect you will find that when you thought you worked ten, or fifteen, or twenty minutes, you've worked two minutes, or four, or ninety seconds.

If you make good use of those fragments of time, then you'll be able to write when you have a stretch of uninterrupted time.

Insulated Time

The half-hours, hours, hour-and-a-halves, two hours you are able to shut out the world—in your room, the library, an empty classroom. Obviously, we have much more fragmentary time than we have insulated time, and it is important that we make use of both kinds of time. For most writers an hour is good, but not good enough. Two hours is plenty; three hours is heroic. During those times unplug the phone, lock the door; do not read, plan, edit, nap, or eat—just write.

The time of day is important. Most young writers start writing late at night but end up writing in the morning—the early morning—when their minds are fresh and the world is least likely to intrude. Goethe said, "Use the day before the day. Early morning hours have gold in their mouth."

The time of day, however, is not as important as habit. Most productive writers—there are exceptions—establish a routine and write at the same time every day. They know the time and the people around them know the time. Alberto Moravia says:

> When I sit down to write—that's between 9 and 12 every morning, and I have never, incidentally, written a line in the afternoon or at night—when I sit down at my table to write, I never know what it's going to be until I'm under way. I trust in inspiration, which sometimes comes and sometimes doesn't. But I don't sit back waiting for it. I work every day.

Do not attempt long, exhausting writing sessions. Few writers are productive in that way. Most writers write regularly for one to three hours every day, and those are considered full-time writers. You may have to try for half an hour to an hour a day.

Once you have produced a draft, fragmentary time can serve you again. I find it better to edit in short bursts. If I edit more than fifteen minutes at a run I tend to be kind, far too kind. In these slivers of time, early and late in the day, I can cut, insert, reorder, and perhaps decide that I need another draft when I have a few hours of insulated time.

PLACE

It helps to have a place where you go to write. It should be a place where you can leave your work lying out and come back to it later, where you have your tools at hand and you have the climate that you prefer.

Ross MacDonald said, "I took my lifelong tenancy in the bare muffled room of the professional writer where I am sitting now, with my back to the window, writing longhand in a spiral notebook." I like to look up from my writing and see a view. Other writers, such as Ross MacDonald, turn their backs to the view. I need music when I write; other writers need silence. Create a place of your own where you can shut the door and be alone.

That's an ideal many students can't achieve because they have families or roommates. It isn't easy to create that internal space, but it can be done, as Lois Duncan points out:

> Now I keep a typewriter with a sheet of paper in it on the end of the kitchen table. When I have a five-minute lull and the children are playing quietly, I sit down and knock out a paragraph. I have learned that I can write, if necessary, with a TV set blaring on one side of me and a child banging on a piano on the other. I've even typed out a story with a colicky baby draped across my lap. It is not ideal—but it is possible.

Writer Donald Graves has been able to write in a dormitory room with pneumatic drill construction going on next door or in a small summer cottage filled with family, friends, and dogs by using earphones and listening to Beethoven at top volume to insulate himself from the surrounding world.

Find ways to detach yourself from the world and go to that place where you can "hear" the writing. Depending on your personality, that place may not be the ideal artist's cabin high in the Rockies. I wrote most of one novel in a park, either sitting in the car or at a picnic table far out of the range of my mother-in-law's voice. I like to write in coffee shops and diners where no one knows me, and where there is a stimulating but unobtrusive background life that I can observe or ignore. When I was an undergraduate, my favorite writing places included the top row of the empty football stadium, a pleasing assort-ment of rocks on the Atlantic coast, a special table in the library, and an empty classroom late at night. Find the places where you can hear your voice as it speaks from the page.

To make deadlines work, you have to learn to let go. There is always another way you could approach the task, always more questions to ask, more sources to explore, more drafts to write. You have to keep moving forward, taking the time you need and the time you have scheduled, no more.

And when is a novel, a textbook, an essay, a short story, a research paper, a report, a proposal, a memoir finished? At the deadline.

■ SHOPTALK ■

Does it matter if I do all my drafting on the computer? Then I can just cut and paste when I want to make changes.

If you're most comfortable working on a computer, then stick with it. But if you find yourself staring at the computer screen for a long time, unable to come up with the next word or phrase or sentence, then switching to a different medium, and/or a different setting may help get you unstuck. Sometimes it's also tempting, if you're working on a computer, to write very slowly and check the spelling and punctuation of each line as you go along. But it may work best for you to write a first draft really quickly, without worrying about these things. If the computer compels you to write everything perfectly, on your first try, get away from it! Try pen and paper, or "talk" your paper into a tape recorder. Just get the draft done.

What if I've got to write the paper tonight?

If you have an hour, take five or ten minutes to collect the information you will need to write. Take a few more minutes to be sure you have a focus, and then a few minutes to put the information in order. If you take ten minutes for each of those tasks, you'll only have invested half an hour. You'll have twenty minutes to write and ten minutes to check over what you've written. The planning will make your draft quicker, often longer, and better.

This kind of quick planning will come in handy when you have to write an essay answer to an exam question or fill out an application that requires long answers. If you have only a limited amount of time, don't give up on planning and focusing. Condense your writing process and put the time you have to good use.

I don't have any problem writing my paper once I get started, but it takes me hours to come up with a good lead or opening. How can I get beyond this?

By getting beyond it. Don't be a perfectionist with your openings. The process of writing will allow you to return to them later. Do what you need now to get going, even if you write an impossibly sappy, dry or silly opening. Just plunge in and start to write. Put someone's name on it and start it as a letter, or write the closing before the beginning. Go with what works.

> I don't write drafts; I just sit down and my writing flows. When I'm through, I've said all I want about my subject. So why should I change?

Because you have probably never found out how much more you have to say. If you never draft and revise, you won't ever see the complexities of the topics you write about. You won't know how much more depth you can bring to your subject. If you're still not a believer, try writing an exploratory draft anyway. See where it takes you. Go about it earnestly and record your progress in your daybook.

> What if I have the opposite problem? I have a hard time getting anything down on paper. I worry before I even begin a writing project, and then I get knots in my stomach when I sit down to do it.

No deadline, assignment, or piece of writing is worth getting sick over. But sometimes it's worth getting mad over! I knew a writer once who used to get paralyzed when she sat down to write in front of an empty computer screen. She'd get sick to her stomach before she had written a word; then she'd get angry for getting sick! By that time she'd march back to her computer and chew it out. Then she'd just write.

> But it's easy for other people to say, "Just write!" If I want to write something really good, it takes a lot of effort. Besides, my grade point average depends on how well I write.

These are valid concerns. Most writers want to write something good, and all writers have to take the consequences for writing well or poorly: Students know that good writing usually results in good grades. Professionals know that good writing results in paychecks.

The problem comes when you let the consequences of writing overshadow the process itself. It's the process of writing that will help you get beyond what is often a paralyzing perfectionism. As you sit down to that blank screen or paper, say to yourself: "This is just an explanatory draft; no one else has to read it. I can do what I want with it, and I can always change it later."

At this point in the process, expect to write badly if you need to. Write quickly to get something down.

> But what if there's absolutely nothing in my head when I want to write?

If you draw a total blank, it doesn't necessarily mean you are paralyzed from fear or an overdeveloped sense of perfectionism; it may mean that you need to go back and do more brainstorming, mapping, focusing, or researching. You may need more information to get you going or a solid angle from which to start. In these cases, you might want to return to some of the activities and suggestions in earlier chapters of this book and use them to jump-start your draft. If you still can't write, it could be that the conditions for writing are simply not good for you. Get up and walk away for a while.

When I get stuck, I don't try to force the writing. I back up, stop, do something else, and try again, perhaps in ten minutes, perhaps the next morning. I'm a morning writer and I find that if the writing doesn't come one time, it will come the next. But be assured that it will come.

But what if I have a paper due the next day? I don't have time to wait for the writing!

Then you will have to force the writing. Even the most well-organized professional at one time or another encounters a deadline bind. At those times, if the writing does not come easily, the writer works to get something, anything on paper.

Look at some of the activities that follow for ideas about drafting. In one of them I suggest setting your clock for a sustained period of time and making yourself write until the alarm goes off. Disciplining yourself like this doesn't mean producing gobbledygook. It means getting said what needs to be said within a given period of time, then going back to revise it. That's what all writers need to do when they are face to face with a deadline.

I'm more afraid of losing control of my paper than of having nothing to say.

The planning and focusing you do before beginning your draft will give you a certain amount of control over what you write. But it's not at all unusual for an exploratory draft to take on a life all its own. This may be frightening, but it's also good. When the draft starts leading you instead of you leading it, it probably means there is some real thinking going on. Since writing allows you to try on new ideas and perspectives, you may have to change your strategy as you articulate your thoughts. You can always go back and fiddle with your focus or an outline so that it accommodates your new way of thinking and seeing.

But what if the draft is literally all over the place and doesn't make sense?

That is still not a bad thing. It's the draft leading you back through a thinking process, getting you to clarify what you want to say. Use some of the suggestions and activities for focusing that follow Chapter 17. A writing partner or group will also be helpful here; other readers can sum up your main points for you, or you can jot down in the margins of your paper what you want to do with each section. That will give you a sense of direction. Then go back and make an outline for your draft and try to stick with it. You can always go back later and develop or pare down areas of your paper as you see fit.

■ **IN THE WRITER'S WORKSHOP** ■

ON YOUR OWN

1. Power through a draft. Read through all of the information, interviews, details, and facts you have collected for it, but don't consult them while drafting. Do as much as you can from memory, and leave a space or asterisk in the draft wherever you think you want to insert more details. For the time being, don't get hung up on particulars.

2. Get a draft down, then write another draft without looking at the original. Include only what you remember or want to remember. Allow the draft to lead you into new areas. Do this again. Then go back to your drafts and select the one you like best, or revise by combining the best elements of each.

3. During your most productive period of the day, set your alarm and write for a sustained amount of time, anywhere from one hour to three. Make sure that you are not interrupted during this period. Think of this time as a business or academic appointment and keep it.

4. Break up your writing time: fifteen minutes before breakfast, a half-hour before lunch, an hour at night, or fifteen minutes before you go to bed. Make sure you write fast and furiously, filling up every minute you have.

5. Put on your favorite classical music—a waltz, prelude, concerto, or symphony—or any kind of music that takes you out of the moment and puts you into a reflective mood. Take a deep breath and "fall" into the music. Vow to write for the length of time it takes for the piece to play, and when it ends, leave your last sentence unfinished. Take a break. When you return, put on a new piece or repeat a melody that worked for you before. Pick up where you left off by finishing the last sentence you wrote.

6. Make drafting part of a larger ritual of physical and intellectual well-being. If you're a morning person, meet the sunrise with tai chi, a cup of herbal tea, and a half-hour or more at your computer. If you work best at night, combine your drafting time with deep breathing exercises and meditation. Visualize productivity and say no to anxiety.

7. If you have writers' block, get a change of scenery; take your draft and work someplace other than your usual writing space. Move from space to space if you need to, making yourself comfortable in each and vowing to write a chunk of draft before moving on.

8. Commit yourself to a certain number of pages each day—whatever seems reasonable. Meet your daily quota and revise what you have at the end of each week.

9. Meet a daily paragraph quota. Determine to write a certain number of paragraphs each day, perhaps five or ten. If you finish quickly, write more or go

back and hone your paragraphs. If you are having difficulty writing, push yourself to meet the quota anyway, knowing that you can revise later.

10. Think of the effect you want each section of your paper to have on your reader, then make a checklist of each part. Start with the words "With this title I want my reader to . . . " "become interested in what I have to say," "laugh," "expect to be surprised," "expect a serious piece," "take me seriously," etc. Move through each section of the piece as you envision it, and anticipate the reader's response.

11. Start in *media res*, which is Latin for "in the middle of things." Don't get hung up on finding a perfect lead, but jump in anywhere. Write a piece of description, a chunk of dialogue or even the conclusion to your story. Develop an idea for the middle of the piece, or select one image or concept you know you can write about comfortably and start with that.

12. Pretend that you're writing in your diary rather than composing a story or assigned essay. Don't try to be deep or complicated. Just get your draft going. Use plenty of time references and words that imply sequence, just as you might in a diary: "That morning . . . " "Later . . . " "After a while . . . " "Then . . . " Let these time words propel you forward; you can always remove them later.

13. Go ahead, break the rule: Tell, don't show! For the time being at least forget about details, description, dialogue, and development. Write your draft in summary form as though it were an encyclopedia entry or an abstract. Then go back and fill in the details, showing rather than telling.

14. When construction workers build a new skyscraper, they erect boards and railings and elevators around it so that they can do their work without falling off. When getting through a draft seems as challenging as building a sky-scraper, let your process become your scaffolding. Analyze your process in the draft itself: "I'm not sure what lead I want here, but I need to start with some-thing, so how about this?" "I thought I knew what to do at this point, but now I'm stuck." "This part of the paper is the suspenseful turning point, so I want it to be good." And so on and so on. When you are through, take down your scaffolding and let your draft stand by itself.

15. Write by ear. Compose sentences that have the right sound to them, the perfect rhythm and voice for the effect you want on your reader. Drum out a rhythm on your desk or daybook before drafting. Imagine what a reflective, inspi-rational, argumentative, persuasive, sarcastic, honest, or upbeat piece might sound like and don't worry yet about how much information or sense your sentences convey. Let the sound guide your writing.

16. Take a significant piece of information from the writing you're working on and list all of the ways it can be documented: quotations, statistics, descrip-tions, anecdotes, and so on. Then develop it, using some or all of these elements.

17. Go back through activities from previous chapters and use any—or many—of the suggestions for collecting information, focusing or writing to see if they will help you get a draft flowing.

18. Jog, walk, swim. As you fall into the rhythm of your body's movements, think about the rhythm of your piece. Let words and lines unfold as you go along. When you have finished, write your ideas down in your daybook. Don't be discouraged if they are incomplete concepts or half-finished leads and sentences; arrange them as potential headings for your paper's outline, and begin gathering information and details for each heading.

19. Experiment with genres if you get stuck. Write a poem instead of an essay, then turn your poem into a complicated recipe. Write up instructions for writing your essay. Make a "grocery list" of pertinent points. Write a letter to your friends telling them about the story you are about to write. Turn your extended story into a play. Then turn your play into a story. Get writing.

20. Draw a picture of your essay. Make it any shape you want, adding width where you want plenty of details and condensing where you want fewer details. Try drawing dark or jagged lines where you want your essay to reflect anger or other volatile feelings, or soft, thin lines for more benign emotions. When you complete your drawing, write one sentence in each part of the sketch that sums up what you want each section of your essay to do.

21. Compose your draft in vignettes rather than paragraphs. A vignette is a short sketch or portrait that stands on its own. Writing vignettes instead of connecting paragraphs will help you focus on details and get a sense of your major points; this method allows you to dip in and out of your story as you plan. Sketch out a list of scenes or incidents that you want to include in your paper. Take one "corner" of each scene or incident, and explore it in detail: a description of your uncle's garden, for example, or the kind gesture of a stranger on the street. Then read your vignettes with an eye toward coherence and connection.

WITH A WRITING PARTNER

22. Ask your writing partner or group to brainstorm questions about your topic and then select at least ten questions they want answered in order of importance or interest. Make an outline for your draft using these questions and major headings.

WITH A GROUP

23. Think of your classmates as business colleagues, and schedule meetings with them twice a week to discuss your draft. Always have a new or revised chunk of writing to show them at the appointed time.

24. Arrange with your teacher to set aside a drafting period in class, a half-hour or so of writing time once or twice a week. Write sections of your draft by hand during this time as quickly as possible. Commit yourself to having a substantial chunk of text to read aloud to your classmates when the period ends.

25. Get an opening paragraph down, and have your partner or group brainstorm questions about what should follow. Write out detailed answers to these questions on your draft, and then decide what parts of these answers you want to keep. If particular questions get you rolling, go with them.

ON THE INTERNET

26. Draft directly to other writers on the Internet. Set up a schedule to e-mail a new section of your draft to someone you meet in an online writer's forum or to a writing partner or classmate.

27. Set up a writer's Web page as a class, or get one of your computer whiz friends to do it for you. Publish a schedule on the page that advertises the "publication" dates of parts or whole drafts. Then take turns as a class or in groups "publishing" pieces of your drafts. Include a way for readers to provide feedback and report to the class on what they say.

Finish Writing

For decades, I blew deadlines, refused to let go of manuscripts, and wasted countless hours and reams of paper over drafts that were never good enough. Now, at 52, I am trying to learn to tell myself "It's good enough," to hit the send button and move on to the next story. It's not easy. To a perfectionist, "good enough" sounds more like an epithet. But lowering my standards is the only way I can achieve my writing dreams of productivity and publication. My writing will probably never be perfect, but perhaps if I'm lucky it will be good enough.

CHRISTOPHER SCANLAN

All art is knowing when to stop.

TONI MORRISON

CHAPTER 22

Writers Help Writers

Writing is a private act with a public result.

The best part of the writing day for me is when I go down to my writing room under the back porch and sit alone before the computer screen. I have had early morning coffee with the regulars at Young's, checked the day's non-writing schedule with my wife, and now I sit alone knowing I will write, but not knowing just what I will write.

I do not follow the instructions of a teacher, an editor, a colleague, a committee, a boss's boss. In an increasingly complex world that forces people to work together in committees, teams, panels, groups, I am on my own. I face a writing task I can perform successfully or screw up on my own. There is no one right way, no one wrong way, but thousands of ways that will work and as many that will not. It is up to me and me alone to find the way that is effective for this task, purpose, and audience. Only the draft tells me what to do.

My acceptance of aloneness that grew in appreciation and delight as I aged probably began when I was an only child and a sickly one at that in an era that allowed weeks of convalescence in a bed. No television, no computers, no computer games. I could read stories and I could tell myself stories; I could nap dream and daydream. I lived my stories, enjoying the long days by myself. That was what I liked about my before-the-sun-was-up paper route even in the crystal cold of a New England winter.

Going Public

But most writing should not remain private. Its purpose is to share, to explain, to persuade, to illuminate, to call attention, to entertain, to make the reader think and feel, and see. Writing is a way of joining and contributing to the human community.

I often found that my shyest students were the ones who said the most yet resisted going public. It is frightening to go public. Writing is self-exposure. We reveal ourselves—how we think, how we feel, who we are—when we write. We all stand naked on the page.

To make the transition from private to public writing, we need to share our writing in process, to receive the response of readers when we can still make changes in our draft. We know what we intended to say but until we hear the reaction of test readers we won't know. Test readers might be compared to a friend who we ask to taste a salad or soup to see if it is properly seasoned. The cook usually asks the question—"does it need more garlic?"—and so does the writer—"do I need more documentation?"

Revealing a draft in process can be dangerous. We need to find helpful test readers who can tell us what works and what needs work with kindness and candor and whose comments make us go back to our desks eager to write.

Finding Good Test Readers

In class we may be assigned to groups of test readers, but most of the time we must find our own test readers—and it isn't easy. The difficulty is that we cannot tell if someone is a good test reader for us until we ask them to read a draft and receive their response. We must make our draft—ourselves—vulnerable and we must be able to survive when it turns out that the reader is not helpful.

While searching for good test readers I have learned there are significant issues that affect my choice:

• *Does this reader write?* I find that the readers who help me the most are themselves writers. They know the writing process themselves. They do not just see writing problems solved, but recognize the problems when they are not solved, when the writer is faced with contradictory options.

There are good readers, editors, teachers who do not write, who read and recognize good writing, but the test readers who help me the most when I am in the process of writing are those who look at my drafts as they look at their own.

• *Is this reader right for me?* This is a clear personality issue. There are many good writers I neither like nor respect, and others I do like and respect that simply rub me the wrong way. It may be a matter of their personality or mine, their style or mine, their way of working or mine, but they simply do not help me. How do I know? Because when I leave them I do not want to write. The good test reader may have delivered an opinion that is difficult for me to accept but I still want to get back to work on the draft immediately. I am inspired to revise.

• *Can this reader help my drafts?* Many brilliant editors, teachers, and colleagues simply make the drafts they read their own. They know what they would do to the draft and how they would do it, but it may not be right for me or my writing task. The good test reader doesn't take over the draft and fix it; he or she is able to enter into my draft, my voice, my way of working and help me see how I can become more myself. The good test reader respects what I am trying to do and my ability to do it.

• *Is this reader right for this stage in my writing process?* I may need a reader who is good at reading a sketch draft or outline and suggesting research options, another who can really evaluate structure, and another who is great at line-by-line reading and questions of voice. I also have readers who are helpful with poetry and others who hate poetry but are good at reading nonfiction.

• *Will this reader give me the kind of reading I need?* My friend, Chip Scanlan, a fine writer, is my best reader and he taught me to tell him the kind of reading I needed. Before that we would share tentative, early drafts and subject them to demanding line-by-line editing. It is vital that writers tell the readers what they need:

- "I know this is rough, but do you think there's a story here?"
- "Here's an early draft; where do you think I need more documentation?"
- "I've written this as a personal essay; do you think it would work better as an argument or perhaps a narrative?"
- "I'm not sure I've got this organized effectively. What do you think?"
- "I like the way this is organized and documented but do you think the voice works?"
- "Before I submit this, would you check the spelling, grammar, mechanics, accuracy, grace to see if I've done anything stupid or clumsy?"

I look for classmates, friends, or colleagues I respect and like, ask them if they will read what I have written. I listen, try never to be defensive—if they don't get it, readers won't—and go back to my writing desk. I don't follow every suggestion—writing isn't a military drill—but if the readers' suggestions are helpful overall and if they made me want to take another crack at the draft, I treasure their help and will return to them again.

Becoming a Good Test Reader

Asked for a reaction to another writer's draft, most of us unholster a red pen and cut. We cruise above the page like a hawk and when we see something to correct, we dive down and do it.

This is what most of our teachers and editors have done. They immediately make right what is—in their opinion—wrong. They take over the draft and make it their own. It's as easy as sitting in the stands and saying the quarterback shouldn't have thrown the ball after his pass has been intercepted. Of course we may be wrong in the context of the game or the season, but we don't admit that.

I have found that the less writing a person has done, the more certain the critical opinion. For professionals, writing is a fascinatingly complex process in which what is wrong on one page may be right on the next. It may be ineffective to use sentence fragments during a paragraph of exposition, necessary to use fragments on the next page to re-create action.

Worse still is the fact that most inexperienced writers want this mistreatment. They believe that writing is a matter of simple right or wrong, that writers follow strict rules that cannot be broken. They expect a teacher, editor, or classmate to fix their drafts so it follows the rules.

"Be honest," they say. "Don't worry about my feelings. I need a tough read." And there may be times when drafts need to be "fixed" on deadline, but it is not the best way to help inexperienced writers learn how to improve their writing skills.

The good test reader invites the writer to set the agenda:

"HOW CAN I HELP YOU?"

"WHAT DO YOU NEED FROM ME?"

"WHAT CONCERNS DO YOU HAVE ABOUT THE DRAFT?"

"WHAT ARE YOU TRYING TO SAY TO WHOM?"

Test readers should not take over each draft and correct it by the readers' standards, but help writers think about their individual writing task and their writing processes so they can learn how to apply the lessons of this draft to future work.

If the writer refuses, at first, to set the agenda, just saying, "Tell me what you think" or "Tell me what's wrong," the test reader should say, "It's not my piece of writing, it is yours, and I want to help you make it better in your way."

There are a number of questions that can help test readers help writers see their own drafts and their own writing techniques more clearly.

"What surprised you?" This is my favorite because it tells me where the writer is and what the writer is learning that I can reinforce with my reaction. What surprised the writer about her draft may be on the page or off, it may be the topic of the draft or the technique used to write it, no matter. We can help writers best when we know where they are, what is their learning point.

My next favorite question is *"What works?"* This usually surprises writers but they need to know the strength in the piece because most effective revision works by identifying and building on the strengths that are in the draft or may even be outside the draft in their command of the subject or point of view towards it.

That question is usually followed by *"What needs work?"* This does not imply failure but allows writers, once they have identified what works, to deal with what needs to be done to support and develop what is working.

Of course our questions must fit our personality and the personality of the writer, but the test reader's responsibility is to help the writer see the strengths and weaknesses and make him realize he has the ability to solve the problems.

Remember the priority of issues to be dealt with is just the opposite of what most beginning writers expect because of what they have been taught in school. They believe that revision means working from problems of spelling, typography, grammar, to questions of structure, documentation, and voice, and then to matters of point of view, audience, genre, subject. The experienced writer reverses the order, first looking at the larger questions of subject, genre, audience, and point of view. There is no point in dealing with the more detailed issues until you identify the territory you are going to explore and the method you will use.

After that is dealt with, it is wise to reexamine the structure, documentation, and voice. Finally when all those concerns are dealt with, the test reader can help find typos, misspellings, grammatical and mechanical details that confuse rather than clarify.

Helping a Writing Group to Help You

When I studied writing in college and graduate school years ago, the writing group was more a test of fire than anything else. Student writers would go public and then everyone would attack. The student writers were not allowed to defend themselves, not even allowed to speak. They simply had to hunker down and take it. It was a literary scrimmage in which everyone tried to break the writer.

I hated it. It didn't help me. Most of the time the group didn't even seem to be talking about my draft but projecting their own writing problems or standards onto my work. They didn't seem to know what I was trying to do or how I was trying to do it. They didn't even care. They wanted me to write like them, each in her or his own contradictory way. The only result was to make me feel I couldn't write.

And, of course, when we read the papers of others I behaved the same way at first, tearing into them like a lion after a kill. That was what I was supposed to do even though I realized it was not helping the writer, often even destroying the writer.

And then, years later I found myself teaching writing. I watched my own students being thrown to the lions and was appalled at the bloody massacre of drafts that had possibilities and the destruction of writers who slunk away, convinced they were hopeless. Then I overheard two writing teacher colleagues say of a wonderful woman writing student that "she didn't have the balls to publish." This was so anatomically incorrect, so sexist, so unhelpful, so revealing that they thought the writing workshop was a macho event, not a matter of instruction, that I said I'd have no more workshops in my classes.

That would have been a loss because writers do need to test their drafts by going public in a workshop. We all know what we hoped to say, but we do not know what our readers have heard and how it affects them until we face them in workshop. We need to know the problems that must be solved, solutions that may solve them, and, above all, to know what works. That's what's most helpful to me when I share in a supportive writing group. They see things that are good where I had only seen bad. But I didn't want to sponsor a kind of critical gang rape of my students' drafts. I didn't know what to do.

Then I read that the poet and writer Kenneth Koch asked the question of the student, "How can we help you?" The next day I changed the rules and announced:

1. The purpose of sharing in a writing group is to help writers.

2. The writers were to set the agenda before the group read the draft. (If the draft was to be distributed before class, always a good idea, the writers would set the agenda in writing at the top of the draft.)

3. The writers would answer the question: "How can we help you?" Now I would add, because of my experience with Chip Scanlan, my favorite test reader, "What kind of reading do you want?" The writers were encouraged to say where they were in the writing process, what they were trying to do, what they thought worked and needed work.

The tone and the effectiveness of the writing workshop changed immediately. The class didn't stop being critical, but they read the draft in the context of the writer's purpose and phrased their responses in encouraging, supportive ways. Often they were more demanding than before, seeing what the writer could do and, in that process, setting the standards higher for a writer.

Even more dramatic was the fact that the writers were not defensive in body language and attitude. In fact, just the opposite: They could be tough, honest, demanding of their own work, and many times the writing group saw more value in the draft than the writer did. Remember that the writer needs to know what works for the reader, so that the writer can build the revision on what works, not on what has gone wrong.

Becoming a Helpful Writing Group Member

To make yourself become a helpful writing group member listen carefully to what the writer says of the draft, its purpose, and the process of writing it. Do not read the draft as if it had to meet some abstract set of standards and do not read the draft as if it were your own.

Read the draft with empathy, as if you were the writer. Your job is not to make writers become you—or Joan Didion or George Orwell—but to become themselves, seeing their world in their own way and sharing what they see in their own voice.

Going Private

After you have gone public by sharing your writing with test readers, you have to return to the loneliness of your writing desk and consider what you have learned. This does not mean following the test readers' instructions blindly. In fact, that should be impossible. You are an individual speaking to a group of individuals. In a recent publisher's review of one of my manuscripts, the reviewers split down the middle, half thinking issue after issue should not be changed because it was so good, and the other half thinking it must be completely changed because it was so bad.

You have to weigh each comment. Here is my scale:

1. I pay close and immediate attention to what readers say that surprises me. Often readers find things in my writing that I didn't see; often they see strengths where I saw weakness. But good or bad, I consider unexpected responses first. They give me a new vision of the piece. I may or may not accept that vision but each one—profound, scary, stupid, weird—illuminates my draft.

2. I next pay attention to the responses I hoped I wouldn't hear. I write a draft and suspect I should do more research but try to get away without doing it. Or I had make an illogical leap, hoping my cleverness would carry the day. It never does. Or I have some tangled sentences that needed untangling. I hope to get them past a reader's eye.

I used to fight to defend what I had written when the teacher, editor, or colleague was so stupid they didn't get it. I don't anymore. I was once egotistical about what I had written and defended it to the death. Now I am egotistical about the fact I can find a thousand ways to write anything. I'll find some way to get what I want to say by the editor.

3. I read the draft with fresh eyes, seeing it anew, and try to make it cleaner, sharper, clearer. My goal is to write with accuracy and grace and become invisible. I don't want the reader to see me, but to see the subject. Writers are truly subversive and they want their readers to think they experienced what the writer has written, that the thoughts and feelings on the page are their own.

I need editors, teachers, colleagues, test readers, but I am my most important reader. It is my brain, my soul that is on the page and the final draft must be the product of my mind and my heart and mine alone.

CHAPTER 23

Learning From Writers

Writing is not a mystical art; writing is a craft that can be understood, shared, learned. The best writers do have talent, but that talent is honed and developed. It is important for apprentice writers to join experienced writers at the workbench, to see how badly they write—good writing is the product of bad writing; the said that cannot yet be said—and see how they find the good within the bad and develop it so that others can understand.

Fortunately there is a great deal of testimony by writers on how they write. The autobiographies and biographies of writers, their collected letters and published notebooks, their case histories and the reproductions of their manuscript pages, interviews with writers such as those published in the *Paris Review* and collected in the series *Writers at Work*—all of these sources document how writers work. You can also invite classmates to share their case histories, asking them to tell you how they have written pieces that you admire. Most of all, you should write your own case histories to discover what you have done when writing well, so that you can reinforce those habits and skills that work for you.

The case histories in this chapter reveal the narrative of writing samples, then the final drafts. You may want to skip ahead and read the final drafts, then go back to see how they were developed. Too few readers have had the opportunity to attend play or symphony rehearsals, watch artists or sculptors at work in their studios, and most of all—since writing is ordinarily a secret art—see writers alone with their pages. We can't open up the skulls of writers, but we can go into their workrooms and observe the process of "making" writing.

Student Case History: Writing to Describe— Sarah Hansen

Sarah Hansen has written an excellent student case history that covers the entire writing process from finding a topic to completing a final draft. Her piece grew out of an assignment to write, with abundant detail, about a familiar place—her hometown.

HOW I WROTE MY ESSAY

SARAH HANSEN

This descriptive essay is the result of eight drafts, conferencing, workshopping, journal writing, thinking, and sharing. It was hard work—sometimes frustrating but mostly rewarding. I have learned to have confidence in my own writing. But I still have not tackled procrastination, and wonder if I ever will.

To come up with a topic, I brainstormed places and people that I would like to describe and that I know a lot about. I picked my hometown, Birch Grove, Illinois, because I have a lot to say about it, and at that point I was confused about my feelings for Birch Grove. My English teacher, Bruce Ballenger, says confusing topics are the best to write about because by writing about them a discovery might be made that will help to end the confusion.

Before I began a first draft, I brainstormed another list of Birch Grove people, places, and events. The list I made ended up in two piles: one bad and one good. This was something I hadn't expected.

I circled the most controversial and the weirdest things on the list. Directly after this, I began to free write about the circled things.

I thought about the paper for a few days then went to the computer to type what I had written during the free write. I added more stuff to it that had been in my head and took the first draft to my conference with Bruce. He liked it. But the point I was trying to make was not clear, because I didn't really know exactly what the point was. Ideas about a hometown are complex. This was the most difficult part of writing this essay: trying to find the point.

Also, my first draft had too much description. I had to find the places where the description didn't fit the purpose of the essay. I actually used scissors and tape on the first draft to cut out unnecessary description. The second draft had less description but was no closer to realizing a point than the first. I was frustrated.

Our writing class had group workshops where we shared our pieces with three or four other students. I read the Birch Grove paper to my workshop group, because I needed fresh perspectives. I also needed some positive reinforcement. All three students liked my paper—that made me feel more motivated to work on it. One woman in my workshop agreed with Bruce and me that the point of the essay needed to be clearer. The most valuable thing I learned from the workshop was that the topic of the essay wasn't clear until the middle. They suggested starting the essay with a paragraph or idea from the middle.

With this in mind, I changed the first paragraph and fiddled around with various parts of the essay. But I was still frustrated with the meaning. I knew that the essay was slowly progressing with each draft, but from drafts two to six, I made little progress finding exactly what it was I wanted to say without sounding boring, clichéd, or obvious. I started to share the essay with a lot of different people. Most close friends tend to like just about anything you do and aren't objective enough and don't give much criticism. Older English majors and my parents and their friends, people that read a good amount of writing, turned out to be the most helpful.

With each successive draft, the second to the sixth, my English teacher and I became more and more discouraged. I couldn't reach exactly what it was about Birch Grove I wanted to say. Did I want to say how I felt; did I want to say something to the people of Birch Grove; did I want to make a point about all hometowns; did I want to make a statement about the world by talking about one hometown? My biggest mistake was not writing in my journal enough. I procrastinated writing about my feelings for Birch Grove, because it was too frustrating.

Around draft four or five, I couldn't look at the paper with objectivity anymore. I was too close to my subject and practically had the words memorized, as did my English teacher. Finally, after draft five, Bruce gave the draft back to me with questions written all over it about what it was I was trying to say. In my journal I wrote answers to his questions. It was this way, by talking to myself in my journal, and by answering questions, that I nearly found what I wanted to say.

I wrote that the good in Birch Grove I had realized by going away far outweighed the bad. The energy of the good things is what makes Birch Grove all right. When people realize this, then Birch Grove will be safe. We decided that this would be the final draft. I thought I was done.

But when my father read the essay out loud that night, I realized what I had wanted to come across did not. In the sixth draft it seemed I had forgotten the racism and the close-mindedness. I intended just the opposite. I wanted to say that I have realized the good in Birch Grove, but that the bad needs to be changed.

The biggest problem I had writing this essay was attempting to find exactly what the meaning was. I also needed to spend more time talking to myself about the essay in my journal. In hand with this, I needed to spend more time writing than thinking about the essay. A good idea can sometimes surprise me as I write, but that rarely happens when I think about my writing without a pen in my hand.

I learned to share my work with as many people as I could who were willing to take the time to read it and give their responses. It is motivating to hear fresh and new ideas. The conferences helped in that Bruce and I would talk about what it was I was trying to say. The discussions helped each draft to come closer and closer. It was also good to hear someone give positive comments about my writing.

Writing a descriptive essay can help with any other kind of writing. Description is about saying things so that other people can see, feel, hear, and smell what you have written. These things are revealed through specific details. It is exactly the same concrete writing that is needed to critique a novel or write a term paper. Sarah's daybook started out with the following entry:

I have to write a paper for a book—a descriptive essay—to be published. I have no idea what to write about—just knowing it's for a book makes me nervous. I've even been avoiding thinking about it. Dad—Heather—East H—commune—expectations—grandma—Birch Grove—Berry Farm—trip to France—second semester at UNH.

She starts out with a writer's apprehension and makes a list of possible topics. She did put a mark like a rising sun after "Birch Grove," and then she wrote a draft that plunged into the subject: "The round and friendly minister of the Methodist Church of Birch Grove, Illinois, was found in Sanderson's three-story department store stealing a large pair of light brown corduroys." In her daybook Sarah wrote:

I showed my first draft of the essay for the book today. Bruce liked it. I was so relieved. He's really helped me to be more confident about my writing. We decided that the point of the paper wasn't too clear. He said that I need to "peel the onion." In class we talked about how the layers of the onion are like layers of ideas and points to an essay or a piece of writing. The deeper into the onion layers you get, the closer you are to your main point. I know a few things that I am pointing out but I don't know exactly how to say them. I think my main point is about how Birch Grove was all bad to me at first, and then, as I went to UNH, I realized the better things about it. But the better things don't excuse the bad things. I'm still confused about it. I don't think this paper is very interesting. I don't think it will keep the reader's interest. We also talked about how there are too many descriptions.

I find this sort of writing to myself important. It helps to put into words what you got from a conference and to identify your feelings about the text and about the process of writing.

The next page in Sarah's daybook showed a typical jumble of doodling and writing. She listed potential specifics as a form of recovering memories and discovering what she may write.

Later she wrote in her daybook:

I've decided to show my paper on Birch Grove to my workshop group. I don't know where to go with it. I have been thinking a lot about the focus of this paper and it's getting me nowhere. Hopefully, they'll have some insight to it that will get me motivated for revising this paper. I spend too much time just thinking—I should be writing in this journal more but don't have discipline—I procrastinate too much.

● ● ●

My workshop group really liked my paper. Lin said it reminded her of her hometown which is cool cause that's sort of a point I'm trying to make—every hometown for every person is both good and bad—end up blaming home-town for everything—have bitterness towards it. A love-hate thing. I don't know that's quite what I want to say though—seems cliché. Brian and _____ both thought that the beginning isn't clear—maybe begin with paragraph that starts, "I moved to Birch Grove, where life offers more, when I was four. . . ." They said as it stands now it's a little unclear what I'm talking about. So I'll try to rework that into the beginning and Brian thought that my point was perfectly said—that I shouldn't add more but said I should make my point clearer. I agree more with _____ cause at this point I don't even know what my main point is. I asked them if they thought it was boring and if it caught and kept their attention. They said it was interesting and kept their attention well so that made me feel better. Asked if there was too much description and they said no.

In all her daybook entries Sarah reveals the way a writer's mind—and emotions—work. I certainly feel the same way about my drafts as Sarah does about hers. To learn to write effectively you need to be open and realize your feelings and how to deal with them.

Later in her daybook Sarah writes:

I'm annoyed with my paper about Birch Grove. I'm sick of it. I'm too close to it and can't see it correctly any more. It seems so trite and boring and cliché. Bruce seems to not like it much either. That's really discouraging. I don't know what exactly I want my point to be that's creative and fresh.

These excerpts from her account reveal the writer at work, what goes on backstage that is essential to the creation of an effective piece of writing. Space limitations here preclude reproducing her drafts, sometimes marked up with her comments, other times with the comments of her readers, but they document the evolution of her essay. In the third draft, for example, Sarah begins, "When I was four, my mother, my dog, and I moved to Birch Grove, Illinois. I've spent all my time there minus the summers which I've spent with my father. Passing the town border a cheap billboard reads: 'Life offers more in Birch Grove.' "

By the fifth draft her lead reads, "Passing over the town border into Birch Grove, Illinois, a billboard, paint peeling off, reads: 'Life offers more in Birch Grove.' When I was four years old my mother, my dog, and I moved to this Midwestern town. As I grew up, I'd pass the fading billboard faded as was along with and my tolerance for BIRCH GROVE, my bitterness and anger seen in a grimace as I thought, 'Life offers less in Birch grave.' faded along with it." By the eighth draft the lead was as it appears below. Writers have to learn by writing and by considering what they have written and how it can be improved.

Here is Sarah's final draft as it was turned in:

SIMPLE BIRCH GROVE

SARAH HANSEN

Passing over the town border into Birch Grove, Illinois, a billboard, paint peeling off, reads: "Life Offers More In Birch Grove." When I was four years old my mother, my dad, and I moved to this Midwestern town. As I grew up, I'd pass the fading billboard, and my tolerance for Birch Grove faded along with it.

The owner of Sanderson's three-story department store found the round and friendly minister, Donald Morison, of the Methodist Church of Sycamore stealing a pair of brown corduroys. Most of the bank presidents and company founders and Mercedes Benz owners of Birch Grove belonged to the Methodist Church on the corner of Third and Main. They put up a big fuss about having a kleptomaniac as a minister. There was great pressure on Don to leave. These influential people weren't seen at Sunday services anymore to listen to Don with his brown, shining eyes give the sermon. Only a few members forgave Don, told him so, and asked him to stay. One Sunday, a woman slowly stood up and told the churchgoers that the Bible says to forgive, and that we should forgive Don, and help him out, because his problem is a disease, just as alcoholism is a disease. Don left the Methodist Church two long months after the incident, and the members are now content to sit in the pews and sing out of the worn, red, cloth-covered hymnals.

Miss Gooch, the assistant counselor at Birch Grove High School, wears her thin, gray-brown hair in a tight curl perm. I was the student council president my senior year, and we were discussing some upcoming activities. Miss Gooch liked to gossip; she asked me how my friend Peggy was doing. Peggy has fair, freckled skin and blond, curled hair—like most other girls at Birch Grove High School. Her boyfriend is thin and has beautiful, chocolate brown skin. What Miss Gooch meant was, "How is she dealing with having a black boyfriend?" Miss Gooch said, "I am not prejudiced, but I don't think the races should intermingle . . . and I hate Mexicans." Sixteen black students and forty Mexican students attend Birch Grove High School, where Miss Gooch is the counselor and student council advisor.

At age eleven, my sister Traci walked to the Save And Shop, three blocks down Walnut Street from our house, to buy groceries. As she crossed the supermarket parking lot, a little girl, not over seven years old, was left alone in a beat-up station wagon. The girl rolled down the front seat window. "Nigger," she said to Traci, my adopted sister, now one of the sixteen black students at the high school. Traci is startled as she looks in the mirror to see her own black face. Her eyes are so accustomed to whiteness.

Sam Ritchel was salutatorian of my class. Now, when I come home for Christmas or Easter vacation, I see Sam wandering around Birch Grove, or staring off in a booth in the Coffee Shop. He's taken too much acid, refuses to get a job, dropped out of the University of Wisconsin, shaves his eyebrows, wears black lipstick, black eyeliner, and black clothing. He listens to Jim Morrison on his tape recorder, and says nothing but "black, melancholy, darkness, despair . . ." In the Weston Elementary School, Sam's nickname was Happy.

I hated everything about Birch Grove. I hated its conservatism, its hypocrisy, its ignorance, its racism, its close-mindedness, and its ugliness. I hated what it did to bright, open-minded people who could not escape. In Birch Grove, I could only think about itchy, depressing, angering things. Times when snotty Claire Saunders knocked over my newly painted three-speed bike in the fifth grade, when the whole of Birch Grove watched *Top Gun* perpetually for weeks after it came out on video, when high school students egged our house five times in two months because my stepfather is the assistant principal of the high school—a fair, kind man who must punish students for skipping a study hall, for smoking in the music wing.

But since I've been at college, far away from my hometown, I can remember eating macaroni and cheese on Kiersten's sunny, white porch with her mother and mine, enjoying the lunch hour before returning back to the third grade. I can remember the annual January snow sculpture competition in front of Prince's Restaurant across from Birch Grove Park. I remember my very first valentine in seventh grade from my very first boyfriend: shy, curly white-haired Jim Morse, a farm boy. The homemade card was caringly shaped and cut out of red, pink, and white construction paper. Two white rabbits kissed on the front; inside, pencil cursive writing read, "I'm glad that you're my valentine, Sarah."

I remember the annual Birch Grove Pumpkin Festival where all of Birch Grove competes in a pumpkin competition, decorating them as a scary monster with orange peels for hair and gourds for arms and legs or a pumpkin phone for goblins and ghosts to use. The Miller family won the grand prize one year and got to go on the *Bozo Show*. There was a pumpkin princess or prince award to the best essay in the junior high, and the grade-schooler with the best scary picture got to ride on the fire engine at the front of the Sunday Pumpkin Parade. I watched the parade from the Abbens' house on Somonauk Street with people from our church, eating warm carameled apples, and drinking hot apple cider sitting on fold-out chairs along the street. The huge oak, maple, and sycamore trees lining the street screamed autumn with their yellows, golds, reds, and oranges.

I remember Mrs. Munter, my junior and senior year English teacher, my most influential teacher, sneaking chocolate M&Ms out of the second drawer down. I remember her strong, clear, enunciated voice demanding and challenging us to accomplish more in her class than we ever had before.

I remember driving along the smooth and winding North River Road just after dusk on a hot summer day, windows rolled down and arms out waving, watching the thousands of tiny blinking lights of the fireflies just above the soybeans and wheat fields. Although I used to hate the flatness of the land, now as I return I appreciate the great big sky and lie in the middle of a cornfield with Steven and Pam, watching the silver-white shooting stars stream across the blue-black expanse.

I see Sean Allen in the store window of Ben Franklin, the five and dime, and wave back knowing he's still the same friendly, simple person he always was and will be. I know that every summer the woman with the wrinkled face will bring out her popcorn stand, and my mother and I'll buy sweet caramel corn and eat the whole bag as we walk slowly home in the hot night air.

Mom says Birch Grove is a good place to bring up children. Maybe it is in some ways. Friendly Sean Allen, the sun on a white porch that makes the skin hum, and Mrs. Munter's deep, resounding voice are as pure and warm as the wealthy churchgoers and close-minded Miss Gooch are tarnished and cold. But even as the sweet-smelling fields, the wide Midwest sky, the leaves of screaming colors that crackle under foot seek to balance this out, I know that Birch Grove still is no place to bring up my children.

Student Case History: Writing to Persuade—Emma Tobin

HOW I WROTE MY ESSAY

Emma Tobin

It all started with a letter. Donald Murray wrote to me one day, asking if I'd be interested in writing a piece for the new edition of his book *Write to Learn*. Thrilled by this proposal, I immediately responded with an enthusiastic "yes." Don asked me to come up with a list of topics and a somewhat sketchy outline for each. Really having no idea what I wanted to write about, this proved to be harder than it at first sounded.

It took a while, but I did get a list. The topics included: comparing gay and lesbian rights to other minority groups' rights, animal rights, how contemporary music affects teens, rock musicals, and age discrimination on the Internet.

A few days later I got an "OK" from Don to go ahead on any of these topics, but he was leaning toward the one on age discrimination on-line—mostly because all the communication we had done was on the computer. I considered this. I had written a more developed paragraph outlining what I would write about on this particular topic, and I felt I would be able to continue writing about it. So I did just that; I had my topic.

I'm an Internet user from pretty far back. I use it for research, communication with friends, and, yes, I do go into chat rooms more than I probably should. But it's from being in these chat rooms that I've noticed the incredible amount of discrimination that goes on. There is almost always someone who is hating someone else about something. It can be anywhere from one fourteen-year-old who is trashing another for being a skateboarder or an entire chat room ganging up on one individual for being a different race. But whatever it is, it's almost always there, in one form or another.

I had lots to say the first time I sat down at the computer to begin writing my paper . . . maybe a little too much. After about a half-hour of furiously pounding away at the keyboard, I finally stopped, looked back, and realized I had three pages filled with jumbled opinions, terrible spelling, some random punctuation, and not a single paragraph. This, I realized, was definitely NOT my essay.

I made several more lame attempts at starting a draft on this topic, until I sat back, realized this wasn't working, and took a new approach. I probably wouldn't have come to this conclusion so quickly if it weren't for Don, actually.

After e-mailing him all of my first attempts, he told me that, while I did have good ideas, they were totally disorganized and not very well focused. Organization has never been a strong point for me, but I was determined to improve.

Don's advice to organize my thinking got me sitting down in front of the screen the next day with a plan just to write a good, solid lead. And that's what I did. I wrote a clearly focused, organized lead, went back, edited it, spell-checked it, and saved it. "There," I thought. "There's the first part of my essay I will actually be able to use."

My paper progressed. I kept writing. I discussed every aspect of age discrimination I could think of. Problem was, I couldn't really think of a whole lot. Where it had seemed that I had a lot of ideas on the topic in my original outline and in my first writing attempts, when I actually decided to get organized, there didn't seem a whole lot to say. I only got about three pages. Dead end. From that point on, I could not think of one, single thing to add, and the only thing I could think to blame was my topic. It was time, I realized, for sane reconsideration.

It was then, in my first exasperated stage, that I came to an on-line article about the law that the government had passed but that had been blocked by the courts in 1996. The law would have made it impossible for teens under eighteen to access a lot of information on the Internet. This, quite honestly, outraged me. I consider myself an adult, and the fact that the government was going to keep one from ANYTHING on-line had me furious. (But also a little thankful because I then had more to add to my piece.)

The first draft was the most difficult. After discussing the law the government was working to pass, I ran out of ideas again and rambled my way through another couple of pages. But there were definite sections that were usable, definite paragraphs, sentences, words even that I liked. So even before I sent the first draft off to Don, I began making changes. I was so embarrassed in fact by my first full-length attempt that I decided to wait until I had a second draft complete to send along with the first, including a note that I knew the first one was not exactly up to par.

But even in the second draft, it again seemed that organization was the key problem. Nothing was in any kind of order that made sense. That's when I decided to come up with a detailed outline that I could follow for the whole essay. I already had the sections written, even if they were a little sketchy. But before I could work on improving them, I needed them to be in place.

Basically, my outline divided my paper into three sections, the first being "What are parents, teachers, and politicians doing to limit teenage [Internet] access?" The second was "Why they shouldn't limit teenage access, and what's wrong with the way some adults view teen Internet use." That was the section that needed the most revision. When I start going off about something I feel strongly about, there's really not much stopping me. I'll ramble for pages before I realize I'm doing it.

The third section was "What I'm proposing." It took me a while to get this one done. To be honest, I didn't know what I was proposing. I wasn't sure what I thought should happen in the end. I guess maybe if I were more sure from the beginning, the piece would have been easier to write.

The main thing I learned about while I was writing this essay was the importance of revision. I certainly did enough of it anyway. Something that I wrote that sounded good one day would sound awful to me the next. An opinion that I had at one point would seem outrageous to me later. I not only had to revise to make the writing better; I had to revise to make my actual opinions different. I kept changing my mind so often on so many issues that it really became difficult to revise my piece.

One thing I changed my opinion on fairly drastically was the issue of pornography on-line. I kept shying away from the topic to begin with. I didn't want to discuss it in a way that made me sound inhuman, just reciting facts and figures, but I also didn't want to get into too many details and make it too explicit. Finding a place in the middle was kind of difficult.

When I started writing this paper, I was sure it was hard to get pornography on-line if you were a teenager, though I really hadn't tried to find out. But when I actually began letting other people (besides Don) read my work, they would read that section, look at me critically, and say "Is that true? Isn't it easy to find pornography on-line?" I would tell them it was in fact true, hoping and hoping that I was right. One day I made the decision to find out for sure.

This is what I discovered: If you want pornography on-line, you can get it regardless of your age. That's when I had to almost totally rewrite that section of any paper. My position changed from "It's difficult to get porn," to "Most teenagers don't really spend their time doing that kind of thing on-line anyway." In general, this is true, but I feel I would have made a stronger point if pornography really WAS difficult to come by . . . which it's not.

The pornography issue definitely tested my revising skills. I was stretched to make a good point, where maybe there was not such a good point to make (or at least not a point in my favor).

It was around this time that I met with Don. Before now, we hadn't conferred in person, only on-line and on the phone. By then, he had read my first and second drafts, and he came to the conference prepared with a list of changes to be made. But, his were very open-ended suggestions. Nothing was "And this part should be more like this . . ." It was more like him telling me how to look for what didn't work, instead of showing me what he thought didn't work. It turned out that, in Don's opinion, my lead didn't work. It had consisted of a sort of sketchy picture of what a typical day for me on-line looks like. "This piece is about safety issues on-line," he said to me. "There has to be some element of danger. Some feeling that something COULD happen." It turned out that he was absolutely right. Conveniently, my second paragraph worked very well as a lead, with a few changes. So in the end, it turned out that the first thing I wrote that I thought could be used really couldn't be used at all.

After working through and reworking an entire essay more times than I can count, I came up with my "third draft" which was really more like my tenth. If I had printed it out and sent my piece to Don every time I made drastic changes, he would have gotten far too many drafts in the end. I was sure that this was it; I had finally produced an essay worth reading.

HOW I HELPED EMMA TOBIN WRITE *HER* ESSAY—DON MURRAY

I invited Emma Tobin to write a freshman English paper for me for entirely selfish reasons. I wanted to work directly with a student assigned to write a college freshman paper. I never expressed any doubts that she would do a good job, because I did not feel any. I found that most students see themselves—and their potential—reflected in the teacher's eyes. Confidence on the part of the teacher and writer is as important as confidence in the writer. Another word for this is *faith*. I had faith that Emma Tobin would produce a good paper.

Teachers who hold opposite views think that such confidence—the student is capable of good work until proven guilty of poor work—pampers the student, that the method is touchy feely. I disagree. My confidence that Emma would produce a publishable paper put extraordinary pressure on her.

I had two principal approaches I would apply that appear contradictory. First, I would give Emma a lot of room to teach herself. I wanted her to find her own subject so that she would be motivated to pursue it. I also wanted her to write *without* instruction so that I would not waste time teaching her what she already knew. I would, however, reinforce her natural writing abilities so that she would know she possessed those skills. Then I wanted to give her a chance to learn to write on her own, knowing that what she taught herself would be truly learned and would remain with her all her life.

I would be available to nudge, encourage, direct, support, rescue, stimulate during her own learning if necessary. When she produced a draft, I would respond with a candid, professional response that would encourage her to solve the problems I spotted in her own way.

She first showed me a long list of topics. Her first one seemed the most likely. It was better thought through, a significant topic that would interest readers of my textbook and could be completed in a few weeks. I nudged her toward this topic, revealing my interest in it, but emphasizing she had to make her own choice; she was the one who had to live with the topic.

Here is her proposal:

AGE DISCRIMINATION ON THE INTERNET

From my experience, the average person in a chat room is a teenager or young adult. Many of us spend more time on-line than adults, and understand how it works better than they do. But still, we are considered "the lower level being" on-line. For example, we are thought to be less intelligent, unimportant, even silly or annoying. Some adults even go so far as to imply or suggest that we "leave the area."

It's a type of discrimination that is not considered "bad" or "unkind" because the ageist person uses the excuse "I was young once too." By saying this, it means they believe that they have the right to dislike us, because they were in our place once. Ageism shows through in everyday life, but much more strongly on the Internet. I believe I could produce a good paper defending teens on-line, but taking the adults point of view, and trying to understand it.

Hands-off criticism can be frustrating for most students. They are used to being told exactly what to do, but instruction external to the piece often doesn't work. Each writing situation has its own context. The writing has its own focus, the point of view of the writer, its own meaning, and a specific form and order that carries that meaning to the intended audience.

The writer doesn't just apply rules; the writer thinks, defining the subject and its writing and solving problems that vary with the writer, the writing task, and the writer's experience with the task. My job was to create an environment that gave Emma the confidence to discover and solve her own problems, certain I would be on hand if she needed me. We all know the basic model for teaching and editing: When a baby starts to walk, we hold out our hands close enough to help, far enough to encourage—and we laugh when the baby falls, cheer when she doesn't, and keep increasing the distance. I gave Emma room, hid my impatience, and waited while she wrote several drafts before she gave me one.

Now I had to give her a professional response. I read the draft quickly and phoned her that it was good but needed work and we made a date to get together. Then I read the draft carefully, doing some line-by-line editing on page two. I did not want to "correct" the entire piece because I would make it mine, and it was her subject and her language. I wanted to show her what I would do but make it clear she had to find her own way to solve the problems I saw in the piece.

Here is her draft:

HOW ADULTS PERCEIVE AND RESPOND
TO TEENAGE INTERNET USE

A newspaper article headline jumps out at me from the page. "Girl Kidnapped from Home by Internet 'Romeo.' " Immediately dropping the comic I was just starting, I turn my attention to the story. . . . Same old stuff. Thirteen-year-old girl leaves her home willingly with a strange man she met online. Girl is underage, becomes sexually active, police get notified by parents, strange Internet guy gets found, girl returns home, admits she made a stupid choice. Story ends with parents saying the problem is solved because their daughter "No longer has Internet access."

This type of story convinces many non-Internet using adults that the Internet is not safe for their kids. Right there is a huge reason why parents don't want their kids hanging out unsupervised on-line. They believe that they are going to get molested or sexually harassed by some screwed up forty-year-old guy lurking on the Net. And if they have no other way of knowing what the Internet is like, then they will become certain that it is a dangerous or risky place for their children to be.

Now I mark up this page.

Pornography. ~~The word certainly catches your attention, doesn't it? It's also a word~~ comes up fairly often in discussion of teens and the Net. Even

> *I cut here to show Emma how to get out of the way of the text. She was running around, waving her arms, calling attention to herself, getting between the reader and the text. I find that I only have to do this a few times for the writer to understand.*

adults who don't worry that teens will encounter sexual predators on-line worry that they will be exposed to inappropriate and disturbing images and information.

> *I wrote in the margin: "Good direct sentence." It is important to point out what works as well as what doesn't yet work.*

Finally, there are some adults who think of the Internet as a big computer or video game which teens waste their time and energy on.

> *I wrote: "Good but that's another point," followed by some words I can't translate. My bad handwriting was an asset; my students had to figure out what I meant. They had to think.*

So what actions are these adults taking to limit teenage access to the net?

> *In the margin I wrote, "Let's discuss rhetorical sentences." Inexperienced writers try to make a connection with the reader in this way but it doesn't work. The questioner knows the answer. It is insulting. Questioner doesn't listen to answer. Nurse: "We want to take our shot don't we."*

Many kids and teens whose families own computers are not ~~even~~ allowed to use chat rooms or the World Wide Web when there are no parents home. Some parents ~~even~~ insist that they sit by the computer and supervise their kids.

> *I cut some unnecessary words and suggested she start a new paragraph below.*

The other place where a large population of teens can use the Internet is at school. ~~Many schools across the country have net access so students can use it for research on the Web and for communication with other classrooms in other schools. Of course, teens could get themselves into the same kind of situation just as easily at school as they could at home. This being what teachers~~ [*I inserted*] BECAUSE OF CYBERFEAR ~~students have~~ many schools limited access, and ~~many schools~~ block all chat room use completely, and strictly limit control [?] Web use.

Here I wrote: "Let's talk about transitions—not needed if information is in the right place."

~~These are some of the reasons that parents and teachers don't want kids on the Internet, but it goes to an even higher level than that.~~ In 1996 the state of Pennsylvania passed a law, the Communications Decency Act, that would make it illegal for any one under eighteen to obtain or access anything online that is considered offensive.

I wrote: "Develop. Clarify."

That obviously includes sexual images and sexual text. Fortunately for teens across America, the law was challenged,

"What was challenged?"

argued before the Supreme Court in the spring of 1997, and eventually over-turned. But this does not mean that the government is through. The law was not adopted because the court thought that it was too vague. ~~It is safe to as-sume that~~ In the near future, HOWEVER, a more specific law ~~will~~ MAY be proposed and passed in other states.

~~The point is that~~ Adults are making decisions to limit Internet access to teens . . .

I did not mark up any more pages, but I did give her the following written response, telling her these were just suggestions:

Response to Emma Tobin's draft:

As I said in the e-mail last night I am glad you are doing this. We have some-thing to work on. I am going to give this a professional, line-by-line reading, and I will be specific about what I think needs to be done. I think it is impor-tant for me to be directive at this time. But I want you to have room to dis-agree, to solve the problems in your own way. I want to be clear so you will understand my concerns but I do not want to be dictatorial.

As I used to tell my students, this kind of careful response is a compli-ment. Most drafts, my own included, do not deserve this attention.

I will have marked the draft in spots to show how I might do it. Do it your own way.

1. **Title.** *You're getting there, but I think it will be helpful if you sharpen the title with some tension or at least an implied conflict.*

   Why Parents Should Fear Cyberspace Why Should Mom and Dad NOT Fear Cyberspace?

   Should Mom and Dad Fear Cyberspace?

   Should Cyberspace Be Off Limits for Teens?

   Is ~~Parents'~~ Mom and Dad's Cyberfear Justified?

   Is Cyberfear Justified?

   Are Teenagers at Risk in Cyberspace?

Play with some more as a focusing device, trying to get to the central issue in as few words as possible. This is too important to be taken seriously: Play.

2. **Lead.** *The lead is well-written but it would not compel me to read on. Nothing happens. If that's your message, the reader has to go on with the fear that something may happen. The first paragraphs may be scaffolding, what you needed to write to get to the lead, and it may be a scene you can use later to allay fears about cyberspace.*

   Your lead may be in the paragraph beginning "A newspaper ~~article~~ headline jumps ~~out at me~~ off the page: "Girl Kidnapped . . ."

3. **Orwell's pane of glass.** *Get out of the way of the information. This is hardest to learn, but you are right on the verge of learning it. Let the information speak. George Orwell said, "Good writing is like a window pane." You should see the subject, not the author.*

   I'll point out what I mean on page two. Good writers always do what you do, writing about what you are going to say. You'll learn just to say it.

   You have to write with authority, in specific terms with specific evidence.

4. **Answer the reader's questions.** *Anticipate the questions the reader will ask and answer them when they ask them.*

5. **Line-by-line editing.** *When your draft is finished—you have your topic, a sequence or order that carries the reader from point-to-point, and you have provided evidence for each point—then you should read line-by-line:*

   Are my nouns specific?

   Are my verbs active?

   Are my sentences, sentences—usually subject-verb-object?

   Is each word the right word?

   Is everything clear to an uninformed, intelligent reader?

   Is my voice clear and tuned to support what I am saying the way a movie score supports the action?

   Have I emphasized what is important, usually placing the most important information at the end or the beginning of the paragraph or section?

   Do I move fast enough to keep the reader reading, slow enough to allow the reader to absorb what I have said?

   Have I given the reader enough or too much information?

   Do I break tradition only when it's necessary for clarity or emphasis?

   Here is her final article:

WHY TEENS SHOULD BE ALLOWED IN CYBERSPACE

EMMA TOBIN

A newspaper article headline jumps off the page. "Girl Kidnapped from Home by Internet 'Romeo.' " Immediately dropping the comic I was just starting, I turn my attention to the story . . . Same old stuff. Thirteen-year-old girl leaves her home willingly with a strange man she met on-line. Girl is underage, becomes sexually active, police get notified by parents, strange Internet guy gets found, girl returns home, admits she made a stupid choice. Story ends with parents saying the problem is solved because their daughter "No longer has Internet access."

This type of story convinces many non-Internet-using adults that the Internet is not safe for their kids. They are convinced that their children are going to get molested or sexually harassed by some screwed up forty-year-old-guy lurking on the Net. And if they have no other way of knowing what the Internet is like, then they will become certain that it is a dangerous or risky place for their children to be.

Of course, there are other reasons why parents might limit their teenagers' access to the Internet. Some think of computers the way they think of video games or television—as a giant waste of time and energy. But for the majority of parents, it is pornography that dominates their thinking about teenagers and the Internet. Even adults who don't worry that teens will encounter sexual predators online worry that they will be exposed to inappropriate and disturbing images and information. For this reason, many kids and teens whose families own computers are not allowed to use chat rooms or the World Wide Web when there are no parents home. Other parents insist they sit by the computer and supervise their kids.

Teens have even less on-line freedom at school. Many classrooms and libraries across the country have Net access so students can use it for research and for communication with other classrooms in other schools. But teachers and librarians worry that teens could get themselves into the same kind of situation just as easily at school as they could at home. Because of cyberfear, many schools limit access, block all chat room use completely, and strictly control Web use.

Many politicians have the same idea: In 1996 the United States Congress almost unanimously passed and President Clinton signed the Communications Decency Act, a law that, among other things, criminalizes "the use of any 'interactive' computer service to 'see' or 'display in a manner available' to a person under eighteen any communication that 'depicts' or describes, in terms patently offensive as measured by contemporary community standards, sexual or excretory activities or organs" ("Complaint," 2). Fortunately, for teens across America, the law was challenged, argued before the Supreme Court in the spring of 1997, and eventually overturned. But this does not mean that the government is through. The law was not adopted because the court thought that it was too vague and that limited adults' freedom of speech. In the near future, however, more specific laws limiting teenage access to information on the Internet may be proposed and passed.

Adults are making decisions to limit Internet access to teens partially out of a misunderstanding of what the Internet has to offer and partially out of an overreaction to sensational stories they've read or heard. Most of these adults just don't have a realistic idea about how most teens spend their time on-line and about what are the relative dangers of an on-line life.

Let's start with the risk of sexual molestation and kidnapping. Even if we admit that there is some risk of meeting a dangerous sexual predator on-line, is this danger greater than the one teens face every day in "real life"? This same parent who won't let a child go into a chat room may let a son or daughter walk to the convenience store two blocks away, where their child may not just talk to a child molester through a screen, but actually encounter one. When looking at the things that can happen to kids and teens on the Internet, some adults seem to forget that these same—or much worse—things can happen off the Internet just as easily. There are dangerous people in the world; there are people on the Internet. Therefore, you are going to end up with some dangerous people on the Internet. It is fine for parents to take that into account, but they need to understand that most Internet interactions are positive and completely safe.

Of course, that's not the impression you get from reading newspapers or magazines. For example, a 1997 *People* magazine story described case after case of teenagers who left their homes to meet up with on-line correspondents. If you read the piece carefully, you see that a majority of the stories were about teens who met up with other teens who turned out to be perfectly safe and friendly. Of course, there were also some stories of teens who met up with middle-aged sexual predators, but in those cases, is the Internet to blame? It's really just juveniles making unwise, uninformed decisions. When a person goes somewhere on their own will, it does not mean that they were kidnapped. Teenagers can make a bad decision to leave home with someone they meet in person just as easily as with someone they meet on-line. Something is definitely wrong in these cases, but the Internet is not the source of the problem. Teenagers who have a desire to run away with someone they have never met must already have a pretty good motive for wanting to leave home.

Adults who want to limit teen use of the Net because of the easy access to pornography also have several misleading beliefs—that pornography is forced on children, that teenagers spend all of their time surfing erotic Web sites, and that older teens would be as traumatized by sexual material as young children are. There is no denying that pornography is available on the Net. There are hundreds or even thousands of Web sites featuring explicit photographs, videos, and stories ranging from soft-core erotica to hard-core child pornography. And even though a teenager has to go through an "age check" and waiver statements to enter most of these Web sites, pornography is pretty easy to get your hands on, if one chooses to do so. But "chooses" is the key word there. When one does end up with sexual content, it is almost always deliberate. You could erase every letter or ad that porn sites send out, you could simply not reply to any on-line users who are looking for someone who wants to "trade pics" (send and receive pornographic pictures), and you could leave any chat area where the topic is sex. If you did not go out of your way to get pornography, you probably never would.

But pornography is not the reason most teenagers go on-line most of the time. While some teens spend some of their on-line time looking at porn, the average seventeen-year-old doesn't come from school, sit at their computer, and start searching for pornographic pictures. Some adults seem to believe that since there is access to pornography on-line that every teenage person in the entire world is going to do all they can to get to it and is going to end up using the computer for nothing else.

But let's assume that some teenagers are spending most of their on-line time viewing pornography. We could still ask what harm is taking place? Is there any evidence that proves that teenagers are hurt by talking about sex with other teenagers in chat rooms or by looking at pictures of naked people on Web sites? Many teens are actually having sex themselves. One would think that if a person could actually have sex, then they could write or read about it. Same thing with pictures. If a teenager has seen (or done) off the Net all the things they see on it, then the Internet is not the problem.

The law that Congress tried to pass in 1996 would keep a person under eighteen from getting their hands on anything even vaguely related to sex. If an eighteen-year-old person can vote, serve in the armed forces, and drive, then certainly a seventeen-year-old can surf the Net. In fact, many seventeen-year-olds are sexually active, some are married, most have jobs, and some are freshmen in college. If our culture gives teens the freedom and responsibility to do adult things, then it's ridiculous to deny them full access to everything on the Internet.

If the Communications Decency Act had been adopted, then it could have been illegal for some teenager to get information on AIDS and HIV, because it is sexual material. It could have been illegal for a homosexual teenager to get any information that they may not feel comfortable asking someone for in person. It could have been illegal for a pregnant teen to get information about pregnancy or abortion. Teens suddenly would have been cut off from a whole world of valuable information.

Let's imagine there is a fifteen-year-old girl named Ann who has just had her first sexual experience. And let's say that she soon begins to worry that she may be pregnant or may have picked up a sexually transmitted disease. Let's assume that she doesn't want to talk to either of her parents about it or anyone at all, for that matter. The thought of going to a doctor or to Planned Parenthood has her terrified, so she looks into the only anonymous source she knows: the Internet.

If the 1996 law had not been overturned, Ann would find once she was on-line that she might not be able to get access to any information on STDs or pregnancy or AIDS. There would be barriers to "protect" her from this information. While adults may think that they are helping Ann by denying her this information on-line, I do not think they understand how wrong they are. Of course, this is exactly the kind of argument that the plaintiffs in the Supreme Court case made to overturn the law. Groups including Planned Parenthood, the

Queer Resource Directory, ACLU, and American Library Association all argued that teens have a need for as well as a constitutional right to this information.

The other problem with adults' perceptions of the Internet is that they not only point out everything that's wrong and exaggerate those points, they also seem to ignore all of the good things that the Internet has to offer teenagers. For example, you never see a story written up on the thirteen-year-old girl who puts out a newsletter every month on animal rights. Or an article on how two fourteen-year-old kids meet twice a week to discuss poetry. And you'll never see anything on the sixteen-year-old boy who has started his own successful graphic design business on the Net. You only see the stories of destruction the Internet has caused.

And what about that side of teenage Internet use that no one could have a problem with: the academic side. It's eleven o'clock at night. You have a paper due the next morning. Frantic for information on the Spanish Armada, you turn to the Internet. There in front of you is an encyclopedia article, plus many other write-ups. You take the notes and produce a good paper without setting foot inside a library. Now, of course, I am not saying this is the best way to get a paper written. One should look in many places and sources of information for a well-rounded piece. But it is a life-saving way to get something done when you have no time. And even when you do have the time, the Internet is an excellent source. They will have information on all the aspects of what you're looking for. What could be better?

Some adults believe that there is no educational side to chat rooms such as those found on America On-line. Totally wrong. Just to get the basics out of the way first, there is really no better way to learn typing than being in an interactive conversation where you have to respond quickly, or your chatting partner will quickly be bored with you. One learns how to argue maturely and effectively and how to relate to people through the written word. Then we come to chat rooms that are especially designed for learning, such as AOL's "Thinkers," a room for pondering life—or really—whatever else is on your mind. Next are chat rooms where you are able to work one-on-one with a teacher on the subject you need help with. Many times I have tackled complicated math work I never thought I could do using someone I found on the Internet as my tutor. The flow of information coming from the Internet is endless. There are so many sides to it, so many possibilities.

For someone like me who has a great interest in writing, the Net has been incredibly enriching. For instance, through AOL's "Instant Novelist" site, I have had a chance to be part of a writing community. You can respond to anything you read, both positively and negatively. When you post a story of your own, it is read by hundreds of little editors across the country, all there to help you improve your work. Many participants develop e-mail relationships with fellow on-line writers. I, personally, do not see one thing that could be considered dangerous about this and most other Internet sites. What I do see are a million ways to learn, to find useful information, and to connect to other people.

When ten-year-old children wind up with pornography in their grasp, we have a problem. But when seventeen-year-old young adults are not allowed access to information that they may need for their education and even health, then we have another problem. Many schools, government agencies, and computer companies are all working now to develop guidelines and new technology to keep kids away from dangerous material on the Internet without limiting adults' freedom to information. Parents can buy "smut-blocker" software, like "Cyper Patrol" or "Net Nanny," which restricts and records a child's use of the Internet. And libraries can now buy Web software and search engines that keep children "from turning up unwanted risqué sites while looking for information on that report on The Chile Pepper through History" (Powers, 2).

But as *Boston Globe* columnist Ellen Goodman has said, the key is to "protect children, without shackling adults." And, in this area, teens ought to be treated as adults. Parents, teachers, and politicians have a good motive: protecting young people from the dangers of the Internet. But they need to step back and distinguish between children and teens. Again, if a seventeen-year-old can work, drive, and attend college (not to mention, have sex and even have children), how can you keep full access to the Internet off that list?

WORKS CITED

Electronic Privacy Information Center, "Complaint," U.S. District Court, Eastern District of Pennsylvania, Civ. No. 96–963, http://www.epic.org./free_speech, p. 2.

Goodman, Ellen. " 'The Boston Solution' to Pornography on the Internet," *Boston Globe*, July 24, 1997.

Powers, Kate. "DO YOU Know Where Your Children Are Surfing?" *Parent Soup: Family and the Internet*, http://www.parentsoup.com.

Rogers, Patock. "Snared By the Net," *People* 48, No. 6, August 11, 1997: 48–53.

Student Case History: Writing to Inform—Tina Winslow

The research paper is the fundamental building block of academic discourse— and it is the composition assignment most dreaded by the students who have to write research papers and the instructors who have to read them. Most research papers are dull, because the students have not yet done research on a topic important to them and the form becomes more important than the message.

Yet students need experience in gathering information, building the information into a significant meaning, and presenting it so that the reader not only understands the message but has access to the sources of information the writer used.

Tina Winslow demonstrates that a student can prove a knowledge of academic research conventions while writing a lively, interesting report that places scholarly material in a human context.

Her assignment was to "Inform readers by completing a five- to ten-page [1,500–2,500 word] research report that will demonstrate your ability to use scholarly techniques to investigate a topic and reveal its significance to them."

She was told to keep a journal that would reveal her writing problems and how she solved them. The student was given time to find a territory, then a topic, sharpening her research question in consultation with the instructor and classmates, then to write several drafts. She was to have at least a dozen sources with footnotes and a bibliography that follows Modern Language Association guidelines. Tina was also referred to the "Tips on Writing to Inform" (p. 310).

The case history shows how she moved from the vague and general to the specific, finding a way to combine several aspects of her topic so that the final article had a clear, documented focus. She moved toward this clarity of vision while achieving an increasing grace. Her work is a demonstration of good thinking as well as good writing, as all effective prose should be.

In her journal she first brainstormed (pp. 228–229) on animal rights looking for a focus line (pp. 229–230) that contained enough tension to spark a research report:

- Animal rights—where is the line?
- Who decides whose rights get to be violated—the chemical industry at odds with the natural order or is it the natural order?
- Would people buy the products if they saw the process it goes through?
- Do animals have rights—historical/religious implications—meat industry—health implications
- Pumping poultry, beef with hormones
- Is the meat industry lying about the health requirements and how far down the line does it go?
- Feel passionately about not eating meat without bias, why?
- No meat has helped achieve my goals to trim down—why? What does meat do psychologically or physiologically that slims people?
- Moods are evened out—hormones in meat?
- No guilt with eating healthy, cheaper
- In small way have stopped poor treatment of animals
- Read a book that describes the process

- People live too much of their life with spurts of unrealistic violence or softened reality
- Would you enjoy chicken if you watched the man rip his feet off because the nails had grown around the bars of the cage back into his feet?

This is an excellent way to begin. Tina doesn't worry about the writing, she is scouting the territory to find a way into her subject, and the journal entries show her ranging across the whole area, looking for the most important material— the material she needs to explore and that her reader needs to know. Her final topic is deeply hidden in her list, and the approach that makes her final paper distinctive does not appear. But this step was essential to her thinking process.

Now let us listen in as she continues talking to herself in her journal. Remember that the direction in which she thinks she is headed is not the direction in which she will go. Elizabeth Bowen said: "The writer . . . sees what he did not expect to see. . . . Inattentive learner in the schoolroom of life, he keeps some faculty free to hear and wonder. His is the roving eye. By that roving eye is his subject found. The glance, at first only vaguely caught, goes on to concentrate, deepen; becomes the vision." In Tina's journal, we catch a rare but important glimpse of the writer in the act of thought, catching her unexpected vision.

- -

JOURNAL

When I think about animal rights many issues shoot through my head. My two kitties waiting on my bed, waking up with a lazy stare that pretty much lays out the law—"You have the right to scratch my ears and why you are at it the bowl in the other room is a bit empty." Those are their rights but they are lucky cause I'm a sucker for a good mew and milk breath. Society's definition of animal rights extends more into our comfort zone as human beings. Not only my comfort zone about what I will use on my body but what goes into my body and the realities that went into mundane things I take for granted. My true experience in this issue began when my roommates a year or so ago were very much into the movement of animal rights. They were adamant about how cruel vivisection was and that it should cease immediately for all products. While I struggle as a compassionate human who has done volunteer work with animals to comprehend the exact reality of vivisection, which in essence needs a proper definition this issue becomes one of limits. Flipping in the handy Miriam-Webster the definition alone of vivisection bothers me inside— "the cutting of or operation on a living animal usually for physiological or pathological investigation" or worse, definition two, "animal experimentation especially if considered to cause distress to the subject." Who gave us the power to take that animal's life? Or worse keeping it alive to test it's reactions. I understand the theory that it's an us or them kind of world but in reality where people are just vain creatures how much does it matter if the deodorant and the makeup don't look just right or don't exist especially when everyone will not be wearing it. It's just a layer of protection anyway.

> *Tina's final paper will not focus on animal rights, but she needs to start here to find her ultimate focus. Her journal reveals the writer talking to herself, and what some people might describe as bad or sloppy writing is good writing here, appropriate to the task. It is courageous of Tina to allow us to see a good writer doing the rough, pre-draft writing that is essential but not usually revealed to a reader.*
>
> *Let's listen further to Tina talking to herself. She is at once the appropriately floundering writer allowing her evolving text to carry her toward meaning and the draftsperson standing back and watching herself working.*
>
> *This split vision—being in the writing act and observing and standing back watching herself in the act—is essential for good writing.*

The paper I want to write needs a focus line. Something that creates a tension. I think if you take the normal person who wasn't attacked by vicious dogs as a child and who was socialized with animals normally and show them the process from start to finish they will understand the brutality of the process. To take something living and breathing and warp it for our needs doesn't seem right. Do the end results, a juicy piece of chicken or tube of lipstick, really make the process OK? In a world filled with lawsuits on product liability, companies are scrambling to find proof that this product when accidently swallowed, poked in an eye or applied incorrectly won't adversely affect humans. If there is so much concern with humans why aren't humans used to test these results and why is there such a lack of concern with humans when their food is concerned. If they don't want to harm people why would they pump pesticides onto the eventual food of cows and poultry, pump hormones into animals for better growth, keep them in deplorable conditions and then wonder why Americans are getting fatter, madder and sicker. It all comes back to a basic respect for other things.

This paper will be about the realities involved in everyday products that involve animals. It could go two ways right now. With vivisection you have the brutality of pictures and there is a plenty of tension about it with animal righters and research industry. When I visited a pharmaceutical company my friend worked in she told me not to even joke about freeing the animals. They had them locked up in a special room you had to have four keys to get into. When I asked her why she didn't mind testing on them she was like well they throw poop on me and are mean but ultimately her argument was humans first, everything else "bah." She didn't realize that if someone put me in a cage and shot me full of drugs I would have a very similar reaction. Mean as spit and proud of it. The other direction of the paper could be on when we eat, what is the process of the food. The chickens and cows we eat aren't exactly running around the yard, they are chemicals through and through from the minute they are born.

Focus lines—potential:

Chemical food—what are we eating? Whose rights are they anyway?

Food industry—provider or killer?

In consultation with her classmates and a conference with her instructor, Tina came to realize she didn't really have anything new to say about animal rights but that she had strong feelings about her new decision to be a vegetarian, a decision that was tested on a cruise with her parents and confirmed two weeks later when her mother—a life-long meat eater—suffered a heart attack. Tina felt uncomfortable about using her personal feelings and her personal experience in a research paper but was encouraged to try to find a way to combine objective research information with personal experience.

Writing is often like a tunnel that is wide at the beginning but narrows as you follow it. Here you will see Tina as the tunnel narrows and she finds her focus and begins to work within it.

OK, focus line:

Solidifying Vegetarianism—the hard way. Or why I am still a Vegetarian today. Or Taming the Taco Urges.

But really the focus although it doesn't sound focused is that the after shocks of my Mom's heart attack solidified never eating meat again for me. I guess I need to trim it into a more readable state but basically this issue to me is like a spark to gasoline. For the record, when I shared this topic with my parents they were not exactly thrilled. To defend my mother, who really wants to know that an incident in her life scared everyone down to their belief foundations. To defend my father, well he just likes to argue. Basically, he wants to vent that you can't be a vegetarian for purely health reasons because he believes that you can be unhealthy, heartwise, and eat no meat. For instance, chicken and turkey and low fat/cholesterol meats can be eaten and still be healthy or did you hear the one about the vegetarian who died of a heart attack. He maintains you are a vegetarian for ethical—not health reasons. My point for my focus is that although I was a brand new vegetarian before the heart attack (Wait till I tell you the taunts that a week cruise with my family brought me a week and a half before my mother's run in with her arteries), the material I read after the scare solidified that I will never again put meat in my mouth. I guess the ethical part is there as back up but after what I learned I see meat and the industry as killers and beyond that totally unnecessary.

(Title)

- Momma, Me, and Meat
- Scaring the Meat out of Me
- Meat Stinks
- A Tube in the Nose Is Meat out of Me
- Vegetarians Unite
- You Don't Get a Chest Pain Eating Broccoli (Unless You Swallow a Stalk)
- Reeducation of My Mouth and My Mom
- Liar, Liar Heart on Fire

- If It Had a Mother I Won't Eat It—Mom
- Moo Cow and Then Shoo
- You Don't Have to Beat Me with a Carrot to Make Me Give Up Meat
- Thicken Your Clogged Arteries with Lies

(Lead)

Understand what will stop me from ever putting meat in my mouth again, was my mother in an ICU bed after her heart attack.

● ● ●

Well that's part of it. But after reading up on heart attacks and what they are about, I realized she didn't have to be in that bed and that keeps me focused in my non-meat eating habits.

● ● ●

(Lead-2)

Nothing made being a vegetarian easier than realizing that my mother having a heart attack didn't have to be a reality.

(Trail)

- mother has heart attack
- already a vegetarian but very new
- in learning more about heart attacks read book after book which detailed what meat is and what it isn't both from heart aspect as well as healthy living aspect
- realization it's a lie—meat industry
- based on what it does to your body, what is in it and the benefits of other types of protein—meat stinks
- I realize this isn't an ethical attack on meat eater's way of life but I personally feel betrayed

(End)

You don't have to not eat meat to be heart healthy but after realizing what goes into the process and how close you are to being a vegetarian why would you eat meat.

(Possible first paragraph)

Through the mist that are tears unshed, I look wildeyed at my mother in an ICU bed with slightly green, thick tubes in her nose. ICU has no room for deep personal talks with the doors flung wide open and everyone's heartbeeps beating loud enough for the staff behind the desks to hear. Her nails are purple as well as her lips. She looks an off color like someone walked in and sucked the oxygen out of her skin. Pale and tired, with wide brown eyes, she pleads with me not to be scared—it's just a minor life threatening procedure.

> *Good writing is promiscuous; writers do not write one draft but many. We do not have the space to show each of Tina's drafts, but we can listen to her journal as she reacts to completing her first draft.*

OK, the first rough draft is out. It's weak in some areas admittedly but I feel better having the thoughts in a rough diving board for better work. I just hate, hate, hate showing other people work that I don't consider finished. The hardest part for me in this critique sessions is admitting that I have to write just like everyone in stages and that the first things out of my typewriter/computer look just like everyone else's. I guess I want to be brilliant and perfect on the first shot. "BULLS EYE! the crowd roared as they tossed the first draft writer roses." But alas, I need more work on the quotations and the integration of paraphrases not to mention documentation style at this early stage is enough to make MLA come out and personally tweak me on the nose. But at least I have exorcised the demons onto paper at this point all while on Tylenol for sinus and cold.

Better flow and tighter in beginning paragraphs, Smoother flow in Paragraph 2. More quotes, direct in Paragraph 3, check for logic flow LOGIC FLOW in paragraph 4 with more sources, more sources and another quote or two. Summary needs more bite.

So . . . round two is done but I have to cut cut cut.

● ● ●

I guess I am going to have to cut the chemicals paragraph but I do this under duress.

> *It was not cut. She found a way to keep it in the piece by making it support her focus on why vegetarianism is important to health. Later, in her journal, Tina debates a cut her peer readers suggested. Ultimately the decision has to be the writer's but she expresses the insecure response to a critical suggestion that is natural in a writer.*

I like that paragraph, I feel it has merit and geez, it grosses me out and I wrote the thing. I was hoping to get my punch in quick and well I guess as a being with somewhat rational thought I realize it doesn't fit in with the mom-had-a-heart-attack motif. I really like the mixture of personal vignettes mixed in with writing of a more research nature. I find it really interesting the process this had been. I started out with animal rights and have it nuzzled, pushed and CUT it down to just vegetarianism.

For next draft:

- Finish getting the references pinned down to MLA style

- Re-arrange the chemical paragraph out of the paper and work out the flow

- Go through with a fine tooth grammar comb and get all of it laying down without obvious cowlicks (pun intended)

A complete case history would reproduce draft after draft, and space prohibits reprinting each one of them. Also, it would probably be boring to all but the most interested students. The important element in the process is the astonishment expressed by the writer in her journal at what she has written, discovering that writing is not recording previous thoughts but thinking by writing. Her understanding of the subject changes as she captures and clarifies meaning through language. This is the most important lesson of her writing course.

Man, oh, man. Whew! Done, finis, end of papyrus! OK, so I feel guilty at being relieved that I'm done with the paper. It is not what I would have conceived at the beginning but it wound it's way down the paper trail to completedom. I wanted a paper that bit and nickered at lies and then spit it out in a huge cavalcade of burning all consuming truth. What I got was a paper that resembled "What I Did over the Summer" tone with a vegetarian twist.

Now, now, I can hear that voice now. (How come this voice always resembles my mother's voice?) "If you aren't happy with the paper then change it." The truth is I will never be happy with the paper. I can put it in my treasure box and dig it up 10 years from now and say (in my knowing and critical tone, of course) "This seems so pedantic and stiff," "What was I trying to say here?"

"Why did I pick that word or phrase?" Hopefully, buried in that chest is also my good critic who reads it and nods her head and whispers, "Because that's where you were. The paper is done I can look at it and see the legitimate course it took. I started off worried by what I would write, how to say it perfectly, WHERE AM I GOING TO FIND THE TIME and now I can look at it and realize I created something.

Each of Tina's drafts clarified what she had to say and allowed her to say it in with increasing liveliness and fluency. At first, she wrote each paragraph separately, moving the information to a position that answered the reader's questions. Then she had to consider the pace and proportion: How much of her mother? How much research information? Throughout the process she had to listen to her peer readers and her instructor but make her own way.

Compare the drafts of the lead in her journal with the final, disciplined example of good writing. She had to go from the bland statement of her first effort ("Understand what will stop me from ever putting meat in my mouth again, was my mother in an ICU bed after her heart attack.") to purple prose ("Through the mist that are tears unshed, I look wild eyed at my mother in an ICU bed with slightly green, thick tubes in her nose.") to the fine, professional beginning that moves the reader ("I look at my mother in the Cardiac Care Unit bed with pale green, plastic tubes in her nose."). In her first draft, Tina moved from her mother to this paragraph:

Defining what a heart attack is, how it occurs and how to prevent it/takes research it's not as cut and dry as eating to much fatty fried stuff, arteries clogging and then the next moment you are grabbing your arm and clutching your chest calling for an ambulance as you go down. In essence, it is an artery clogging that causes heart attacks but as more and more research is done, it's about a whole lifestyle. Several papers can be written on the technical medical reasons behind a heart attack, why meat is morally wrong, what is wrong with the meat industry but the focus for this paper is on why eating meat and dairy products is unhealthy for the body. Every fork of meat and dairy product have harmful chemicals present, a meat and dairyless diet automatically trims weight off people and a vegetarian diet makes having a heart attack hard to do. Accordingly the premise that being a vegetarian while only one aspect of the whole heart attack chain reaction and still a controversial one, is one worth merit and consideration.

As Tina said in her journal, she is embarrassed at readers seeing her early drafts, but it is important for students who imagine that others write well the first time to observe how real writing emerges, draft after draft, until the final draft has this excellent paragraph:

The first step is to look at meat and dairy products for what they really are. Meat and dairy are primarily vehicles for fat and cholesterol. Most of the established health organizations, as well as the Surgeon General, recommend reducing the fat in your diet to 30 percent (Robbins, *May All* 89). Studies indicate that this number should be even lower to prevent cancer, strokes, diabetes, hypertension and heart disease risks, and to eliminate or drastically reduce cholesterol (Robbins, *May All* 89). But Dr. T. Colin Campbell, director of one of the most comprehensive and informative diet and health studies ever undertaken (Chen et al.) and on the committee that set the 30 percent guideline, states it would have been impractical to recommend less than 30 percent, as most people would have to drop the animal foods from their diet and go vegetarian (Robbins, *May All* 90).

Every piece of information, whether it comes from personal experience or library research, moves the meaning of the paper forward. The result is a moving, significant, well-documented research paper that both pleases and educates the reader. Here is her final draft:

TAKE A BITE OF LIFE

TINA WINSLOW

I look at my mother in the Cardiac Care Unit bed with pale green, plastic tubes in her nose. CCU has no room for personal whisperings with the doors flung wide and everyone's heartbeeps beating loud enough for the staff behind the desk to hear. Her nails are purple as well as her lips. She looks an off color as if someone sucked the oxygen out of her skin. Pale and tired, with wide brown eyes, she pleads with me not to be scared: it's just a minor lifethreatening illness.

The initial prognosis was a minor heart attack, which calmed everyone until the tests revealed three of her arteries were more than 65 percent blocked. This new prognosis, terrible and threatening, was the one thing that would force change into my Mom's life so dramatically and so thoroughly. Having married a Nebraska "meat and potatoes man" her response from the beginning was not one of compromise but rather pouty resistance to a new way of life forced upon her.

Even with a monitor recording her heartbeat she was upset by the chicken and pasta they gave her for lunch.

"It is so bland."

"Mom, you're in a hospital."

"But you think they could put some cheese on this stuff."

"Mom, you just had a heart attack."

I had just become a vegetarian shortly before my mother's heart attack and I discovered through the research I did—both before becoming a vegetarian and after my mother's heart attack—that a diet with no meat and dairy products automatically trims weight and reduces the chances of a heart attack. I also learned that a vegetarian diet prevents the harmful ingestion of chemicals that are present in meat and dairy products and provides a good defense against disease. With benefits like these, being a vegetarian seems the only logical choice for a healthy life.

The first step is to look at meat and dairy products for what they really are. Meat and dairy are primarily vehicles for fat and cholesterol. Most of the established health organizations, as well as the Surgeon General, recommend reducing the fat in your diet to 30 percent (Robbins, *May All* 89). Studies indicate that this number should be even lower to prevent cancer, strokes, diabetes, hypertension and heart disease risks, and to eliminate or drastically reduce cholesterol (Robbins, *May All* 89). But Dr. T. Colin Campbell, director of one of the most comprehensive and informative diet and health studies ever undertaken (Chen et al.) and on the committee that set the 30 percent guideline, states it would have been impractical to recommend less than 30 percent, as most people would have to drop the animal foods from their diet and go vegetarian (Robbins, *May All* 90).

Even chicken, the most common alternative consumers choose when trying to cut fat from their diet, derives 35 percent of its calories from fat and that's without the skin (*PETA Guide* 1). Beef, on the high end of the scale, has about 22 grams of saturated fat in an average 8-oz. serving (*PETA Guide Compassionate Living* 17). And as Dean Ornish points out in his book *Reversing Heart Disease,* "eating fat makes you fat" (255).

Why does eating vegetarian naturally cut weight and reduce the chances of a heart attack? According to Martin and Tenenbaum, authors of *Diet against Disease,* most of the fat we eat is in the form of meat and dairy products, so reducing our fat consumption in these areas will reduce the total fat and saturated fat in our diets (16). Conversely, vegetarian foods are primarily complex carbohydrates and are hard for your body to convert into fat (Ornish 257), so the less cholesterol you eat, the lower your risk of developing coronary heart disease (Ornish 263). As advised by the Physicians Committee for Responsible Medicine, a diet without meat and dairy products makes low cholesterol easy "since cholesterol is found only in animal products such as meat, dairy and eggs" (2). Your body also makes all the cholesterol it needs naturally so "it's the excessive amounts of cholesterol and saturated fat in the diet that lead to coronary heart disease" (Ornish 263).

Two months after becoming a vegetarian and two weeks before my mother's heart attack, my entire family went on a cruise. I guess on a cruise, where every meal is supposed to be about reckless abandon without regard to waist size, waste or what you're eating, a vegetarian feeling uneasy isn't going to be the most popular topic.

"What do you mean the French onion soup made you sick?"

"Mom, once you don't eat meat, your body gets used to not having it and I didn't think about French onion soup being made with beef broth."

"There is no way broth can make you sick."

My mom, looking concerned but unbelieving, eyed me suspiciously and tried to make light of it.

"Look, honey, I just ate a whole side of cow, tail and all and I'm fine. How can a soup broth made of beef make you sick?"

The vegetarian target on my forehead grew as my mother's tone drew my entire family's attention at the dinner table. That week spent with my family trapped on board a floating buffet table, just two weeks before my mother had a heart attack, was a study of open hostility at the mention of not eating meat or cheese. My mother—at the head of that committee—was unbelieving that meat could be so harmful. "My quirky daughter, what's next?" seemed to be the question asked without realizing she was less than fourteen days away from a full-blown heart attack—not realizing that it was also the same thing making us both sick.

But it is not just the fat and cholesterol we need to be aware of in meat and dairy products: "Most of us, with images in our minds of the cows of yesteryear, could hardly believe the extent to which the meat industry today relies on chemicals, hormones, antibiotics and a plethora of other drugs" (Robbins, *Diet New America* 109). The image of a cow chewing on grass in a field is an image of the past as is the pecking and scratching chicken of the barnyard, and the loving mother cow letting the farmer squeeze milk into the pail. They are all misconceptions of what meat and dairy consumers are actually internalizing each time they consume these products. Today's cows used for meat are fed a diet with the strict purpose of fattening them up the cheapest way possible (Robbins, *Diet New America* 110). "It is impossible to raise animals in intensive confinement without continual reliance on antibiotics, sulfa drugs and other substances" (*Fund Facts* 2).

Chickens are also fed a diet of chemicals to produce more fat and thus more profit. With "over 90% of today's chickens" fed arsenic compounds (Mason and Singer 56–58) and virtually every chicken raised in the United States being fed a diet of antibiotics, it is hard to believe chicken is being sold as a health food (Robbins, *Diet New America* 65). Furthermore, "up to 90% of federally inspected poultry is infected with salmonella bacteria" (*PETA Guide* 1). Chicken is not health food as presented to Americans everyday.

The ad campaign "Milk: It Does A Body Good" is also a lie. With the introduction of the Bovine Growth Hormone (rBGH), milk, cheese, butter, ice cream, yogurt and infant formula are now being contaminated without the U.S. Food and Drug Administration testing the long-term health effects on consumers (*Vegetarian Voice* 12). Furthermore, the FDA admits that "use of rBGH in cows may lead to increased amounts of pus and bacteria in milk" and that "powerful antibiotics and other drugs used to fight increased disease in rBGH-injected cows may lead to greater antibiotic and chemical contamination of milk and dangerous resistance to antibiotics in the human population" (*Vegetarian Voice* 12). And because these drugs present in these forms of meat and dairy products "form toxic residues in animal tissue, they pose a harm to human consumers" (*Fund Facts* 2). In other words, what they eat, you eat.

After her heart attack, I tried to help my mother understand the vegetarian lifestyle—which means no meat and dairy products of any kind.

"Tina, you can pick the chicken out."

"WHAT!? Mom, it's tortilla soup with shredded chicken not to mention it's in a chicken broth."

"Well it's got lots of vegetables in it. Maybe you can pick those out."

"It's OK, Mom, I'll just make a cucumber sandwich and be fine."

"But I did put in extra veggies for you."

"And for you, too, Mom, you get the benefits, too."

Since the heart attack she has resigned herself to retiring the *Cooking Beef: A Recipe a Day* cookbook and has even had lessons in low-fat cooking, but it hasn't occurred to her that as she moves away from fat and cholesterol she is also moving into vegetarianism. We are making progress, though. After realizing that fat and cholesterol make eating meat and dairy so bad for us, she also understands what makes them a double jeopardy for everyone.

Meat and dairy products add chemicals, saturated fat, and cholesterol to a diet. So what will vegetarian foods add to a diet? Beyond reducing fat and cholesterol as previously discussed, a diet without meat or dairy products will reduce cancer risks, reduce protein levels, and add fiber. A vegetarian diet higher in fiber than meat-based diets "helps to dilute, bind, inactivate, and remove many of the carcinogens and toxic substances found in our food supply" (McDougall 120). Due to these properties and other considerations involving fiber "a diet high in fiber helps prevent colon cancer as well as cancers of other parts of the body" (McDougall 120). "An additional benefit of a [vegetarian diet] is that it contains generous amounts of substances with 'anticancer' properties" (McDougall 128). Some of these include Vitamin A, Vitamin C, Vitamin E, and minerals. Thus a vegetarian diet, "complemented with vegetables and fruits, provides a multitude of overlapping mechanisms for preventing cancer and keeping us healthy" (McDougall 130).

According to Martin and Tenenbaum, "there is no known nutritional need for the amount of protein we eat" (27). Americans typically eat roughly twice the amount of protein as the Recommended Dietary Allowance sets for healthy people (Martin and Tenenbaum 27) and much of this protein comes in the form of meat and dairy products. Too much protein lowers the body's ability to naturally absorb calcium and "as surprising as it sounds, one major culprit in osteoporosis may be protein" (Barnard 19). Furthermore, high protein "intakes have been found to contribute to progressive kidney damage" (Barnard 24). Through eating more whole grains, fruits, and vegetables, which naturally reduces saturated fat—and maintains the same level of protein intake—an alteration in the ratio of animal to vegetable protein inevitably will occur" (Martin and Tenenbaum 26). The shift allows more reasonable protein intake without the fat.

I couldn't believe it. My mother was defending my beliefs to my aunts. It was a humorous and satisfying scene.

"Tell them, Tina, what is that Bovine Hormone thing you were telling me about. GROSS, pus in my milk."

"Well, the milk farmers put . . ."

"And what about McDonald's cows eating the rain forests" she interrupted.

"See to support the cows used in . . ."

"And the chicken, Tina, tell them about cholesterol in chicken. The whole industry of meat has hoodwinked us all. It's all a mass market sell."

I know she hasn't eliminated meat entirely but I have watched her over the past four months gently guide herself and our family from taco salad, hamburgers, and sausage to red beans and rice, lentil soup, and other vegetarian meals as she discovers the hidden benefits of vegetarianism on her own.

The choice of a vegetarian lifestyle with all the perceived sanctimonious philosophy can be traced back to the simple fact that eating meat and dairy products is bad for you. A constant reminder to me is remembering someone I love with a monitor on her heart now sitting across from me laughing as she puts another bite of life into her mouth.

WORKS CITED

"Altered Bovine Hormone Makes Milk, Dairy Products Even Riskier." *Vegetarian Voice* 20.3 (1994): 12.

Barnard, Neil, M.D. Food for Life: *How the New Four Food Groups Can Save Your Life.* New York: Crown, 1993.

Chen, J., et al. Diet, *Lifestyle, and Mortality in China: A Study of the Characteristics of 65 Countries.* New York: Oxford UP, Cornell UP, and the China People's Medical, 1990.

Fund for Animals, *The Fund Facts:* Animal Agriculture Fact Sheet #2. Houston: Fund for Animals, 1992.

Martin, Alice A., and Frances Tenenbaum. *Diet against Disease.* Boston: Houghton Mifflin, 1980.

Mason, J., and P. Singer. *Animal Factories.* New York: Crown, 1980.

McDougall, John, M.D., and Mary McDougall. *The McDougall Plan.* Piscataway: New Century, 1983.

Ornish, Dean, Dr. *Dr. Dean Ornish's Program for Reversing Heart Disease.* New York: Ballantine, 1990.

The PETA Guide to Animals and the Meat Industry. Washington, D.C.: PETA, 1993.

The PETA Guide to Compassionate Living. Washington, D.C.: PETA, 1993.

Robbins, John. *Diet for a New America.* Walpole: Stillpoint, 1987.

Robbins, John. *May All Be Fed: Diet for a New World.* New York: Avon, 1992.

Student Case History: Writing to Analyze—Julie Schum

Read the following student paper by yourself, ignoring my commentary, then read it with me as I demonstrate what a writer reads in the writing. It was written in an undergraduate course in critical analysis of literature for Dr. Brock Dethier when he was on the faculty at the University of New Hampshire. The student, Julie Schum, is a science major who wants to be a writer concentrating on science and environmental issues.

KATE'S RESISTANCE TO DOMINANCE BY PETRUCHIO
IN *THE TAMING OF THE SHREW*

Julie Schum

I had one strong response upon reading Kate's submissive speech at the end of Shakespeare's *The Taming of the Shrew*: I don't buy it.

> *This is an academic paper, an excellent literary research paper, but the writer's voice is established in the first sentence. The writer has a strong point of view and her own unique way of expressing it. I hear her voice as a promise of a strong and lively point of view.*

Something seemed funny about the strong female character, who had been the star of Shakespeare's play, her scalding wit an equal match for any of the male characters', suddenly forsaking her independent nature and calling upon all women to become submissive to men. I didn't believe her. I wasn't convinced. Her words were telling me one thing, while her actions and the fact that hers is the voice delivering the critical and longest speech in the play seemed to contradict that message.

> *The author makes a statement, then immediately documents it. I sense an order that will take me through a reading of a play I haven't read in decades. I feel I will have a guide that will make each point clear and give me time to consider it.*

My reading of *The Taming of the Shrew* left me with the feeling that Shakespeare's purpose in the play was not to encourage men to dominate women and women to be submissive to their husbands. Shakespeare was dealing with an issue facing his audience at the time. The play seems to be a reflection of the cultural change from a time when women kissed their husbands' feet as part of the wedding ceremony to a time when many women chose not to marry and to speak up for themselves in the patriarchal society. To the audience of the 1590s, Kate's final speech would have sounded old-fashioned, possibly reminiscent of the good old days, but would not be interpreted as a message to women to be submissive or for men to abuse their women into submission.

> *The author puts her topic into literary, historical, and social contexts. I feel sure that she has something important to tell me and that she will satisfy my hunger for accurate, specific information that will stimulate my thinking.*

Lynda Boose points out in her article "Scolding Brides and Bridling Scolds," . . .

> *I'm relieved. This isn't just going to be the author's opinion off the top of her head. She is going to cite objective, scholarly authorities to support her position.*

. . . that Kate's statement,

> . . . place your hands below your husband's foot.
> In token of which duty, if he please,
> My hand is ready, may it do him ease" (V.2 176–178) . . .

> *Good. I do not have the play in front of me, but I am going to be given evidence from within the text so I can hear the lines and see if they support the writer's thesis.*

. . . is an allusion to an actual pre-Reformation marriage ceremony in which the bride must kiss her husband's feet in an act of submission and obedience, a ritual which was removed from the Book of Common Prayer in 1549.

> *The lines from the play are put in context. My guide through the piece—the author—is answering my questions as I ask them.*

Boose believes Shakespeare used the patriarchal, outdated reference in Kate's speech because, "on the one hand, it inscribes the concluding Kate and Petruchio marital relation as an anachronism; and yet, on the other, by idealizing and romanticizing that model, it imbues it with the nostalgic value of a vision of social order imagined as passing away" (195–6). By this interpretation, the audience would have taken the taming of Kate as exaggerated, an old-fashioned ideal of submissive women, not as a model Shakespeare was encouraging them to follow. Men in the audience may have cheered Kate's final speech, but most would have done so with a sense of fantasy and nostalgia, knowing that they would never see their wives making such a speech. Seeing Kate's speech in historical context gives me a different perspective on the injustice of the speech and its impact on women's role in society. Knowing that the audience was probably not convinced by the explicit theme of taming women allows me to see beyond the blatant sexism of the plot to the more implicit themes of the play.

> *Here the author skillfully leads me to her conclusion and then, in the next paragraph, establishes and defines—definition is very important—an important theme.*

One of these themes is the importance of language and the ability of women to have power through speaking. Kate is considered a shrew because of the language she uses and her disregard of what is socially acceptable for her to say. Bianca, on the other hand, plays the role of the socially acceptable woman—she is silent. Karen Newman makes the observation in her article "Renaissance Family Politics and Shakespeare's *The Taming of the Shrew*" that, ". . . Kate refuses her erotic destiny by exercising her linguistic willfulness. Her shrewishness, always associated with women's revolt in words, testifies to her exclusion from social and political power. Bianca, by contrast, is throughout the play associated with silence" (90).

> *Each point is made clearly and then documented. I am instructed in writing and rewriting this chapter by the author's skill in this process.*

The contrast in the speech of the two sisters is shown clearly by comparing Petruchio's courtship of Kate to Lucentio's courtship of Bianca. In the first exchange between Kate and Petruchio (II.1 182–271), Kate is the instigator of the quarrel and gets the better of Petruchio through puns which mock his attempt to treat her as an object of exchange. She uses words to resist his efforts to dominate her. Newman agrees that, "[Kate] takes the lead through puns which allow her to criticize Petruchio and the patriarchal system of wooing and marriage" (94). In the exchange between Bianca and Lucentio (III.1 31–43), Bianca simply repeats the words Lucentio says to her. Newman feels that Bianca is conforming to the accepted role of women by not speaking. She says, "[Bianca's] revelation of her feelings through a repetition of the Latin lines [Lucentio] quotes from Ovid are as close as possible to the silence we have come to expect from her" (94). Kate is considered a shrew because she uses wild language and linguistic wit to resist being treated like a commodity. Bianca is favored by suitors because she is quiet, complacent, and submissive. In this instance, language is the tool Kate uses to break away from being traded among men by her father.

> *Go through the rest of the research paper by yourself, with a partner, or with several of your classmates, noting just what the author is doing, paragraph by paragraph. Read it aloud and hear the writer's voice. Outline it to see the logical trail she carves through the material. Write out her thesis and the points she makes to see the significance of what she is saying.*

As Petruchio tries to tame Kate, a major tactic he uses is intentionally misunderstanding what she says. By changing the meaning of her words, he takes away her power to be independent. After the quarrel when Petruchio and Kate first meet, Petruchio negates Kate's power by telling Baptista that Kate has agreed to marry him and that she loves him when they are alone (II.1 278–310). Baptista believes Petruchio, and Kate is powerless to fight against being treated like an object by her father and Petruchio. She must marry Petruchio, who forced himself upon her and defeated her independence by ignoring her ability to speak.

Petruchio intentionally misinterprets the meaning of Kate's words again when she wants to stay at the wedding feast (III.2 198–238). Kate clearly tries to resist his power to control her by saying,

"The door is open, sir, there lies your way,
You may be jogging while your boots are green.
For me, I'll not be gone till I please myself" (III.2 209–211).

Petruchio ignores her will, and the fact that she's angry about being humiliated at the wedding, and claims that he is rescuing her from thieves, saying,

"Fear not, sweet wench, they shall not touch thee, Kate" (III.2 237).

He says this in the same breath that he calls her

"my goods, my chattels, she is my house,
My household stuff, my field, my barn,
My horse, my ox, my ass, my any thing" (III.2 229–231).

His tactic of dominating Kate in this scene is to rob her of her independence as a human being by ignoring her words.

Petruchio's strategy continues when they reach his house. Newman says, "Kate is figuratively killed with kindness, by her husband's rule over her not so much in material terms—the withholding of food, clothing, and sleep—but the withholding of linguistic understanding. As the receiver of her messages, he simply refuses their meaning; since he also has material power to enforce his interpretations, it is his power over language that wins" (95). Kate still struggles to maintain her independence through words. In the scene with the tailor, Kate tells Petruchio that she will not be silenced:

"Why sir, I trust I may have leave to speak,
And speak I will. I am no child, no babe.
Your betters have endured me say my mind,
And if you cannot, best you stop your ears.
My tongue will tell the anger of my heart,
Or else my heart concealing it will break,
And rather than it shall, I will be free
Even to the uttermost, as I please, in words."

As Petruchio withholds food and sleep from Kate, she becomes more willing to be civil to him, realizing it's the only way she'll stay alive. Still, she doesn't lose her wit and her confidence to be outspoken and contradict Petruchio.

The conversation between Kate and Petruchio on the way to Padua is a relief to me. It shows that Kate has not been conquered in the sense that she still has her wit and her ability to speak. Newman says this exchange shows Kate is having fun playing along with Petruchio's games (95–96). She refers to the pun Kate makes when saying to Vincentio,

"Pardon, old father, my mistaking eyes,
That have been bedazzled with the sun" (IV.5 145–6).

"Sun" in this case, is a pun referring to Petruchio, who referred to himself as his mother's "son" earlier in their conversation.

Kate retains her sharp verbal abilities through the end of the play. Even when Kate gives her monologue on how to be a good wife, it is Kate who is speaking and telling the audience what she feels. She has retained her individuality at least to the extent that she contradicts the other two wives and addresses the audience with the longest and most climactic monologue in the play. Newman says, "Kate's having the last word contradicts the very sentiments she speaks" (99). Newman also notes that even though one shrew is tamed, two more reveal themselves: "Bianca and the widow refuse to do their husbands' bidding, thereby undoing the sense of closure Kate's 'acquiescence' produces" (100).

Because Kate does not lose her power to speak, it seems that Shakespeare is showing us that Kate is not ultimately defeated by Petruchio. The play leaves the audience with an uneasy feeling that the conflict of men not being able to dominate their wives is not resolved. This is further supported by the historical context of Kate's final monologue and how the contemporary audience would have responded to that as a fantasized, unrealistic basis for the situation to wrap up. Historically, this play reflects the feeling of English society in the 1590s. According to Newman, "The period was fraught with anxiety about rebellious women" (91). Other historians have identified the era as a "crisis of order" which was based on a fear of women rebelling against their submissive role in the patriarchal culture (Newman 90). Boose adds that there was a sudden increase in witchcraft trials and other court accusations against women documented in this time period. There was also an increase in the instances of crimes that are typically female, "scolding," "witchcraft," "whoring," "brawling," and "dominating one's husband" (184). These historical records of punishment show the strength women were showing in beginning to overcome their submissive role in society and the magnitude of the threat these women posed to men.

Boose observes, ". . . what is striking is that the punishments meted out to women are much more frequently targeted at suppressing women's speech than they are at controlling their sexual transgressions" (184). This social phenomenon is reflected in *The Taming of the Shrew*, when Kate is considered a shrew because she speaks freely, and in the way Petruchio tries to dominate her by suppressing her ability to speak.

Also in the play, there are several references to Kate that could imply accusations of witchcraft. After Kate yells at Baptista for making deals with Bianca's suitors, Hortensio says,

"From all such devils, good Lord deliver us!" (I.1 65).

When Baptista scolds Kate for attacking Bianca, he says,

"For shame, thou hilding of a devilish spirit" (II.1 26).

Kate is associated with the devil, probably like many women in England at that time, because she is a threat to male authority.

The punishments that Kate receives from Petruchio—public humiliation at her wedding, humiliation at the wedding feast—also resemble the historical customary punishment of "scolds" and "shrews." Boose refers to these as Kate's "shaming rites" (192).

Looking at the play from this historical perspective shows that Shakespeare's purpose in *The Taming of the Shrew* was to reflect what was going on around him in society. The audiences who saw Shakespeare's play probably recognized Kate's outspoken, shrewish behavior in women of their time and identified with Petruchio's quest to dominate them and restore the order that society once knew. Many men probably cheered Kate's final speech wishing their women would adopt such attitudes. But, by showing the audience Petruchio's inability to truly dominate a shrew, the play showed the present and future of the gender struggle—that for one tamed shrew there were two more untamed, that the days of a woman professing her submission and inferiority to her husband were gone. Despite the content of Kate's final monologue, it seems the primary theme of *The Taming of the Shrew* is that men should beware because the shrews will not be tamed.

> *Note the strong ending written not with rhetorical flourishes but with solid, specific information that weaves all the strands of the research paper together and leaves at least this male thinking about women today and the women in his life—his wife, his daughters and granddaughter, his women friends. Shakespeare speaks to us today because he dealt with the fundamental issues of men and women, then and now.*

WORKS CITED

Boose, Lynda E. "Scolding Brides and Bridling Scolds: Taming the Woman's Unruly Member." *Shakespeare Quarterly* 42 (1991): 179–185, 194.

Newman, Karen. "Renaissance Family Politics and Shakespeare's *The Taming of the Shrew.*" *English Literary Renaissance* 16 (1986): 86–100.

Shakespeare, William. *The Taming of the Shrew.* Ed. G. R. Hibbard. London: Penguin Books, 1968.

The author's teacher, Brock Dethier, wrote at the end of the paper: "*A.* Excellent. Best research paper I've seen this semester." It is a superb example of academic writing that is more than that—simply good writing—and we can all take instruction and inspiration from good writing.

Case History of an Essay

Donald M. Murray

Friday, December 15

At 5:00 P.M. I am given the assignment to write an essay that will interest college students "seventeen to forty-five."

My first reaction, as it always is—that I have nothing to say. Then I feel those subjects that first come to mind—the Battle of the Bulge in the winter of 1944–45, my wife's and my unequal aging, the role of caretaking in a marriage—do not seem appropriate for this audience. They reflect my immediate concerns: the snow outside reminds me of my first battle, my concern for my aging wife and my lack of qualifications as a male nurse. All those are and will be legitimate subjects for my "Now and Then" column in the *Boston Globe*, but they do not seem appropriate for this assignment.

I make myself remember that the subject will come, in my case, not by forcing, by hard, focused thinking; but it will rise from a dreamy corner of my brain if I assign it to my subconscious; what topic can I explore that may interest seventeen-to-forty-five-year-old college students?

I notice that I say explore. I "write to learn" and I want to discover something by this and every writing task. The topic may not be new to me, but I hope to write something more than I have written—or thought—before.

As I drive with Minnie Mae to Applebee's for dinner I realize that a corner of my mind is asking itself what did I need to know. The word *failure* drifts by but a car is cutting me off, so I pay attention to my driving. After ordering, while Minnie Mae goes to the restroom, I allow my mind to drift and find I'm back in school as a high school student, failing, and realize no one taught me how to fail. In writing down these notes the idea is more developed than I want it to be. I don't want my conscious telling my unconscious what it has already said. I want to allow that important, dreamy kind of thinking, to take place before I write. I take out the three-by-five card I always carry with me and write "failure." That is enough to remind me of the potential topic.

Saturday, December 16

I get up at 5:30 A.M. On Saturday morning I pick up two old friends and we go out to breakfast. I feel the idea of failure being turned over like compost in the back of my brain and recognize I have a topic: importance of failure . . . still learning to fail . . . can't write unless willing to fail . . . risk and failure . . . ought to teach failure . . . hurt children only teaching success. I could interview my friends, one is a sculptor, the other a scientist, and both teachers. That would be a good way to approach the subject but I choose to keep it to myself, to play with the ideas in my mind without interference from anyone else. We talk hockey, the cost of health care, politics, and engage in our familiar male banter.

I have the choice of following what I call a linear or straight-line approach to the topic or a nonlinear, circular, approach. Using a linear approach I would:

- Look for quotations on failure.
- Seek articles and books on failure.

- Interview people who I think would have something significant to say about failure.
- Search the Internet.
- Make formal notes on my failures and what I have learned from them.
- Start playing with sketch outlines.

I have done all those things in the past and may do many or most of them later, but I have learned to follow the advice of the novelist Virginia Woolf who wrote, "As for my next book, I am going to hold myself from writing it till I have it impending in me: grown heavy in my mind like a ripe pear; pendant, gravid, asking to be cut or it will fall." I will go on to other work, other living, and allow the topic to ripen.

Sunday, December 17

It is a good topic but I realize that I have dealt with the topic too often. I feel I will discover new things to say, but I have to consider other topics.

I am working within restrictions. My audience is college students "seventeen to forty-five." I want to write a personal essay, an internal exploration of what I don't know I know rather than a formal research paper, since I may be able to use it as a column or publish it in a local journal that welcomes my essays. And I am restricted by the life I have lived. This will be nonfiction although I write fiction and poetry.

I brainstorm:

- Why I write fiction? Fiction truer than nonfiction, imagined more realistic than reality?
- The older I live the more I wish I had known my grandfathers who died before I was born—and their four grandfathers, and their eight grandfathers, and their sixteen grandfathers who lived far back in the mists of Scotland. I think I am more influenced by them than I know.
- I have just edited a memoir. The stranger in the mirror.
- My secret childhood, a healthy schizophrenia that saved me.
- A quote I want to explore:

From THE ART OF POSSIBILITY, Zander and Zander, Harvard Business School Press, 2000

"Frank Sulloway, a former research scholar at the Massachusetts Institute of Technology in the Department of Brain and Cognitive Sciences, [*Born to Rebel* (New York: Pantheon Books, 1996)] suggests that we think of 'personality' as a strategy for 'getting out of childhood alive.' Each child in a family stakes out her own territory of attention and importance by developing certain aspects of her character into 'winning ways.' One child may be sociable and outgoing, another may be quiet and thoughtful, but both are aimed at the same thing: to find a safe and identifiable niche in the family and the community and to position themselves to survive. Anxiety regulates behavior and alerts the child to the dangers of being one-down, unattended to, or at a loss.

"The survival mechanisms of the child have a great deal in common with those of the young of other species, save for the fact that children learn to know themselves. They grow up in a medium of language and have a long, long time to think. A child comes to think of himself as the personality he gets recognition for or, in other words, as the set of patterns of action and habits of thought that get him out of childhood in one piece. That set, raised to adulthood, is what we are calling the calculating self. The prolonged nature of human childhood may contribute to the persistence of these habits long after their usefulness has passed."

- How I survived childhood?
- Did I survive childhood? Still trying to escape.
- Try to look back and see myself as a teen-ager.
- My Tilton year. The person I became my freshman year in college.
- What I learned from my war.
- Good war. Term used about my war that I hate, but there was good for me in what I learned about the world and myself.
- One trait. Desperate risk taker. Confronted the dragon.

My subconscious is back on the hunt. It will continue tomorrow as I drive to Boston to see a doctor and back. (Another topic: Seventy mile-per-hour writing. The writing before writing.)

The danger of having an imagination.
The imagined reality.

- And that circles back to the imagined self.

Monday, December 18

I come to my desk harried and harassed. I have to go to Boston to a doctor. I have a number of Christmas tasks and errands to do and an alp of correspondence that needs answering. And I can't even remember what I've been writing about here. This doesn't worry me. I have it written but I need to make myself calm, quiet. We have to make ourselves ready to receive writing. I take deep breaths, I make my body relax, perhaps my mind will follow.

Now I can look at what I had written yesterday to see if anything surprises me. Is there a line I have to follow? No, but . . . Writing often lies in the buts. In this case: No, but I see an image of a skinny kid with glasses in a maroon woolen sweater with a striped stocking hat and—can it be?—corduroy knickers, turning off Hancock street in Wollaston, Massachusetts. There is a trolley car screeching past in the background. He would be sixteen in 1936 and allowed to wear long pants so it must be before that. He is coming home to tell his parents he's gotten a job. They will not care. That isn't the problem but what I find mysterious is why he went to apply for the many jobs he worked as a teenager. How did he, an almost pathologically shy kid, have the nerve . . . [My *Globe* editor calls to go over a column and I do some rewriting, making three phone calls to get it right. No problem with interruptions. I have stopped in the middle of a sentence. I'll be able to tune to the voice of that draft.] . . . to march in and ask for the jobs, acting, he hoped, confident that he could do a job he didn't know he could do. What did he learn? How much has it, did it, mark his life since? What was his peculiar self-image, a bookworm who thought he was stupid in school, one boy at home and another on the street? What was held back, what is held back?

This has, of course, become interior freewriting, a sort of pre-discovery draft that may lead me to what I need to write. And I notice that in writing this I have grown calm, patient, lost to the world in following the words that may lead me to a territory to explore.

Tuesday, December 19

A distracted morning of care for Minnie Mae, responding to the editor of a book I'm working on, responding to the editor of *Write to Learn*, and being interrupted by phone calls, yet I have a feeling from two notes I made on my three-by-five card at the doctor's in Boston yesterday that I can plunge in.

The note was: *How I saw myself*

> "see"
> I watch a skinny 15-year-old kid with glasses running for home. Hancock street in Wollaston, Massachusetts. It is 1939, at the end of the Great Depression and months before the Germans invade Poland and World War II begins. A yellow-orange trolley car screeches by in the background as he turns at the Amoco gas station and climbs the stairs, two at a time, to the second floor apartment his parents rent in the two decker.
>
> He checks in on his grandmother who lies paralyzed in the middle bedroom. Her eyes are closed and her mouth gaps open. He steps close to her. She is still alive and goes to the kitchen where his mother sits by her cup of tea staring at some world in which she lived.
>
> He tells her he lost his paper route because he had been sick and had to spend so much time in bed. But now he has a job at Miller's Market after school on Friday and all day Saturday. He knows she heard him, knows she will use this information to order fancy food she cannot afford, but is not surprised by the silence. They hurt each other with not speaking, turning away, going in the next room as he does to escape into a library book.
>
> His sleeping porch bedroom has a ceiling of National Geographic maps. The Arctic is right over his head. That is where he will go if he does not have his war.
>
> This is how he sees himself.

shy

dumb

(bored)

introverted

ugly

weird

confident

writer

(football plays and girls)

I have to stop and meet someone for lunch, but I hear a voice and see a direction I will take when I get back to the draft. Then I will start by layering, writing over what I have written and pushing on, loosely following the trail I have made in my list.

[later] Driving this afternoon I hear my parents and my teachers criticizing my lack of concentration, one of my strongest points.

Wednesday, December 20

My mind keeps wandering back to this piece with a change:

1. how I was seen
2. how I saw myself then
3. how I see myself now

I don't formally outline but I do note potential sequences as I have here.

Now I want to plunge in, writing over or layering what I have written and moving forward.

I watch a skinny 15-year-old kid with glasses, darting between the cars on Hancock Street in Wollaston, Massachusetts and he races home. It is 1939, at the end of the Great Depression, months before the Germans invade Poland and World War II begins. A yellow-orange trolley car screeches by in the background as he turns the corner by the Amoco gas station and climbs the stairs, two at a time, to the second floor apartment his parents rent in the two decker.

He checks in on his grandmother who lies paralyzed in the middle bedroom. Her eyes are closed and her mouth gaps open. He steps close to her. She is still alive and he goes to the kitchen where his mother sits by her cup of tea staring at some world in which she lived.

He tells her he lost his paper route because he had been sick and had to spend so much time in bed. But now he has a job at Miller's Market after school on Friday and all day Saturday. He knows she heard him, knows she will use this information to order fancy food she cannot afford against his 50-cent a full day salary, but he is not surprised by the silence. In his family they hurt each other by what they do not say, by turning away, by suddenly standing up and going to the next room.

He goes to his sleeping porch bedroom that has a ceiling of National Geographic maps. The Arctic is right over his head. That is where he will go if he does not have his war. He opens again Admiral Byrd's book *Alone* in which he tells how he survived winter in the Antarctic in solitude.

I am this boy and I remember how others saw me and how I felt about myself. Mother criticized my posture, my enunciation, my clothes, my hair and my overall ugliness. And I agreed with her, feeling I was unattractive.

She joined my father, my uncles, and my teachers in calling attention to my lack of concentration and I thought that my principal moral flaw.

People worried about my being an introvert, a loner, shy. So did I. I preferred reading to hanging out on the corner by the drugstore, I was self-conscious and self-centered, awkward at meeting strangers.

My vulnerability to childhood sicknesses made me feel weak, not strong. My uncles led the chorus that said I was spoiled. My mother told me again and again I was lazy. My father, mother, ministers, teachers, classmates and streetmates were critical of my weirdness, thinking my sense of humor unfunny and certainly unpolitic.

I was funny looking, awkward, clumsy, scared, stupid, lazy, strange: a teenager. And I believed that the way I was seen was accurate.

But now, sixty years later I see that skinny kid hustling work, motivated by what I am not sure. He is not lazy and deep down he knows it. He does think he is stupid, but he'll make up for that by good work habits and he does.

dumb in school—reader—bored

concentration

meeting people

strong—man's work

snapshot photo store "hunk"

Thursday, December 21

My stomach is in knots with all I have to do this morning before we drive to New York. I need to have a quiet moment writing. This serves me as prayer or meditation serves others, a calm out-of-the-world moment in which I concentrate or focus on a quiet task of making or discovering. I can either layer again or pick up where I stopped.

Writing is, above all, a matter of faith, and reading this over I have lost faith in it. It seems a dung pile, nothing less. But I have learned that the solution to this feeling is to enter into the writing task, forgetting the grand angst for the moment of line-by-line making.

This evening at the moment of melancholy as the sun goes down but the evening dark has not closed in I hear the voices of my childhood from the grave. My mother, of course, is the loudest telling me to stand up straight, to enunciate clearly, to dress properly, to be obedient.

My father stands at a distance, watching me to see if I will stand up to mother as he cannot; my uncles telling me I am spoiled, to grow up and be a man; my teachers telling me to concentrate not to stare out the window; my classmates thinking—I think—I am not only funny looking but weird.

> *I am surprised to be writing a new beginning. I heard it and allowed it to write itself. It may frame the piece better, it may be a new piece, it may be . . . what I do not know. I am involved in the frightening fun of writing, saying what I do not expect, what may be what I do not want to hear or what may clarify the confusions of a long-lived life.*

December 22

It is a busy day with computer problems but riding home after a family dinner at a Japanese restaurant, I thought I could take a quick look at a possible ending.

> They were wrong and I am grateful they were. What people told me I was made me work hard to prove they were wrong. It might have taken only a few A's, a couple of hugs at home, to satisfy the hunger that has driven me toward a life better than I could have imagined when I raced home to tell mother I had a job at Miller's Market.

> *Many novelists say they know the end before they begin. I don't usually work this way and certainly this ending has only come after I had pretty much completed the draft. Tomorrow I will get up early and finish it.*
>
> *What I've learned:*
>
> - *Much writing is done away from the page.*
> - *Once I have the tension and the voice I can stop and return at any time.*
> - *Writing can be done in small fragments of time during a busy and distracted life.*

December 23

This has been one of those hours-on-1-800-numbers-with-computer-problems days and now I will try to do a complete layering draft as much as to calm me down as to complete the assignment.

> ~~This evening at the moment of melancholy as the sun goes down but the evening dark has not closed in I hear the voices of my childhood from the grave. My mother, of course, is the loudest, telling me to stand up straight, to enunciate clearly, to dress properly, to be obedient.~~
>
> ~~My father stands at a distance, watching me to see if i will stand up to mother as he cannot. my uncles telling me i am spoiled, to grow up and be a~~

~~man, my teachers telling me to concentrate not to stare out the window. my classmates thinking I think I am not only funny looking but weird.~~

I have been worried about using a frame—my experience is that it is better just to get to the story, and that opinion was reinforced when my possible ending referred back to the material after the frame. The frame also tells too much while showing too little and expands many issues rather than focusing on one issue.

I watch a skinny 15-year-old kid with glasses, darting between the cars on Hancock Street in Wollaston, Massachusetts as he races home. ~~it is 1939 at the end of the Great Depression and only months before the Grmans invade Pland and Wrld Wr II begins.~~

I'm not sure the depression and war stuff is necessary, not sure it moves the essay forward.

I am that boy, now a 76-year-old man, and I hear a yellow-orange trolley car screeches by ~~in the background~~ as ~~he~~ I turns the corner by the Amoco gas station and climbs the stairs, two at a time, to the second floor apartment his parents rent in the brown shingled two decker.

He checks in on his grandmother who lies paralyzed in the middle bedroom. Her eyes are closed and her mouth gapes open. He steps close to her. She is still alive and the boy goes to the kitchen where his mother sits by her cup of tea staring at some better world in which she lives in memory of imagination.

He tells her he lost his paper route because he had been sick and had to spend so much time in bed, but now he has a job at Miller's Market after school on Friday and all day Saturday. He knows she heard him, knows she will use this information to order fancy food she cannot afford against his 50-cent a full day salary, but he is not surprised by the silence. In his family they hurt each other by what they do not say, by turning away, by suddenly standing up and going to the next room.

I enter into that boy I was so long ago and am surprised by how he sees himself. He believes what his parents, his uncles, his teachers have told him: that he is lazy, that he lacks the ability to concentrate, that he is a shy introvert who cannot meet people, that he is unattractive, even ugly.

The fact is that part of him still believes what had been drilled into his head with unceasing repetition. Yet that boy racing home is clearly not lazy. He has sought work on his own without the support, counsel, or suggestion of his parents.

At Miller's Market he will work long hours—often from 5 am on Saturdays when they go to market until close to midnight and Mr. Miller, going outside and looking up and down street for potential customers, sees none and reluctantly shuts the store.

This skinny, bespectacled boy will do a man's work, hauling in huge bags of potatoes, staggering under sides of beef, lugging in large boxes of canned goods. He answers the phone and takes orders, sells at the vegetable bins and behind the counter, takes over the canned goods inventory, arranges the fruits and vegetables displayed on the sidewalk and in the store, becomes the maker of Scots all-beef sausages.

His teachers, well most of them, tell him he is dumb yet he reads far beyond the assignments . . .

December 24, 2000

[picked up the next morning while waiting to go to breakfast with son-in-law and grandsons.]

His teachers tell him not to read beyond the assignments, not to look out the window and daydream but to concentrate, to pay attention, to focus, not to let his mind wander.

He believes them although he reads fat adult books when he is in elementary school, carries on a game of monopoly with his friends that last months, develops a stamp collection that includes hand-drawn colored maps of each country, starts a collection of sayings about the writer's craft that will become a book 52 years later.

In fact, as a writer he has lived on his ability to daydream, to look out the window and see what others didn't see, to find the unusual in the commonplace. And his power of concentration, his ability to write in the city room and anywhere else, to shut out the world beyond the story is amazing—and sometimes painful—to those who live close to him but on the other edge of his consciousness while he writes at the computer or in his head at the supper table.

I switch back and forth between the boy I was and the old man I am, remembering how I felt because I carried many of the childhood beliefs all my life. Others saw me as a risk taker, a paratrooper, a freelance writer while having a family, a job switcher who gambled on his future. Yet I saw myself as a conservative, a person who played it safe.

I was told I was weak and I was seen as a coward on the playground because my mother told me that if I really believed in Jesus and did not hit back the bully's hand would be stayed. It wasn't, and I played football, boxed, fought in my war yet still felt I was weak and a coward until the young trainers at the health club are amazed at what I can lift at my age and I accepted that I could do what had to be done in the face of danger.

I stop and do a word count: 798. I should be closer to 700. I add that ending I had drafted and read the piece to see what I can cut or sharpen and to see if the fragments I have written at different places hold together as a logical, consistent essay that says something worth saying.

They were wrong and I am grateful they were. What people told me I was made me work hard to prove they were wrong. It might take only a few A's, a couple of hugs at home, to satisfy the hunger that has driven me toward a life better than I could have imagined when I raced home to tell mother I had a job at Miller's Market.

Now for the final line-by-line reading:

I watch a skinny 15-year-old kid with glasses, darting between the cars on Hancock Street in Wollaston, Massachusetts as he races home.

I am that boy, now a 76-year-old man, who ~~and I hear a yellow-orange trolley car screeches by in the background as he/I turns the corner by the Amoco gas station and~~ climbs the stairs, two at a time, to the second floor apartment his parents rent in the brown shingled two decker.

He ~~checks in on his grandmother who lies paralyzed in the middle bedroom. Her eyes are closed and her mouth gapes open. He steps close to her. She is still alive and the boy~~ goes to the kitchen where his mother sits by her cup of tea staring at some better world in which she lives in her imagined memories.

He tells her he lost his paper route because he had been sick and had to spend so much time in bed, but now he has a job at Miller's Market after school on Friday and all day Saturday. He knows she heard him, ~~knows she will use this information to order fancy food she cannot afford against his 50-cent a full day salary, but he is not surprised by the silence. in his family they hurt each other by what they do not say, by turning away, by suddenly standing up and going to the next room.~~ but she says nothing and the boy feels the familiar disappointment. She thinks he will lose the job as his father has lost so many jobs.

I enter into that boy I was so long ago and am surprised by how he sees himself. He believes what his parents, his uncles, his teachers have told him: that he is lazy, that he lacks the ability to concentrate, that he is a shy introvert who cannot meet people, that he is unattractive, even ugly.

The fact is that part of him still believes what had been drilled into his head with unceasing repetition. Yet watching that boy I was racing home I realize he is not lazy. He has sought work on his own without the support, counsel, or suggestion of his parents.

At Miller's Market he will work long hours—often from 5 A.M. on Saturdays when they go to market until close to midnight and Mr. Miller, going outside and looking up and down street for potential customers, sees none and reluctantly shuts the store.

This skinny, bespectacled boy will do a man's work, hauling in huge bags of potatoes, staggering under sides of beef, lugging in large boxes of canned goods. He answers the phone and takes orders, sells at the vegetable bins and behind the counter, takes over the canned goods inventory, arranges the fruits and vegetables displayed on the sidewalk and in the store, becomes the maker of Scots all-beef sausages.

His teachers, well most of them, convince him he has a serious problem of concentration. ~~is dumb. Yet he reads far beyond the assignments. His teachers tell him not to read beyond the assignments, not to look out the window and daydream but to concentrate, to pay attention, to focus, not to let his mind wander.~~ He believes them although he reads adult books when he is in elementary school, carries on a game of monopoly with his friends that last months, develops a stamp collection that includes hand-drawn colored maps of each country, starts a collection of sayings about the writer's craft that will become a book 52 years later.

In fact he has astonishing~~, as a writer he has lived on his ability to day-dream, to look out the window and see what others didn't see, to find the unusual in the commonplace. and his~~ powers of concentration, ~~his ability to writes~~ in the city room and anywhere else, shuts out the world beyond the story in a way that is amazing—and sometimes painful—to those who live close to him but remain on the other edge of his consciousness while he writes at the computer or in his head at the supper table.

I switch back and forth between the boy I was and the old man I am, remembering how I felt because I carried many of the childhood beliefs all my life. Others saw me as a risk taker, a paratrooper, a freelance writer while having a family, a job switcher who gambled on his future. Yet I saw myself as a conservative, a person who played it safe.

I was told I was weak and I was seen as a coward on the playground because my mother told me that if I really believed in Jesus and did not hit back the bully's hand would be stayed. It wasn't, and I played football, boxed, fought in my war, yet still felt I was weak and a coward until the young trainers at the health club are amazed at what I can lift at my age and I accepted that I could do what had to be done in the face of danger.

They were wrong and I am grateful they were. What people told me I was made me work hard to prove they were wrong. It might have taken only a few A's, a couple of hugs at home, to satisfy the hunger that has driven me toward a life better than I could have imagined when I raced home to tell mother I had a job at Miller's Market.

Another reading before I send it off to my editor:

I watch a skinny 15-year-old kid with glasses, darting between the cars on Hancock Street in Wollaston, Massachusetts as he races home.

I am that boy, now a 76-year-old man, who climbs the stairs, two at a time, to the second floor apartment his parents rent in the brown shingled two decker. His mother sits by her cup of tea at the kitchen table staring at some better world in which she lives in her imagined memories.

He tells her he has a job at Miller's Market after school on Friday and all day Saturday. He knows she heard him, but she says nothing and the boy feels the familiar disappointment. She thinks he will lose the job as his father has lost so many jobs.

I remember how the boy sees himself. He believes what his parents, his uncles, his teachers have told him: that he is lazy, that he lacks the ability to concentrate. Part of me still believes what had been drilled into his head with unceasing repetition. Yet watching that boy I was racing home I realize he is not lazy. He has sought work on his own without anyone's encouragement.

At Miller's Market he will work long hours—often from 5 A.M. on Saturdays when they go to market until close to midnight when Mr. Miller, going outside and looking up and down street for potential customers, sees none and reluctantly shuts the store.

This skinny, bespectacled boy will do a man's work, hauling in huge bags of potatoes, staggering under sides of beef, lugging in large boxes of canned goods. He answers the phone and takes orders, sells at the vegetable bins and behind the counter, takes over the canned goods inventory, arranges the fruits and vegetables displayed on the sidewalk and in the store, becomes the maker of Scots all-beef sausages.

His teachers convince him he has a serious problem of concentration. He believes them although he reads adult books when he is in elementary school, carries on a game of monopoly with his friends that last months, develops a stamp collection that includes hand-drawn colored maps of each country, starts a collection of sayings about the writer's craft that will become a book 52 years later.

In fact he has astonishing powers of concentration and is able to shut out the world beyond the story with a painful detachment from those who live close to him when he writes at the computer or in his head at the supper table.

I switch back and forth between the boy I was and the old man I am, remembering how I have carried the myths of childhood inside me all my life. Others saw me as a risk taker, a paratrooper, a freelance writer while having a family, a job switcher who gambled on his future. Yet I saw myself as I had been seen as a child, a boy paralyzed by fear.

I was told I was weak and was seen as a coward on the playground and believed my reputation even when I played football, boxed, fought in my war, and impress the young trainers at the health club at how much I can lift at my age.

I am angry at all who made me feel inadequate when I was young and angry at myself for believing them so long. Then I remember how hard I worked to prove them wrong. It might have taken only a few As, a couple of hugs at home, to satisfy the hunger that has driven me toward a life better than I could have imagined when I raced home to tell mother I had a job at Miller's Market.

> *I do a word count: 617. That's more like it. Compare this draft from the last one and you will see how much I have cut and changed, but what you will not see is the joy I felt as I worked at my craft, using language to clarify my relived life.*

Would I have preferred to write a draft of the essay at one sitting without interruptions?

Yes. But my life intruded. My wife has some serious medical problems I had to deal with. We had to pack and travel to visit a daughter and her family. I lost control over the time I had to write and I had two major computer problems that have yet to be solved. I can't use the CD drive that I need to use and the screen frequently flickers and goes blank.

Would it have been better if I had not had to write it this way?

I don't know. I think it would have been different because it would have not had as much rehearsal time in my head.

What have you learned?

1. I have learned about my life, exploring how the opinions of others affect our image of ourselves.

2. I have learned once more that I can write in small fragments of time despite distractions and interruptions.

CHAPTER 24

Revive a Dead Draft

The teacher or editor or test reader declares the final draft DOA—Dead On Arrival. It lies flat on the desk not breathing.

You are hurt, angry, frustrated. You worked harder on this piece than any other you have written, done more research, more planning, more drafting, more revising, more editing, more . . .

Virtue is no more a defense than laziness, lack of effort, sloppiness. You read the draft again. The patient does not breath, but what can you do?

When I look at one of my prose corpses, I first try to blame someone else. The editor is a lousy reader, the assignment was stupid, the deadline too close, the standards too strict, the requirement too long or short and then I take a deep breath and read my "perfect" draft quickly and coldly the way a reader will.

Now I agree that the draft is dead, but I do not know what to do. I followed the rules, worked hard and look what happened. An hour ago I thought my paper was the best essay ever written. Now it seems hopeless. I cannot write. Others have talent. I have none. Even after a lifetime of publishing, this happens more often than I like to admit. It is part of the territory of insecurity and false security writers inhabit.

First aid for a lifeless draft is possible. Dead draft is a disease that strikes even the most experienced writers. I have to remember that I have brought many rhetorical corpses back to life. It can be done and I know how to do it. There is a sequence of techniques writers perform that will revive the draft. Guaranteed.

First I make myself the triage nurse who is calm in the face of tragedy. I make myself distant, professional as the nurse does who decides what has to be treated first when an accident victim arrives at the Trauma Center.

THE DRAFT ENTIRE

I read the entire draft that I thought was final as a stranger reader who just wants to be informed not impressed by the brilliance of the writer.

Does the topic need to be refined? Does it need more research? Should it be a different genre, a critical essay instead of a personal one? Is it far too long so that the reader loses interest or so short the reader is unsatisfied?

Most often I have to do one thing: LIMIT the topic. The draft needs a tighter focus, a clearer point, a narrowing of subject matter so the topic can be explored in great depth. If I have control over the title, I sharpen the title.

"The Problem Of Athletic Scholarships" becomes "Paid To Play? Play Hurt."

This is a piece I could write because I got to a junior college on an athletic scholarship in 1942, and over sixty years later my right knee is still throbbing from my being clipped on the kickoff—and no substitutions then.

I look at the dead lead: "There are many financial, social, academic and physical costs to paying students to play what were once amateur sports." Would you read on after reading this lead or the next one? "Operations on 27 knees, 24 ankles, 14 shoulders, 3 wrists, two hands, 11 arms, one neck were one cost of the football program last season. That doesn't count the concussions, fractured ribs, and torn muscles that must be included in the price players pay all their life for a 'free' scholarship."

Now I have a choice about genre within this topic. Is it a student newspaper exposé, an article for the alumni magazine, an argument against athletic scholarships, an interview with one or more injured players, an attack on the sport of football, a case history of one or more student athletes, a personal essay? It even could be a short story, a poem, a nonfiction book proposal. Any of those choices would give new energy and focus, breathing life into the corpse who is now barely breathing.

THE DRAFT IN SECTIONS

Now I am ready to read the draft more slowly, section by section. These sections may be marked with a topic heading—Knee Injuries—or just be a group of paragraphs with similar information. I read the article chunk by chunk to see if there are paragraphs or groups of paragraphs that add nothing to the forward motion within this new, limited topic. There are always such chunks and surgically removing them livens the corpse.

I look for the paragraphs or sections that really work, holding my interest or making me want to know more—and develop them. Instead of removing obstacles to a lively draft, I breathe life into the draft by making what is best better.

Then I examine the paragraphs to see what ones need more specific information or that might become anecdotes or little documenting stories. I make sure that most of the paragraphs follow my 2-3-1 rule: The second most important bit of information at the beginning, attribution and the less interesting material in the middle, the most interesting emphasized at the end.

This may be the best time to make an outline to make sure that one thing leads to another. Usually this means giving the reader information that makes the reader want to know what comes next, what does the information mean, how does it affect the people in the piece or the reader.

And as the corpse starts to breathe more strongly, I look at the documentation. Have I fallen into the habit of repeating the form of the documentation using just anecdotes or quotes or statistics? They should be varied so that the most convincing points are documented by the most appropriate form of documentation.

THE DRAFT LINE BY LINE

Finally I read the draft line by line. I read it out loud to make sure I can "hear" the draft as readers will hear. My ear will make me cut, add, reorder, whatever is necessary to serve the reader. I don't look for correctness. My reading is for effectiveness: what communicates what I have to say with clarity and grace.
I look for:

- *Jargon* "One thousand workers were *outplaced*." becomes "One thousand workers were *fired*."
- *Vague generalizations* "To best serve the justified concerns of the stockholders, the Board of Directors initiated an in-depth utilization study improve the productivity ratio." becomes "The owners wanted larger profits so they let workers go and increased the demands on those left."
- *The passive voice* "It was decided by a sub committee of the Board of Trustees that . . ." becomes "Management decided to . . ."
- *The verb to be?* "The new CEO will be speaking at . . ." becomes "the new CEO will speak at . . ."

And here is my secret. Corporations paid me to clarify their public statements and I felt all I did was to eliminate the "lys," "ings," "woulds" and the "that's" for a good fee indeed.

As I go through the draft line by line, I cut what can be cut, add what must be added, and change the order of clauses to make the piece tight, quicker, more direct. Indeed less IS more.

CHAPTER 25

Revise

Joan Didion tells me: "My writing is a process of rewriting, of going back and changing and filling in. In the rewriting process you discover what's going on, and you go back and bring it up to that point." Writer after writer, female and male, journalist and poet, master or apprentice, traditional or experimental, tell me that writing is rewriting. The first draft is the beginning not the end.

And yet all my English teachers in junior and senior high as well as in college and graduate school, taught me to plan so carefully that I knew what I was going to say and then said it. I remember most papers being written in class. The teacher's response was the same. My papers were "corrected." Little was said about content, the term "voice" was never used, but the red pencil, like a heat seeking missile, focused on spelling, punctuation, diction, grammar.

The same was true of my newspaper editors. They expected me to produce publishable copy to deadline—and I did. My first draft was my final draft. All through school, college, and even on a metropolitan newspaper, I was a first draft writer.

I was given better and better assignments, even served a stint on rewrite where I wrote 35 to 45 first draft stories. I was ambitious. I wanted to publish magazine articles, even books. I sent off a query proposal to *The Saturday Evening Post*, and got the go ahead to send them an article which was then every freelancer's ambition. I thought I had done just fine. I would be published and go on to write magazine pieces and books.

Instead of praise for my first draft, I received a 7,000-word criticism of my 5,000-word piece from Bob Johnson, *The Saturday Evening Post* editor, who followed up the letter with a phone call. He was coming up from Philadelphia to Boston so he could spend the day giving me criticism he couldn't fit in his long letter.

His letter and eight-hour seminar made me realize the truth of what I had read but not practiced: writing was rewriting. I began to see the end of the first draft as the true beginning of the writing process. For years after Bob Johnson's visit I wrote three drafts and edited each one ten times—30 readings in all. Now, 49 years after Bob's visit I do write my newspaper columns in one draft most of the time, but almost everything else is read and reread, written and rewritten many times. I delight in this process of discovery and clarification.

Few moments are more exciting for me than coming to my computer and seeing a draft on the screen that needs revision. I am a surgeon eager to get to the operating room, a lawyer going to court, a football player just before the kickoff, a farmer cultivating acres of corn. I have a job to do and it is a job that I both know and continue to keep learning.

I am going to produce a rough first draft in response to a real writing assignment I have been given, then introduce a strategy for revising it—a logical, easy-to-understand, and easy-to-use method of revising—that can be applied to any writing task: a term paper or critical essay, lab report or office memo, thesis or letter of sympathy, case history or poem, scholarship application or take-home exam. Poets and screenwriters, historians and Supreme Court justices, marketing executives and clinical psychologists, novelists and engineers all have to think by writing and rewriting—and then rewriting again.

This piece of writing starts with an assignment from Diane Koski of the University of New Hampshire Foundation, a fund-raising organization for the college where I am both an alumnus and a retired faculty member. She asked me to write a letter telling how the university has changed in the past fifty years that might inspire financial support from my classmates. This is exactly the sort of assignment that might be given to a volunteer for a nonprofit group, lawyer, sales manager, grant seeking scientist, hospital administrator, minister, priest, or rabbi, anyone who has to produce a piece of writing designed to attract money. I've done this sort of writing professionally, and I am doing this one as a volunteer—a reluctantly drafted volunteer. Out of guilt and a sense of duty, I agreed to a task I did not relish but felt I must do.

I always start the same way, talking to myself in my head and in my daybook. I'm a visual person, as most writers are, and I see in images or pictures: myself as a soldier climbing down from the train that no longer runs, marching down Main Street, coming back to Durham after the war, twenty-one and a streak of white in my hair; particular classrooms in Murkland Hall, teachers such as Gwynne Daggett and Carroll Towle and Sylvester Bingham and Bill Hennessey and their offices; and my first wife. I walk around with that movie running through my head, and then I begin to hear fragments of language—proper names such as T-Hall, the main administration building once described by a student of mine as "a Victorian missile ready to lift off"—and phrases—"an educated man can sit alone in a room and be happy." That was to me, a lightning strike in the middle of a boring lecture on this campus. Finally, I start to write a discovery draft, beginning with description as I usually do.

When I first returned to teach at the university, the English department chair, who was a literature teacher, not a writer, ordered me NOT to teach the description essay in freshman English since it was not sophisticated enough for college students. But description, the mother of all writing in my opinion, is where I start writing if I have no obvious beginning.

In this case I am trying to discover what I find special about my educational experience as a student and a teacher at the University of New Hampshire. I train my memory's eye on the day I first arrived in Durham. I was on a troop train in 1943, during World War II.

> The train pulled into the station in Durham, New Hampshire, the one that is now an ice cream parlor. We were marched up Main Street where GIRLS AND MORE GIRLS, REAL LIVE CO-EDS lined the street. I didn't know then that my first wife was among them, and I did not know that Durham would be my home—with my second wife and our three daughters, one of whom would be buried in the Durham Cemetery when she was only twenty.
>
> I wanted to be going overseas, not to school. My father wanted me to have my war, and I did too. So did my church. "Onward Christian Soldiers, Marching as to War." I didn't know I would become a paratrooper and survive combat. That I would return to school, marry the co-ed. If we had lived together, as my daughters and their husbands did, before marriage, we would never have married.
>
> Before I graduated I was insulted when the head of the English department suggested I should become a teacher and teach six courses a semester for $900 a year. I didn't know I would become a professor at this campus. I don't remember the classes so much as the professors' offices, conferences with Carroll Towle, his corncob pipe and his enthusiasm as he attacked my drafts.
>
> (And my conferences with his son years later.) Gwynne Daggett, his sleeves rolled up above his knotty biceps, his hands clasped behind his head, and his delight in ideas, attacking and defending, questioning, doubting, caring. When I was a teacher years later, I don't remember the classroom as much as my office and meeting all my students every week. One on one. I remember my learning as much as theirs. My teachers, I realized then and now, were still learning with me.

Now I have a first draft, one page, 299 words. It is a jumble that jumps around in time and topic, an example of freewriting that isn't close to a polished letter to alumni, but I sense there is something there I can build on. I am an experienced detective. Sometimes the topic or approach is obvious. I see it immediately and that is it. Other times it is not obvious, and I follow an organized search plan I call a strategy for revision. It was, at first, instinctive, but now I have made it into a chart so I can share it with others. It provides a logical approach to revision. If you study the chart you will see that the writer first looks within the draft itself, then looks ahead to new drafts, finally looks back to the original assignment. Revision is, after all, thinking, a process of discovering new meaning.

THE STRATEGY OF REVISION

1. LOOK WITHIN FOR THE SURPRISING:	2. LOOK FORWARD FOR THE CHANGING:	3. LOOK BACK FOR THE EXPECTED:
Word	Purpose	Purpose
Line	Meaning	Meaning
Distance	Distance	Distance
Voice	Genre	Genre
Focus	Audience	Audience
Details	Evidence	Documentation
Sequence	Order	Logic
Purpose	Pace	Pace
Meaning	Proportions	Proportions
Genre	Development	Development
Audience	Voice	Voice

I move quickly through the strategy of revision, skimming over some points, lingering over others, moving back and forth between the three forms of revision, as you will when you are experienced with the entire process. But to understand the strategy, you should, at least once, examine an early draft, point by point, to see the full potential the strategy can reveal in a draft. That is what I will do to see if my discovery draft has the potential for me to fulfill the assignment of a fund-raising letter. I scan the text, reading quickly.

LOOK WITHIN FOR THE SURPRISING

Word

I hesitate over "GIRLS!" I realize, now that my consciousness has been raised, that the word *girls* hearkens back to an era I could remember and explore in a column. No other word really sparks my interest.

Line

"Onward Christian Soldiers" catches me, because it was one of my favorite hymns when I was young. I didn't hear the irony of a killing, militaristic Christianity until

I saw my first dead German soldier and his belt buckle, which proclaimed that God was with the Wehrmacht, Hitler's army. "I don't remember classes as much as the professors' offices" also catches my eye. That may lead to something.

Distance

I'm remembering my first view of the campus reflected through the many lives I would live in Durham. Should I stay at that distance—the assignment would seem to demand that—or would it be more effective to move in close, put the reader with me on campus in 1943?

Voice

"I remember my learning as much as theirs" has a certain melody or music I can imagine developing as I write.

Focus

The focus is on the meetings, one-on-one, with my professors. That may be the focus of the next draft.

Details

I need more details like Towle's corncob pipe and Daggett's pride in his biceps.

Sequence

I sense a sequence or implied narrative that could run through the piece: discovery that my students were learning with me and later discovering that I was learning with my students.

Purpose

To get alumni to see what is special about this intimate form of education, to encourage them to celebrate and support it—with cash.

Meaning

At a university, faculty and students learn together.

Genre

This piece looks like an essay, more than a letter, a personal reflective essay that puts our alumni experience in a positive educational context.

Audience

I could target a different audience—the readers of my column, teachers who read my articles and textbooks—but here the audience will be alumni.

It took me a few minutes to zero in on this draft and find the approach I can use to produce a fund-raising alumni letter. Writing is always a matter of selection, choosing the road to go down, and making choices all along the way. Today I have found, within my discovery draft, my approach to the assignment—I will write about students and teachers learning together—but I must, to avoid problems as I write this piece, at least check the other two strategies of revision.

Next, I look ahead to see what may need to be changed.

LOOK FORWARD FOR THE CHANGING

Purpose

In reading these 299 words, I might have decided to write about the relationship of men and women ("girls") in the 1940s, or a militaristic Christianity, or the importance and techniques of teaching writing by conference.

Meaning

Any of these issues may have a new meaning that I might feel the need to explore. In fact, I think I will celebrate—in a column—the benefits of feminism for an old man who now has women friends.

In fact, I am going to start next week's column right now, while the words are eager to flow:

> The other morning I marched down Durham's Main Street, which runs through the middle of the University of New Hampshire, and was both a retired professor taking his constitutional and an eighteen-year-old soldier marching down the same street in 1943.
>
> What I remember is not the itchy winter uniform, the green lawns and brick buildings, but the GIRLS! that lined the sidewalk.
>
> Today I do not see girls but women.
>
> The girls were mysterious, alluring, threatening, different. The women to whom I nod or wave, with whom I stop to chat today, are colleagues and friends.

Once I have this much written, I can go back and finish it when I have time.

Distance

As I get back to thinking about my fund-raising letter, I might zoom back and forth, almost line by line, from present to past and back, making a virtue of one of the weaknesses of the discovery draft.

Genre

I see poems and short stories in this draft that I may develop later.

Audience

There could be a general audience—old-timers who would be nostalgic, young people who would be astonished, feminists who might be pleased, old fogies who might realize the benefits—to them—of the feminism they have attacked.

Evidence

I could go to school records which might document curriculum arguments for or against conference teaching, or rules and regulations that would document the very different treatment of men and women at UNH then and now. I might interview women who have lived these changes.

Order

I might not start with my parade down Main Street but with the scene, after I returned, of the Military Arts Ball, which no longer takes place in Durham.

Pace

I might saunter through the past or speed from present to past and back.

Proportions

I will always have the question of how much past and how much present.

Development

I must have enough information—descriptive details, facts, documentation— to make the past clear to the young, the present clear to the old.

Voice

My voice must, as always, be appropriate to the subject, the audience, and myself. I must be aware of language—girls, dates, balls, curfews.

Again, let me remind you that these lists are just quick checklists to protect you from wasting your time on fruitless revision, allowing you to concentrate your energy where revision will be rewarded. Finally, it is important to look back to what was expected. If you are rewriting a novel, you may want to betray your expectations, but if you are revising a screenplay for a Hollywood producer, a marketing report for a corporate vice president, a thesis for an academic committee, or a fund-raising letter for an alumni officer, you'd better be sure you can fit your discoveries to their expectations.

LOOK BACK FOR THE EXPECTED

My focus on individual education can fit the purpose of showing alumni a consistent strand that deserves their pride and their funds despite all the changes at their university.

Meaning

It is significant that university faculty continue to learn and share their learning with their students.

Distance

It is appropriate for me to move back and forth in time, as long as the time shifts clarify the meaning I am communicating for my readers.

Genre

The essay format of the letter will work, I think.

Audience

My audience is clear. Men and women who graduated fifty years ago.

Documentation

My documentation is personal and anecdotal, which is appropriate for this piece of writing.

Logic

The emphasis on individual learning is logical, it makes sense.

Pace

I shall have to make sure the readers are kept moving forward fast enough so they will continue to read, slow enough so they will absorb what I have to say.

Proportions

I will have to make sure there is little—but enough—of a fund-raising appeal, surrounded by mostly informative material. I will also have to make sure there is enough reflection to recreate the past but much more on what is going on at UNH today. That is what we hope they will support.

Development

I will have to develop each part well enough that the reader can relive or live it.

Voice

My voice should not be pushy. I should simply recount what I have experienced at UNH in a way that encourages them to support the school. (Fifty-two alumni responded with $5,265.)

Here is the revision I submitted:

I first came to Durham in 1943 when an Army sergeant counted cadence as we marched down Main Street. I returned from Europe in 1946, surprised to have survived combat, and experienced an unexpected intimacy of learning with Carroll Towle, Gwynne Daggett, Bill Hennessey, and others who met with us in class, in their offices, in their homes and ours, in the corridors of Murkland, and on the sidewalks of Durham.

I lived the glorious triangle of university learning:

An individual teacher,

a senior learner

A test to be understood,

a question to be asked,

a problem to be researched

An individual student,

a junior learning

In 1963 I was invited to return to the university to set up a journalism program, and I reentered the triangle of learning as the senior learner, meeting with each individual student every week in the method of Carroll Towle and the pattern of freshman English which is still taught by class and conference.

Since retiring from the faculty nine years ago, I have continued to live in Durham, observing the evolving university firsthand. I have cheered the hockey and football teams, applauded the academic honors won by faculty and students, watched the new buildings rise on a campus I still find beautiful, but most of all, I have celebrated the evidence I have found that the triangle of learning goes on: An individual professor and an individual student learn from each other as they confront a specific intellectual question.

This individual learning is expensive but central to the university. It is the way that faculty continue to learn, that students discover how to learn, and that society benefits from their combined learning.

Visit the campus and you see buildings, but if you are fortunate enough to live here you may catch a glimpse of what goes on in the seminar room, faculty office, laboratory: a belief doubted, an answer that finds a question, a principle challenged, a theory tested, a pattern explained, a problem solved that gives birth to a new question.

In room _____ at the Whittemore School of Business and Economics, Dr. _____ meets with _____ . They are fascinated with _____ and study the puzzling results of a survey that contradicts expectations. Now they have a problem to solve that may change the way _____ look at _____

In a laboratory in_____ , _____ uses a _____ to test and retest a_____ taken from Great Bay the day before. She calls over Dr. _____ who runs his own tests, and then they sit down to study computer printouts that may some day lead to _____ .

[And so on for the School of Health Studies and Human Services and the College of Liberal Arts]

Four individual students and four individual faculty members focusing on four significant questions. Radiating out from them are the intellectual interactions of _____ full-time and part-time faculty members with _____ undergraduate and graduate students.

Of course there are large classes, but the center of what goes on at the University of New Hampshire is that grand triangle of individual learning. I give to support what happens when an individual instructor and student learn from each other, and I hope you will join me.

The alumni office did the research that changed, developed, and filled in my blanks, and the letter was published pretty much as I had drafted it. But it was not a first draft; it was a revision constructed after exploring a discovery draft.

Notice that I passed up many topics in that discovery draft: my desire to go to war and what happened when I did; marriage, divorce, remarriage; the births of three children and the loss of one; what I studied in school and how it affected my life; what it was like to return and teach where I had been a student; teaching my teacher's son; profiles of Towle or Daggett; an essay on what makes a good teacher—all those topics and more embedded in 299 words. But I had an assignment, and so I concentrated on what might help me fulfill that assignment.

Sometimes I practice an unconscious revision. Once we have written, we have captured a vision of the world. Several years after writing that letter I was invited to write a column for the university magazine on what goes on at a university, and this column was, in effect, a revision of the piece above although I never looked back and didn't realize the connection until I was rewriting this chapter. Here is the "unconscious revision:"

• A LANDSCAPE OF WORDS •

I live at the edge of that mysterious organism we call a university, nine-tenths of a mile from the classrooms in Murkland where I was a student, the same distance from Ham Smith, where I taught for 24 years. As I watch faculty and students apparently arriving or leaving early, or read news stories about research grants I do not understand, or listen to anecdotes that illustrate Henry Kissinger's statement— "Campus politics are so vicious precisely because the stakes are so small"—I, like so many politicians and taxpayers in this state, find myself wondering, "What does go on in Durham anyway?"

A few times, waiting to meet an old colleague, I've lurked outside a classroom in Ham Smith, hoping to observe what indeed goes on, even to catch a glimpse of the central activity of a university. Perhaps I will see on a student's face the look of surprise and delight when confusion comes clear. I may hear a question that hangs above a seminar table until it attaches itself to a student's mind for a lifetime. I may even find the mystery that is a university when a professor pauses during a lecture, surprised at a truth that has tumbled unplanned from her lips.

But of course, I do not capture, see or hear what happens in a university. The central act is invisible—a sudden, unexpected falling in love with learning that happens so quickly, so easily that neither the student nor the teacher knows that a life has been changed.

I came to UNH first as a soldier in 1943 and returned from combat in Europe three years later, surprised to be alive. I carried little with me but the dream of becoming a writer—a dream that seemed so wonderful, so removed from the ordinary person I was, that I imagined it to be impossible. Yet in Durham, I found professor Carroll Towle, who seemed to think my dream possible. Gwynne Daggett, Sylvester Bingham and others demonstrated lives lived in the landscape of language. Just as important, I joined a community of pilgrims who followed the same impossible vision.

I remember no moment of grand illumination, but in four semesters and two sessions of summer school, my dream became a vocation. I left UNH a writer and have, ever since, lived a life of words. It might have happened somewhere else, but I doubt it. It happened in the mixture of hope and knowledge and obsession that is not only tolerated but encouraged in a university.

I returned to UNH 15 years later to teach. I worked hard at my new craft, but the more I learned to teach, the more mysterious this central mystery of the university became. It seemed the longer I taught, the less I taught, and the more my students learned. In fact, I did not teach so much as encourage. In my classroom, my office and my home, students found themselves part of a community that did not laugh at their dreams and allowed them to teach themselves the craft to which they, like their instructor, would forever be an apprentice.

I never quite knew what worked on my page or in my classroom, but I am amazed, looking back, how many students left with a vocation for writing. I knew it was happening, but I could never quite see it, never be sure what had happened and when.

The other afternoon, I was invited by John Lofty to meet with his class on the teaching of English. The students and I wrote together, then talked our way across the landscape of words that had become their teacher's life and mine.

What happened? What did I teach? What did they learn? I do not know.

What goes on in a university remains a mystery. I leave John Lofty's class and cross the boundary between gown and town. At home, I again observe antics of the university community with amusement, amazement and, often, a critical eye. But each morning, at 79 years of age, I return to the lifelong apprenticeship that began when I returned from war to the mystery we call a university. I still do not know exactly what happened to me at the University of New Hampshire, but I am grateful each morning that it gave me the courage to write what I do not yet know.

Two Key Questions

Another approach to revision is built on two key questions:

WHAT WORKS?

WHAT NEEDS WORK?

Years ago, before I had a computer, I would write at least three drafts for a magazine article and revise each by hand at least ten times. To discover what I was doing so I could teach it to my students, I pasted each typed draft on a much larger piece of paper, revised, then wrote in these large margins what I was doing, why I was doing it, and how. I surprised myself. I thought I was fixing failure and correcting error but discovered that, most of the time, I was strengthening success. I was building on the elements in the draft that worked, making them stronger, rather than correcting error.

Once I found what worked and developed those elements, I went on to what needed work. I found that many of the errors, problems, or failures in early drafts disappeared as I revised by focusing on developing the strengths of the article. Those that hadn't disappeared could then be addressed.

What is failure to one writer is opportunity to another; what doesn't work for one writer may work for another. I am reminded of what novelist Fay Weldon said:

> What others say are your faults, your weaknesses, may if carried to extremes be your virtues, your strengths. I don't like too many adjectives or adverbs—I say if a noun or a verb is worth describing, do it properly, take a sentence to do it. There's no hurry. Don't say "the quick brown fox jumped over the lazy dog." Say, "it was at this moment that the fox jumped over the dog. The fox was brown as the hazelnuts in the tree hedgerows, and quick as the small stream that ran beside, and the dog too lazy to so much as turn his head." Or something. Writing is more than just the making of a series of comprehensible statements: It is the gathering in of connotations; the harvesting of them, like blackberries in a good season, ripe and heavy, snatched from among the thorns of logic.
>
> Having thus discouraged the apprentice writer from overuse of adjectives, I turn at once to Iris Murdoch and find she will use eighteen of them in a row. It works. What is weakness in small quantities is style in overdose. So be wary of anyone who tries to teach you to write. Do it yourself. Stand alone. You will never be better than your own judgment, and you will never be satisfied with what you do. Ambition will, and should, always outstrip achievement.

Remember Fay Weldon: Ask "What works—for you?" Ask "What needs work—from you?" Then ask what the reader needs.

The Revision Checklist

Revision is not editing. They are two separate activities, and keeping them apart makes the task of preparing a final draft much easier.

The following diagram shows how the emphasis changes from revision to editing:

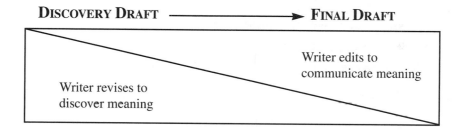

Revision is re-seeing the entire draft so that the writer can deal with the large issues that must be resolved before she or he deals with line-by-line, word-by-word issues involved in editing.

In reading for revision, it is important to step back and scan the draft so that you can see it as a whole. In this way, you will notice such things as the relationships between the sections of the draft that you cannot see when you are concentrating on the relationship between a particular verb and an individual noun.

Make your own revision checklist. Mine is in the list below. The list is long, but many of the questions can be answered in an instant. Because you have explored, focused, planned, and drafted, you have solved most of these problems in advance. This is a checklist to see if any problems remain that must be solved before the editing that produces the final draft:

CHECKLIST FOR REVISING

Subject

- Do I have something I need to say?
- Are there readers who need to hear what I have to say?

Focus

- Does the draft make a clear, dominant point?
- Are there clear, appropriate limits to the draft that include what needs to be included, exclude what is unnecessary?
- Do writer and reader stand at the appropriate distance from the material?

Authority

- Are the writer's credentials to write this draft established and clear?

Context

- Is the context of the draft, the world in which the story exists, clear?

Voice

- Does the draft have an individual voice?
- Is the voice appropriate to the subject?
- Does the voice support and extend the meaning of the draft?

Reader

- Can you identify a reader who will need to read the draft?
- Can you see a reader who will want to read the draft?
- Are the reader's questions answered where they will be asked?

Genre

- Is the form of the story the best one to carry the meaning to the reader?
- Does the draft fulfill the reader's expectations of that form?

Structure

- Will the lead attract and hold a reader?
- Does the ending resolve the issues raised in the draft?
- Is there a clear trail through the draft?
- Does each point lead to the next point?
- Does each section support and advance the meaning?

Information

- Is the reader's hunger for specific information satisfied?

Documentation

- Does the reader have enough evidence to believe each point in the draft?

Pace

- Is the reader carried forward toward the intended meaning by the flow of the draft?
- Are there points where the draft needs to be speeded up to keep the reader from abandoning it?
- Are there points where the draft needs to be slowed down so the reader has time to comprehend the meaning of what is being written?

Proportion

- Are the sections in appropriate proportion to one another to advance and support the meaning of the draft?

Quantity

- Where does the draft need to be developed?
- Where does it need to be cut?

Move through the checklist quickly, scanning the draft and then revising part or all of it as necessary until you have done all you can do—or until the deadline is upon you. Then begin editing the final draft.

CHAPTER 26

Edit

In 1957 I picked up a new issue of *The New Yorker* and read an article by the great essayist E. B. White, about his writing teacher Will Strunk. In that article, which later became the introduction to *The Elements of Style* (William Strunk, Jr., and E. B. White), he quoted Strunk as saying:

> Vigorous writing is concise. A sentence should contain no unnecessary words, a paragraph no unnecessary sentences, for the same reason that a drawing should have no unnecessary lines and a machine no unnecessary parts. This requires not that the writer make all his sentences short, or that he avoid all detail and treat his subjects only in outline, but that every word tell.

I can still feel my excitement as I typed out those words on a three-by-five card and thumbtacked it above my typewriter. The card turned from white to yellow to tan. Its edges curled and the type started to fade before I threw it away decades later. By then it was printed on the inside of my forehead where I could see it every time I sat down to draft, revise, or edit. It is still there.

There are few satisfactions for this writer greater than editing a final draft—word by word, space by space, line by line. As Diane Ackerman says,

> Most of a writer's life is just work. It happens to be a kind of work that the writer finds fulfilling in the same way that a watchmaker can happily spend countless hours fiddling over tiny cogs and bits of wire. Poets also love to fiddle with a word here, a word there—small spaces for hours. And when I'm working on a poem, I'm working harder than I've ever worked at anything in my life—I'm concentrating harder. But it's enjoyable. Not something I would describe as fun—it's more like rapture, a kind of transcendent play.

Fiddling around with a piece of writing is so satisfying because the subject comes clear. I like to make my copy simple, easy—like the flight of the seagull. Each editing makes the writing more natural. Editing—ironically—makes each draft more spontaneous.

I'm going to write a few lines about a cliché topic—Father's Day—and then see if editing will reveal the meaning to me and then, to you the reader.

> I never expected to be a father. My own father was at work or church most of the time. Even when he was home, he seemed at a distance a stranger in a house dominated by women—his grandmother and her daughter. I didn't really know what a father was supposed to do. Then I had a daughter, and I found I knew what to do.

Editing is simply a matter of adding, taking away, moving around, and making sure the result was clear. Do I have something to say? I can't edit until I have specified a topic, since all editing is aimed at developing and clarifying the topic. No topic, and editing is a waste of time. In my sample, I do have a topic—discovering how to be a father.

I also need a structure, a design, and order. I have that. I have an embedded narrative—how I passed from not knowing a father's role to knowing. Now I can edit. I move some of it around:

> My own father was at work or church most of the time. Even when he was home, he seemed at a distance, a stranger, in a house dominated by women—his grandmother and her daughter. I never expected to be a father I didn't really know what a father was supposed to do. Then I had a daughter, and I found I knew what to do.

I put in and take out:

> My own father was at work on the road buying silk stockings, women's corsets, or ladies gloves or at the department store making sure they were sold at a profit. If he wasn't on the road he was at church, a deacon trying to fulfill the orders of the prophets. When I was young, I didn't know the difference between profits and prophets. Both ruled our life. Most of the time. Even when he was home, he seemed at a distance, a stranger in a house dominated by women. I never expected to be a father; I didn't really know what a father was supposed to do. Then a nurse handed me Anne, my first daughter, wrinkly red and howling. Then I had a daughter and I found I knew what to do. No thinking, just instinct. I held her against my shoulder and rubbed circles around her tiny back. Her howls became sobs, her sobs moans, her moans, silence. She slept, and I became a father.

That's all. In most cases, editing means putting in more than taking out, moving around, simply clarifying.

I have worked for the past few years with editors on some of the best newspapers in the country, and I've found that these editors make the same mistake most teachers—and their students—make. The mistake is to plunge in and start editing language first, working from the written line back to form and then to meaning. It simply doesn't work.

Proofreading and Editing

Proofreading is what most people think of when editing is mentioned, but it is only a small part of editing. It is important to correct spelling, to check facts and names and quotations, to conform to certain stylistic standards of mechanics and usage, to clean up typographical errors. But editing is that and much more.

Editing is the honing of thinking, making meaning rational and clear, accurate and graceful. Editing is the final clarification of meaning. You choose one word and reject another word in relation to meaning. If the meaning isn't clear, the choice will be arbitrary and often wrong. There are no rules for word choice unrelated to meaning. Also, when you choose to write a short sentence or paragraph, it is usually for emphasis, and unless you know what you want to emphasize you won't know whether to make the sentence or the paragraph long or short.

When you edit, you repeat steps from the revision checklist, but your reading is different. When you revise, you read to see what needs to be done in the next draft; when you edit, you are the reader's advocate, preparing the final draft for your readers.

Editing Priorities

Effective editing is usually the result of three separate and distinct readings, each with its own pace, strategies, and techniques. The highly skillful editor or writer may be able to perform all three readings simultaneously, moving from the large global questions of meaning to structural questions of order, and to line-by-line questions of voice. But those interrelated skills are best developed by separating the reading—reading first for meaning, next for order, and third for voice.

Of course in each case the writer has to keep an eye open for the audience, standing back and making sure that what is being said and resaid on the page is clear to the reader.

This seems to be a slow process, but the first reading is usually a very fast one—a quick flyover of the territory to make sure that there is a single dominant meaning and an abundant inventory of information to support that meaning.

If there is no subject, no dominant meaning, no inventory of information, it is a waste of time to do more revising and editing. Stop immediately. Find a subject. Find its meaning. Find the facts to support that meaning.

The second reading looks for form and structure. It is a bit slower, but not much. The piece is still read in chunks to see if the sections support the main point and appear when the reader needs them.

If there is no form to the writing, no order within that form that leads the reader to meaning, read no further. It will be a waste of time. Stop. Choose a form and establish an order within that form.

At the end there is the third reading, a slow, careful, line-by-line editing of the draft to be sure that it is ready for a final proofreading. Here the writer cuts, adds, and reorders, paragraph by paragraph, sentence by sentence, word by word.

The process of three readings may sound tedious, but it shouldn't be. In each case you'll have the excitement of discovery, of finding a meaning that you did not expect to find and defining a change to make it become clear. Writing gives you the satisfaction of craft, the feeling you have when you lean your weight into the corner and make your bicycle swing gracefully where you want it to go. Writing is similar to hitting a tennis ball, baking bread, building a sturdy shelf, sewing a dress, planting a garden. It is a process of making, and it is fun to make something well, to handcraft a piece of prose that will carry meaning and feeling to another person.

Editing Marks

Most computer editing is invisible, but those who print out their drafts and edit with a pen or pencil will find it helpful to mark up the draft according to the traditions of the editor's trade using the symbols on page 280.

In the box on page 281 are some of the most helpful editing marks for the third, careful, line-by-line reading. If you are reading "hard copy" (draft pages you have printed out, not a computer screen) you will find these marks helpful in editing your drafts or the drafts of a classmate in a peer-editing session.

During the first two readings I sit away from the desk, if I

am not using a computer, in an easy chair and use a

clipboard or a bean bag lap desk. I read the draft quickly, as

a reader will, and do not mark anything within the text. I

do not correct spelling or typos, change words, revise, or

edit. Instead, I make marks in the left margin:

✓   A check for something that works,

★   a star for something that works well,

C   a C for something that needs cutting,

⌐↑   an arrow that suggests movement,

⟨⟩   a two-headed arrow to indicate the need for expansion,

→◄—   two arrows pointing at each other to show what needs to be

tightened,

?   and a question mark for further consideration.

These marks allow me to move through the text quickly.

Editing Checklists

The Quick Edit Checklist and Expanded Edit Checklist that follow are built
on the editing system that uses three readings—one for the topic, one for development of the topic, and one for language that communicates the topic. Of
course the actual process of revising and editing will not be so neatly contained.
Change of focus leads to change of language, and change of language can
change the topic; still, the master list is a way of proceeding logically and efficiently through a series of confusing writing problems.

paragraph	¶The craft of editing depends on reading aloud.
capital	the craft of editing depends on reading aloud.
lowercase	The Craft of Editing depends on reading aloud.
close	The craft of edit ing depends on reading aloud.
separate	The craft of editing depends on reading aloud.
transpose	The editing craft of depends on reading aloud.
punctuate	The craft of editing depends on reading aloud ⊙
insert	The craft of editing depends ᴏⁿ reading aloud.
take out	The craft of editing depends on reading aloud.
cut	~~The craft of~~ editing depends on reading aloud.
restore	~~The craft of~~ editing depends on reading aloud.
move	Insert The craft of editing depends on reading aloud.

Large inserts should be numbered or lettered and an

arrow should be marked in the margin of the text

where it is to be placed.

→ move Insert A here

Each writer has his or her own strengths and weaknesses. Eventually you should adapt my checklists to your own style, problems, and solutions.

Many times writers edit against deadlines, without time to carefully revise and edit. Remember that you have to deal with the first item before going on to the second and the second before the third. Here is a checklist for that situation:

THE QUICK EDIT CHECKLIST

- State the single, most important message you have for the reader in one sentence.

- List the points that support the message in the order the reader needs to receive them.
- Read the draft aloud to be sure the text is accurate and fair, and that the music of the language supports the message you are sending to the reader.

When you learn that the first draft is not the end result of the writing process, you will plan to allow time—at least as much as comes before the first draft—for reading, revising, and editing. The quick checklist is designed to help in the three readings for subject, structure, and language, but don't be surprised when you have to move back and forth through the checklist as solutions breed problems, and new problems demand new solutions.

THE EXPANDED EDIT CHECKLIST

This list is long, but remember that many of your answers will come rapidly, in a second or less. You are scanning the draft to catch the problems that have survived the writing process and must be solved before the draft is final, ready to face a reader.

- State the single most important message you have for the reader in one sentence.
- Does the draft deliver on the promise of the title and lead?
- Does your message have significant meaning you can make clear to the reader?
- Is the message important, worth the reader's time?
- Does your message contain the tension that will provide the energy to drive the reader forward?
- Is your message focused? Do you have a clear point of view toward the subject?
- Is the message placed in a significant context? Will that context be clear to the reader?
- Does the message have limitations that help you control and deliver the information?
- Do you have an abundance of information upon which to build the draft? Can you answer the questions the reader will certainly ask?
- Is that information accurate and fair?
- List the points that support the message in the order the reader needs to receive them.
- Is the form, the genre, of the draft appropriate to deliver the message to the reader? Will it contain and support the meaning of the draft?

- Does the structure within the draft support and advance the principal message?

- Does the order in the piece make the reader move forward, anticipating and answering questions as they arise?

- Is the structure logical? Does each point lead to the next in a sensible sequence?

- Is there a narrative thread that carries the reader forward? Will the sequence or narrative stand up to a doubting reader?

- Is the draft too long? Too short?

- Are the proportions of sections within the draft appropriate to the information they deliver? Are there sections that are too long? Too short?

- Is the draft effectively paced? Does it move fast enough to keep the reader reading, slow enough to allow the reader to absorb what is being read?

- Does the draft go off on tangents that take the reader away from its principal message? Does it include elements of good pieces of writing that do not support the current message but may be developed on their own later?

- Is each point supported with evidence that will convince the reader?

- Is the draft written at a distance that will involve the reader but also allow the reader to consider the significance of the message?

- Read the draft aloud to be sure it is accurate and fair, and that the music of the language supports the message you are sending to the reader.

- Does the title catch the reader's attention, and does it make a promise to the reader that can be fulfilled by the draft?

- Does the opening accomplish the same thing?

- Is each piece of information accurate and fair and presented in context?

- Does the reader need more information? Less? Can anything be cut? Must anything be added?

- Does the reader finish each sentence having gained information?

- Can the draft be heard by the reader? Does the music of the draft support and advance the meaning of the message?

- Does the draft reveal rather than tell whenever possible? Does the draft call attention to the message rather than the reader?

- Does each paragraph and each sentence emphasize the appropriate information?

- Does the sentence length vary in relation to the meaning being communicated, with shorter sentences at the most important points?

- Does the draft depend, at important points, on the subject-verb-object sentence?
- Is the draft written in the active voice whenever possible? Is each word the right word?
- Have all sexist, racist, and ethnic language and stereotypes been eliminated?
- Has private language—jargon—been replaced with public language the reader can understand?
- Has worn-out language—clichés and stereotypes—been replaced with language that carries specific meaning to the reader?
- Is the draft primarily constructed with verbs and nouns rather than adverbs and adjectives?
- Has the verb *to be* in all its forms been eliminated whenever possible? Excess *would*s, *what*s, and *ing*s?
- Is the simplest tense possible used?
- Are the tenses consistent?
- Are any words misspelled?
- Are the traditions of language and mechanics followed, except when they produce ungraceful language or change the meaning of the draft?
- Is the draft attractively presented, so that nothing gets between the reader and the message?
- Does the closing give the reader a feeling of closure and completeness, yet stimulate the reader to continue to think about the message that has been delivered?

Develop your own editing checklist, building on your own strengths and weaknesses in writing. Do not forget that this final stage of writing is still focused on discovery of meaning; as you edit, you learn more about your topic and make what you have to say come clear to the reader—so clear and easy to read that the reader may believe the writing was spontaneous.

■ SHOPTALK ■

When I write a paper, I'm usually pretty satisfied with it the first time around. I figure that what I've written down is what I want to say. So why revise?

Writing well is thinking deeply. Real thinking, like thoughtful writing, happens in layers. We think on the surface, and then we dip below. Surface thinking helps us get done what needs to get done everyday. This kind of thinking is perfectly fine for routine writing tasks, such as making lists or composing notes to our siblings or roommates. This is superficial writing and there's no need to revise it.

But thoughtful writing requires a more complex analysis of ideas, images, and concepts. That's why we layer writing through drafting and revising, to get below the surface to the core of analysis. That's where the surprises and insights are; that's when and where we really start to see. Until you explore layers of thinking through writing and rewriting, you will never know exactly what it is you want to say or are capable of saying.

> In the past when teachers asked me to revise, they just wanted me to clean up a few sentences and check my grammar and spelling. Why can't I do that now?

You can. Go ahead and fix mistakes, correct your grammar, be conscious of your spelling. A note of caution, though: Cleaning up and correcting are proofreading; they are cosmetic remedies rather than methods of thinking. They do not constitute revision, at least not in the way I use the term. Revision is just what it says: re-vision, or seeing again through rewriting. Seeing deeply means writing deeply, and to write deeply means to think deeply. This is what revision is all about.

Correct grammar and spelling are important, but it's probably no use fixing up what you've written in a first draft if your ideas and how you write about them are likely to change during the process of revising. While it doesn't really matter if you "clean up" earlier or later, it may make more sense to save this step until the end.

> Is it OK if I do all of my revising and editing on my computer?

You should do what works for you. But . . . sometimes, because a draft looks so neat and clean up there on the computer screen, it's hard for the writer to really mess with it, to really re-see it, rather than just rearranging a few commas and changing a word here or there. It might be better to print out your draft and cut it into pieces, or mark it up with colored pencils, or do something that helps you see the draft in a new way. Then you can go back to the computer and truly revise.

> How do I know what needs to be revised in my paper? Where do I start?

If you are not used to revising, it is a good idea to roll up your sleeves and plunge right in. Move things around, change your focus, write from another perspective or angle. Experiment. As you transform your draft, you begin to see the various possibilities of each piece of writing. You also demystify your writing so that you aren't afraid to mess with it. This kind of mucking around with what once seemed solid and fixed will help make the revision process seem less daunting.

As you look for different ways to revise, you also want to work closely with a writing partner in class or read your drafts aloud in a group workshop. Ask for feedback, and practice giving feedback to other writers. This exposure will help you become a more apt critic of writing, not to mention a better revisionist.

What if I gather too much feedback? How do I revise?

Learning to cull through comments and suggestions is an essential writer's skill. Different readers read differently. While there is often a consensus in writers' workshops about what needs to be done with a paper, it is just as likely that your readers will disagree in their suggestions. You will never be able to satisfy all of them. But you will have a sense of what you like or don't like about the suggestions you receive. Pick and choose from them; don't try to incorporate all of them into a revision. You'll only get muddled and end up confusing your readers.

Try to weigh feedback and suggestions against your own intentions as a writer. Trust your own intuitions about your writing and how your draft speaks to you. Ask specific questions of your readers about what you've accomplished and hope to accomplish in the draft. That way you will be sure to get feedback that is useful to you. You will also remain in charge of your writing.

My writing partner or classmates tell me that I don't have to change a thing, that everything is clear and makes sense to them. So I guess I don't have to edit, do I?

That depends. If you have edited thoroughly before asking your classmates to look at your work, it could be that your writing is ready to go. It might seem like an empty task to edit once more. Maybe you simply don't need to.

Or it could be that you need to imagine a wider audience for your work, a readership more varied than the one composed of your classmates. Imagine a newspaper or magazine that might publish your work, and think of the audience you might have. Is your piece ready for publication without further editing? Would your main images and ideas be absolutely clear to all of your readers?

Sometimes your classmates will understand what you write about because you share similar experiences with many of them: You may all be close in age, or live and work within the same school environment. For this reason, they may not need images or ideas clarified. They can simply "relate" to what you write. But someone who does not occupy the same realm of experience as you and your classmates may require more clarification. Keep these readers in mind as you edit.

Why can't I just run a grammar and spell checker on my computer?

Go ahead. These tools are useful. But they are no substitute for reading a draft for meaning. Your computer cannot do that. Sometimes it will even give you the wrong grammar suggestion for the meaning you want. You may purposely use long sentences to imply seriousness or formality, and your grammar-checking software will advise you to cut them in half. Other times you might want short, concise sentences or purposeful fragments, and your program will tell you to correct or lengthen your sentences.

Since you edit as much for the voice of the draft as for meaning and correctness, you will want to listen to your writing rather than depend on your computer to tell you if it's right or wrong. Spell check final revisions, but don't count too much on grammar checkers and other writer's programs to edit your piece. They make assumptions about what is standard writing and who are standard writers. You have your own voice, and your writing reflects that voice. There is nothing standard about it.

How do I know when I'm done editing?

When the deadline arrives. I once took a survey of all the people in my department at the university who had written books. They had all revised or edited their books after the manuscripts had been accepted. There is no natural end to the editing process. As Paul Valery said, "Writing is never finished, only abandoned."

What if I don't have time to edit?

Sometimes when you have to turn in writing that you do on the spot, you won't have time for extensive editing or revising. This possibility is particularly likely when you're writing answers to essay questions on exams. The trick in situations like this is to plan before writing.

With essay answers and other kinds of on-the-spot writing, you should take a few minutes to sketch out an outline or structure for your answer before you begin, since you will not be able to go back and reorganize when you finish. You will also probably want to edit as you write, or schedule a few minutes at the end of your available time to go back and make whatever changes you can while keeping your paper reasonably legible.

If you are in the habit of editing your work anyway, you will develop an eye and ear for what's right or out of place in your writing. Reading and editing closely while you have time will sharpen your editing skills for those occasions when you don't.

Will writing a case history really help me with the kind of writing I will do in other classes than my writing class?

Writing case histories means reflecting, analyzing, and interpreting. Since writing is learning and thinking, a case history is a microcosm of the educational process itself. It replicates everything you do in school: taking subjects apart, examining their components, holding them up to the light, exploring them, and then putting them back together and viewing them from an enlightened perspective. You follow this process in almost any class—whether it be math, science, English, history, or economics.

> But won't picking apart my writing ruin my spontaneity? If I analyze my writing too much, I'm afraid I'll start to sound boring and stilted.

Athletes play hard, putting body, soul, and mind into their work. Writing a case history is like being an athlete who reviews videotapes of a game in order to improve his or her performance. Fast forwarding, rewinding, or pausing at crucial points in the tape, the athlete analyzes key parts of the game and reflects on what he or she sees, taking stock of what went right or wrong in a game, what worked and what didn't. This kind of analysis does not ruin the athlete's ability to enjoy him or herself on the field; it allows the athlete to act spontaneously while engaging the mind.

When you write a case history you are like the informed athlete. The more you analyze and reflect on the process of writing a piece, the more informed about your own skills you will be as you approach writing tasks of different kinds. You will know what you do best and what you need to work on. You will know what methods work with one type of writing and not with another. This knowledge will make you a more confident writer, one who can adapt skills to almost any assignment. The more confidence you gain, the more spontaneous and creative you will be.

> How can I write a case history if I haven't kept track of the way I wrote the piece? I can remember some details, but memory alone won't help me write a complete history.

Often we tell or write stories about ourselves or others from memory. In fact, writing itself is a way of reclaiming memory and bringing it into the present.

While your case history may not be "scientifically" accurate if based solely on memory, it will still allow you to reflect, to think back on how you write and what you have learned.

As you sit down to write your case history, you will probably find that you have much more to go on than memory alone. If you have followed this text and completed some of the activities in previous chapters, you will have a variety of sources to interpret and analyze. You may also have kept a daybook or journal, or your writing partner may have kept notes on stories and essays you have written. If you have worked extensively with a partner or writing group, you might want to interview them to get their perspectives on your writing process and the pieces you have written throughout the semester. Look also at any comments your teacher has written on your papers. If you have had conferences with your teacher, you might want to think back on those conversations, as well.

■ IN THE WRITER'S WORKSHOP ■

ON YOUR OWN

1. If you keep a diary or journal, go back to entries that describe a significant period in your life. When you originally wrote these entries, you wrote them for yourself alone; now envision a readership—your classmates or the readers of a newspaper column you might write. How would you change these entries for your readers? What would you keep and what would you omit? Consider how your own perspective on the events or period you wrote about may have changed over time: What do you know now that you didn't know then? What experiences have you had that allow you to read these entries differently than before?

2. Go to a favorite outdoor site and write about it, double-spacing and keeping wide margins. Put the piece away for two weeks and then return to the site, changing your perspective by sitting in a new place to write. Look again at your surroundings, jotting down any extra details that you may have missed the first time. Then note in the margins and between the lines of your paper what you would want to develop or change. As you re-see your environment, how might you revise your paper? How might your focus change according to your perspective?

3. List at the top of the draft at least three of the seven writer's senses—seeing, hearing, touching, tasting, smelling, imagining, and remembering. Then go back through your paper and expand the areas that bring these senses into play, incorporating into your draft the details that pertain to each sense. As your paper expands, you may want to go back and pare down other sections where you summarize or tell instead of describe and show.

4. Start with the first full paragraph of your second page, and drop your entire first page altogether. You may have to revise the opening sentence of this paragraph a bit, but use it as the start of your revision. If you wish, incorporate bits and pieces of your original first page into the rest of your story. Then reread your draft to see how it changes. Does your new beginning confuse the reader, or does it invite her with an interesting lead? Do you still need what preceded your new beginning, or can the revised paper stand on its own without that material? What changes in the body and conclusion of the draft will you have to make in order to accommodate your new beginning?

5. Copy your draft onto a computer disk or hard drive, or photocopy it for safekeeping. Then take your original copy and drop a bomb on it! Demystify it, break it up, fragment it, "discombobulate" it. Try a bit of dialogue here, expand descriptions there, cut paragraphs and sentences in the middle, rewrite the conclusion as the lead or the lead as the conclusion. Try different fonts. Incorporate poetry into the story. Rewrite whole scenes or incidents from another person's

viewpoint. Take risks and have fun with your draft. (Remember: You still have a copy of your original version!) When you finally have a working draft—a fragmented piece in progress—share it with a group. Have each person pinpoint at least three new areas of your draft that intrigue him or her. Choose from these to find a basis for a more coherent revision.

6. Take a piece of writing, your own or someone else's, and cut it in half. Replace multiple words with one when one will do. Make war on needless adjectives. Cut back on prepositional phrases. Pare to the bone.

7. Choose a descriptive piece of writing with vivid and specific imagery and make it vague. Replace concrete adjectives (limp, sallow, square, sharp) with abstract adjectives (awesome, boring, beautiful, ugly). Then read the passages aloud to see how they change. Close your eyes and try to picture the images. Which adjectives work? Which don't?

8. Keep two verb lists in your daybook, one for strong, active verbs (yank, scoop, sweep, hurl), and the other for passive verb forms (was yelled at, is made clear, was held by). As you read textbooks, stories, poems, signs, essays, instructions, novels, drafts, or e-mail messages, write down strong, interesting verbs on the active verb list, and then write a sentence next to each using the verb in the passive voice. Jot down passive constructions on the passive verb list, and write a sentence for each, changing the passive voice to active. Once a week, select two verbs from both lists and discuss them with your group. Explain how the active and passive voices convey different tones and meanings.

9. Read your paper backward, sentence by sentence, starting with the very last one. This technique allows you to pick out mistakes you might normally gloss over when reading logically from beginning to end, front to back.

10. Reflect in your daybook about writing a particular piece. Don't go back yet to your notes or conversations with your writing partners; instead, write from your "gut." What were your strongest feelings about the piece? What did you love about it, hate about it? What in it pleased you or frustrated you? Where did you get stuck and how did you move on? How did you feel as you started the piece? Continued it? Finished it? How do you feel about the piece in retrospect?

11. Compare and contrast the first draft of a paper you wrote with a final draft. Make a copy of your first draft on your computer and triple the space between lines. In the margins and spaces, note where you made significant changes to the draft as you revised it. Retrace the steps you took to get from first to last draft. How and why did you make the changes you did? What effect did those changes have on the final draft? What did you learn about your writing process while revising the final draft?

12. Use the headings of your original outline to build a case history. Under each heading retrace your steps in writing the paper, and review how you

adhered to or digressed from your outline. Explain why. Did feedback from your writing partner or group influence your decisions? How many revisions did you do before you made the changes? At what point in the outline did you become stuck? Where did you find it easy to move forward? Think of your outline as a series of stepping stones to your final draft; explain how you used or skipped these stones or moved them around as you wrote.

13. Draw lines down the centers of two sheets of paper in your daybook. At the top of the first sheet write, "Things that Worked." On the left-hand side of this sheet, list the parts of your essay that you had fun writing or that you found easy to compose. At the top of the second sheet, write, "Things I Found Difficult." On the left-had side of this page, list all the parts of your essay that seemed hard to write or that frustrated you. On the right-hand side, reflect on the reasons for your difficulties and how and when you overcame them. Use these observations as the basis for your case history.

14. Write a case history of a laboratory problem you have solved in a science class. Trace your steps with the procedure, and recall how you thought the problem through, where you got stuck, and how you finally resolved it. Adapt the same procedure to a successful essay you have written, tracing your journey from draft to draft. Then write a few paragraphs examining the similarities and differences between the two case histories.

WITH A WRITING PARTNER

15. Work with a partner to re-see (re-vise) selected portions of your draft. Read aloud passages that are meant to convey specific images, and ask your partner to listen without reading along. Pause between selections and have your partner describe to you what he or she sees or doesn't see from your reading ("I see..."; "I wish I could see..."; "I don't see enough of..."; "I don't get a full picture of..."). Have your partner jot down specific questions that will help you re-see portions of your draft. ("What color hair did your friend Tom have?" "What kind of furniture did the scary room have?" "How did the girl move when she was scared?")

16. Divide your draft into sections, leaving ample room between each. Write in the blank spaces between each section, answering the following questions: "What do I want to achieve in this section of my draft?" "What have I achieved?" "What more do I have to do to this section in order to reach my goal?"

Follow the same procedure above, but list only what you hope to achieve in each section. Then pass the draft on to a partner, and let him or her decide whether you've achieved your goals. Have your partner suggest ways of revising your draft to better accomplish what you want.

17. During the first week of class, write an essay about your impressions of college. Exchange the essay with a classmate to keep until later in the semester. Before the semester ends, have your partner read your essay aloud to you. As you listen, note what changes in perspective now that you are a seasoned college student as opposed to someone who is brand new to campus. What things would you want to develop, downplay, or change in your original essay? How do time and space help you revise what you wrote earlier?

18. Collect troublesome sentences from your own work. As your writing partner, group, or teacher helps you recognize wordy, unclear, or grammatically weak sentences, add them to your list. Select one or two sentences from the list daily, and work with a partner to revise them.

19. Choose five sentences from any of your drafts and rewrite them in at least five different ways: Make them concise, vague, descriptive, awkward, short, ungrammatical, whatever. After each rewrite, incorporate the sentences back into the drafts they came from, and discuss with a partner or group how they change the original paragraphs.

20. Have a partner read through a couple of pages of your draft and then write one sentence in the left margin next to each paragraph briefly summing up what the paragraph is saying. If your partner has trouble summarizing a paragraph or misreads your meaning, rewrite the troublesome passage, working to clarify each sentence.

21. Write a collaborative case history with your writing partner. Trace how you helped each other as you wrote, what kind of feedback you got, and how sharing your writing influenced your final drafts. Interview one another and share notes from your daybooks, drafts, outlines, and freewrites. Vow to be as honest as possible with each other about what worked and what didn't.

22. Choose someone you know who absolutely hates to write, and study his or her process of composing a single essay for a class. Ask the writer to describe the difficulties he or she has with writing. What obstacles did the writer encounter? Did he or she overcome them? If so, how? If not, why? Using the writer's drafts and interviews, compose a case history.

Now choose someone who is in love with writing, and repeat this activity. Then write a case history comparing the avid writer to the frustrated writer. See if you can pinpoint specific features of both writers' processes that made writing particular pieces good or bad experiences for them.

WITH WRITING MENTORS

23. Write a case history of an editorialist or columnist for a local or school newspaper. Ask if you can sit in on meetings in which editorials or columns are discussed. Then interview the writer several times over a period of weeks and at

every stage of writing. Ask the writer to save drafts and proofread copies of his or her work. Interview the writer's coworkers—other writers, editors, support staff, and so on—about the writer's process and about what they know about how the writer works.

24. Write a case history of writing projects by your roommates or friends. Ask to see drafts of essays they have written for their classes. Interview them about the steps they took in writing their essays. Observe them in action and ask them to reflect—either by talking or on paper—about their writing processes. Have them tell you what they liked or disliked about writing their essays, what worked and didn't work, and why.

WITH A GROUP

25. Give copies of the second half of your draft to your class. Ask them to write a couple of paragraphs each describing what they imagine the first part of the draft to be like. Then pass out copies of the entire draft and discuss ways that their readings of the draft's conclusion may help you revise the first part.

26. Hand out copies of your paper and read it aloud to your class. Then pass around a piece of paper and ask your classmates to compile a "what if?" list: "What if you dropped this opening paragraph and began here?" "What if you forgot this part about your aunt and wrote just about your grandmother instead?" "What if you took the wonderful sentence in the middle of paragraph five and made it your focal point?" Choose one or more of these "what ifs" and use them to revise your paper.

27. As a class, list on the board as many vague or abstract sentences as you can: "It was sure a bright day." "The room was really nice." "The poem was pretty boring." "It was the most exciting moment of my life." With a partner, select five of these vague sentences, and make them vivid and descriptive. Read them aloud to one another to see if you get the picture.

28. Brainstorm a list of clichés in class, and write them on the board. Then exchange papers with a writing partner and go through line by line in search of clichés. Add more to the list on the board as you find them. Circle them and have the authors write replacement phrases or sentences.

29. Compile a booklet of case histories with your writing group. Have each member write a history about an essay he or she composed in a particular genre—a reflective essay, a persuasive essay, a research essay, and so on. Don't let any two members select the same genre. When the case histories are finished, exchange them within the group, read them as editors, and prepare them for "publication." Make sure to include final drafts of each member's genre essay with his or her case history.

INTERVIEWING OTHERS

30. Research your own case history as a writer of a particular piece. Consult your daybook and go back to comments your classmates or teacher wrote on earlier drafts. Interview your writing partner, your groupmates, your dorm neighbors, friends, or parents—anyone and everyone to whom you talked about your piece. Ask them what they remember about your writing process and what you told them about your topics. Review the activities that you completed in this text that may have helped you as your wrote your piece. Sort through outlines, maps, brainstorming lists, and freewrites as ways of tracing your writing process.

31. Write a case history of one particular step in your writing process (finding a subject, focusing, drafting, revising, etc.). Choose a step that you always have trouble with, no matter what you write. Using your notes and conversations with classmates, reflect on the ways you approached this step, the obstacles it presented, and how you negotiated those obstacles. Interview classmates about their own experiences with this step and then reflect on what you have learned about it.

ON THE INTERNET

32. Many OWLS offer guides to grammar, citations, and other writing concerns that might be of use as you get down to the nitty-gritty of editing. For example, go to The Deadly Sins Checklist at <http://www.ccc.comment.edu/grammar/sins.htm> on the Capital Community College's Guide to Grammar and Writing site. And if the editing starts making you a little crazy, go to Word Play at <http://www.wolinskyweb.net/word.htm>, Sites that Feature Fun with Words.

33. Visit a writer's discussion group online and trace one writer's journey through a single essay or story. Read all of the writer's posts, and keep a list of the writer's main concerns and how she or he resolved particular problems. Think of the writing process and outline in this text, and ask yourself how each concern relates to a particular step in that writer's process. Then use this list to begin compiling your own case history.

Writing After Graduation

The work is hard, the perks are few, the pay is terrible, and the product, when it is finished, is pure joy.

MARY LEE SETTLE

I have discovered that rejections are not altogether a bad thing. They teach a writer to rely on his own judgment and to say in his heart of hearts, "To hell with you."

SAUL BELLOW

You Want Me to Write What?

Think of yourself as the person everyone calls on when they can't get their computer to work. If you are like me when you have computer problems, you suffer a combination of anger, a sense of failure, acute frustration, stupidity, even rage. All the Mr. or Ms. Fix-its I have called on are calm. They don't see it as a problem but as a problem to be solved, the more difficult the better [they are usually paid by the hour].

Now that you have your own writing process you can be the person who solves writing problems. Even if you've never written a marketing report, a social work case history, an appeal to a foundation for help, an article for your local newspaper, don't panic. Remember you have a writing process that can be adapted to many writing tasks. The greater the challenge the better. You should even welcome the challenge of those you never expected to perform. An engineering report, a sales analysis, an accident report, a scholarship application, a poem, a legal brief, an essay are all constructed of common elements and with similar skills.

When you have come this far in the study of writing, you have experienced all the essential skills you need to write effectively. If you now learn the basic elements from which writing forms are constructed, you can prepare yourself when a professor asks for a critical essay, a science teacher assigns a lab report, a history instructor demands a term paper, experience inspires a poem, the concert committee assigns you to write a press release, a foundation invites a grant proposal, an employer asks for a sales report, or a supervisor wants an analytical report on a manufacturing process.

The ability to adapt your writing process to new writing tasks will serve you well after college. One study revealed that electrical engineers do far more writing after college than English majors do. As you live and work in an increasingly complex and shrinking world, you will find yourself communicating in writing with supervisors, subordinates, colleagues, clients, customers around the globe.

Specific writing tasks may change, and the messages they produce may, in your lifetime, be sent and received by technological devices we cannot yet imagine—I never imagined a fax or modem or e-mail—but the demand for clear writing will increase as we work with people over great distances.

You know the logical steps to follow when faced with a new writing task. Listen to the assignment, and ask questions if you do not understand the purpose of the project or what the person giving the assignment expects. It is helpful to study examples of similar assignments. Each writing form has its own traditions, but you may depart from them for reason; if you do not know the tradition the reader expects, however, you cannot depart from it in a way the reader will accept.

If you give yourself a writing task—a letter applying for a job, a note of sympathy, a journal narrative of an important event in your life, a memo redefining your job, a poem—you need to listen to yourself and then, playing the reader, question yourself to determine your expectations.

Writing forms or structures may appear arbitrary, but they have all been constructed, as houses are constructed, in response to logical, predictable demands. Houses need roofs and walls, doors and windows, rooms and hallways to satisfy the needs of people who live in them. The design of the house will change if it is to be built in northern Maine or southern Arizona, if it is in Manhattan or on a farm in North Dakota twenty miles from town. But each house is a variation on a common need.

The same elements occur in every writing task. Traditions are simply the records of how writing has been constructed in the past to solve special problems, the way a house in Minnesota may have a peaked roof so snow will not collapse it, and one in Arizona will have thick walls and extended eaves to make it cool and keep out the noonday sun. If you look at the problems a writing tradition attempts to solve, you will understand the tradition and be able to adopt or adapt it to solve your writing problems. The following sections review the questions to ask when you confront a new writing task.

Why Write this Assignment?

The writer needs to answer that TOUGH question. To choose, adapt, or develop a form, the writer needs to know the purpose of the writing to be done. There are important general reasons to write. Writing is the most disciplined form of thinking. Writers have to make the writing clear to themselves if they are to make it clear to readers. The act of writing demands content that is accurate, documented, authoritative, persuasive.

A written text can be read and understood over distances of time and place. It can be read and reread, shared, examined, revised, edited, considered, and reconsidered by many people. It provides a continuous point of reference.

In most literary works the purpose for writing is less clear to the reader, sometimes even to the writer in the beginning—to celebrate an experience, to explore an event, to understand a character, to examine an emotion, to tell a story, to entertain—but most writing does not produce literary works; it usually has a clear purpose—to persuade, to inform, to explain.

The reasons people write vary greatly. The writer may want to get a passing grade in history or share her historical research with other historians; the writer may want to report on families who have multiple social problems for a course in social work or persuade the government to concentrate all its services on a few problem families; the writer may want to recruit students for a junior-year abroad program or to persuade an employer to adopt a new sales approach.

A good way to understand the purpose of a piece of writing is to define what you expect the reader to think, feel, or do after reading it: "I want the reader to respect our Franco-American heritage"; "I want our government to concentrate on those few families in town who are the breeding ground for most of our social problems"; "I want students to sign up for a junior year in Siberia"; "I want my boss to try a new sales technique." A clear purpose helps the writer define, limit, and focus what the writer has to say and often predicts the form that will fulfill the writer's purpose.

WHAT IS MY MESSAGE?

Writing is thinking, and writers discover what they have to say by saying it. The message cannot be entirely predicted, and so the writer not only chooses the form of writing according to the message, but adapts that form to fit the evolving meaning.

Some writing tasks, such as poetry, are highly inventive, with the message discovered during the line-by-line drafts. But most writing tasks in the academic and working world have a clear purpose: to identify, define, and develop a historical trend; to report on the results of a biological experiment; to analyze a piece of literature; to explain a new software program; to suggest solutions that may solve a traffic problem at the supermarket checkout counter.

Sometimes a word will reveal my message to me in the private way of a writer's language—"advantaged"—or more likely a phrase—"the disadvantages of being an advantaged student"—occasionally a sentence—"I came to realize my disadvantaged students had an advantage." Too often an editor, early in a project, will demand a clear, specific, conclusive statement of intent, a thesis statement, but I disliked teachers holding me to statements that I had to make before I had completed my research and before I had thought about the topics by writing drafts.

The message statement is not a contract. It is a goal, a possibility, a target, a starting place. Some such tasks might be:

- To document the role of French Canadian priests in the exploration and mapping of North America.

- To argue that social services should concentrate on the families in a community that have the most physical, emotional, social, educational, and financial problems.

- To recruit students for a junior-year-in-Siberia program sponsored by the Russian department.

- To propose that an automobile dealer consider the no-salesperson approach, where each car has the final price posted and there is no negotiation.

WHO IS MY READER?

The message statement usually implies the audience: The first message above implies a history instructor or an audience of American historians; the next a sociology professor or a legislative group or agency that controls a budget; the third, college students who have enough money to spend a year abroad; the fourth, the owner or manager of an automobile dealership.

It is important, as you can see, to limit or target a specific audience. A sociology professor teaching an undergraduate course would require a different form and voice from a professor of social work in a graduate program. If the professor is in political science, still another form might be required. If the writer is appealing for a change in the law or a change in agency policy, the form of the appeal will again be different.

WHAT EVIDENCE WILL PERSUADE MY READER?

When you have decided on the purpose, the message, and the reader, you can anticipate the reader's needs.

Readers are hungry for information. Specific, accurate information gives your writing authority. The reader says, "This guy's done his homework; this guy knows his stuff." Readers need documentation; they need evidence to be persuaded. Writers need to remember to write with information, no matter the writing task. Readers read, above all, to be informed.

WHAT VOICE WILL KEEP THE READER INTERESTED
AND MAKE THE READER BELIEVE WHAT I HAVE TO SAY?

The reader responds, above all, to voice, to the individual who stands behind the page. We each have our natural voices that are reproduced in our writing, and we need to develop and control those natural elements that are composed from ethnic and family heritage, environment, and practice in speaking and listening. Voice is also a matter of intellectual, social, and emotional style.

Your challenge as a writer is to hear your voice then tune it to the topic and the audience. As you plan to write, you should compose fragments, perhaps sentences and paragraphs, in your mind and on your journal pages, listening to make sure that the music of the language supports your meaning and communicates to a stranger.

Each writing challenge you answer should be fun—and will be a chance to learn, making your tool book more and more full of tools ready for the next challenge.

CHAPTER 28

New Tasks, New Forms

When I was in high school I imagined that there was a committee equally divided between women English teachers and editors. They were all old and they met secretly, dressed in Supreme Court robes to decide what was correct. Once they decided, it was absolute, no appeal, no questions. These were The Rules.

When I became a publishing writer, I discovered I was the committee. My job was to communicate information to readers as clearly and gracefully as I could. The critical question was not "Is it correct?" but "Does it work?"

It works when the teacher or editor through which it passes and the readers who read it understand. If they are entertained, so much the better; but first, like Sgt. Joe Friday says, "Just the facts, M'am."

Many tasks you are asked to perform will require new forms, in other cases you will be asked to follow a company, government, or academic discipline form, but even there you should adapt the form when it is necessary to produce clarity and grace.

What Form Will Carry My Message and Its Documentation to My Reader?

To write this section, I looked in memory for the basic writing tasks I have done and came up with four tasks that have their own basic structures. You can do the same thing when faced with a writing task: Look within your experience and the demands of the job, then decide how to do it. Of course my "inventions" were discovered by the Greeks centuries ago, but we have to keep creating a rhetoric that serves our task, our audience, our time.

These are the basic writing tasks or problems the writer has to solve. The writer's purpose defines, in part, the solution or form, and these forms lie behind the writing in other genres—screenwriting, poetry, science writing, historical writing, business and political writing. The writer begins with the tasks writers most frequently face:

To describe

To analyze

To inform

To persuade

Of course, these forms overlap. Description may be necessary to persuade, informing may involve analysis, and so on. The writer creates the form that fits the task, adapting the formal elements to the immediate task, inventing each time from the materials that have been invented before.

Most writing tasks are not so neat that you can run into the warehouse and grab a pretested, prepared writing form. Each task is different, and you need to adapt traditional forms to the new task and sometimes design a new form. It is really a simple task.

Write to Describe

Description is the basic form of writing, but when I first taught freshman English it was outlawed in our program as being too simple for academic discourse. Simple? That was the opinion of those who did not write. Description is not simple, but it is fundamental and the best way, I believe, to lay the foundation of the writer's craft. At first, you use description to capture a place or a person, then places with people, then people interacting with others, and you end up describing ideas, theories, concepts, thoughts and feelings, propositions and conclusions, speculations and facts. All forms of writing contain descriptive elements that make readers see, think, feel, react.

Writing description can introduce you to the discipline of recording information, ordering it into meaning, and communicating that meaning to readers. All the elements of effective writing—accuracy, concreteness, meaningfulness, context, development, form and order within a piece, emphasis, documentation, flow, grace, style, reader awareness, proportion, pace, voice—may be called upon when you write description.

TIPS ON WRITING DESCRIPTION

- *Be accurate.* The writer has to earn the reader's trust. A single error in fact or an accurate fact in the wrong context can cause the writer to lose the reader's trust.

- *Be specific.* Readers hunger for concrete details. The specific carries authority with it. Don't use words such as *beautiful* and *ugly* that carry no meanings out of context. What is beautiful or ugly to one person is the opposite to someone else. Give the reader specifics, and the reader will feel or think the reaction to it. Don't tell the reader what to think or how to feel; make the reader think and feel by using specific images.

- *Create a dominant impression.* Establish a focal point, and relate all your details to that point, developing and supporting it. If you walk into a trauma center, your eye goes to a stretcher or to a team of people working on someone or to parents sitting and waiting. Everything in your description must flesh out the dominant impression.

- *Establish an angle of vision.* The reader should see the trauma center from a particular angle: from the waiting room or the swinging doors of the ambulance bay, from the patient's bed looking up, from a nurse or doctor's eyes looking down. This position can move, but it should move slowly. Think of how a professional moves the movie camera and how the amateur blurs the screen by panning too quickly.

- *Determine the correct distance.* Stand at an appropriate distance to reveal what you want to say. Zoom in close for intimacy and immediacy; draw back to put the subject in context; move back and forth so that the topic is revealed effectively.

THE NARRATIVE ESSAY

Narrative—storytelling—is the most important form of description. Narrative allows the writer to describe historical and current events, processes and travels, searches and researches, biographies and autobiographies, reflections and investigations, actions and reactions that take place in the river of time.

We think of narrative as primarily a fiction technique, and when I first started teaching, narrative was not allowed in freshman English. Yet writing narrative is an essential skill for a nonfiction writer, too. In fact, all effective writing has an embedded narrative; the reader may not be aware of it, but the implied story keeps the reader's interest and moves the reader forward, toward the writer's meaning.

Narrative also satisfies the reader's fundamental hunger for story, chaos ordered into meaning. Readers who would not read about a subject on their own will make the effort if it is told in the form of story: the boring financial or scientific story is un-bored if you read the account of a fiscal battle or a scientist's struggle to make a breakthrough.

TIPS ON WRITING NARRATIVE

- *Time in a story is not a clock.* The second hand does not move evenly, click by click, toward the minute; the minute hand does not move evenly, click by click, toward the hour. Time in a story is distorted, as it is in life. We spend a great deal of time telling of a moment in great detail, then skip to the next moment that is important to the story. When I was in the infantry, we used to say that combat was days of boredom with minutes of terror. That comment also describes the use of time in a narrative.

- *Show, don't tell.* This fundamental rule of dramatic writing applies to any narrative, whether it is fiction or nonfiction. The reader likes to have the story revealed, and it takes a while for an inexperienced writer to show what is happening rather than telling the reader what is happening—and what to think and feel. Narrative makes the reader think and feel for himself or herself. I write fiction, and when I make the transition to narrative, I find myself seeing the event I am describing as a movie. I do not say the character is scared; I show his hand shaking, his eyes open wide and looking around, his hesitant step and quick retreat back through the door.

- *Build with scenes.* The basic narrative unit is the scene, just as in a play or movie. The scene includes character, action and reaction, and setting. At the end, at least one of the characters is changed.

- *Characters interact.* Character, not plot, makes the story go. One person says or does something—or says or does nothing. "I love you," she says. He stands up, nods to the people at the next table and leaves the restaurant. There is an action and a reaction, and now the story will grow as she acts or he returns and she leaves and so on. His response to her statement comes from the nature of his character and is a revelation of his character. The action—his departure—is driven by character. That is what interests the reader: not his leaving but how could he respond in this way? The reader wants to see how she will respond and her response comes from the nature of her character and is a revelation of her character. Story is built on character; story is driven by character; character determines action.

- *Dialogue is easy.* Beginning writers are often afraid of dialogue. I remember what Elizabeth Bowen wrote: Dialogue is action. It is what people do to each other.

The only exercise I assign is one to teach dialogue. Here is the situation: She is meeting him to tell him she is pregnant; he is meeting her to tell her that he does not want to see her anymore. Write that scene entirely in dialogue. Not names, no he-said's or she-said's. Just speech in quotation marks, one speaker to a paragraph.

Write to Analyze

As we describe, we analyze. We cannot help but evaluate what we have seen, taking it apart to see what makes it work. Analysis is as important to the writer's toolbox as the wrench is to the mechanic. Analysis helps you understand an idea, an event, a feeling, a text. Analysis is a work of the mind more than the emotions.

Do you remember Graham Greene's profound question? "Isn't disloyalty as much the writer's virtue as loyalty is the soldier's?" Writers are blessed and cursed with this disloyalty. Disloyalty allows them to stand back from themselves—and their families, friends, churches, jobs, organizations—dissect what is happening to see what forces are at work. Writers suffer from this distancing, always standing back and questioning their motives, what they do and do not do, how they and their families, friends, neighbors, colleagues act and react. Writers question the world; nothing is sacred.

Writers are take-aparters. They x-ray, analyze, and look for causes and effects, theories, patterns, systems. The only defense of the writer's lonely trade is that writers are also put-togetherers. They construct their own analyses, new buildings of meaning that bring order, sense, and reason. These new constructions will face analysis from others as the intellectual world struggles to understand.

The principal elements of effective analysis include a clear and fair statement or description of what is to be taken apart, a logical process of dissection complete with evidence at each step of the way, a tone or voice that is appropriate and convincing, and a conclusion that constructs a new meaning.

TIPS ON WRITING ANALYSIS

- *Read the text.* The writing may be a novel, documentation of a new personnel procedure, a sociological report, the film of a football game, a marketing plan, an environmental report. Read it quickly all the way through, then read slowly, step by step, to make sure you understand what you are analyzing—or what you don't understand.
- *Respond.* Respond to what you are analyzing—an essay, a manufacturing procedure, a historical theory, a medical treatment, an engineering report, a political speech, a movie—by taking into account your personal

reaction. Too often, analysts stand back, not allowing themselves to connect what they are analyzing to their own experience, not realizing that emotion and personal thoughts are appropriate factors in analysis. When I analyze a historical account of a military event, I make use of my experience in combat; when I analyze a news story, I make use of my experience as a newspaper reporter.

- *Discover the focus.* To begin analysis, the writer should understand the central meaning of the process, event, discovery, law, theory, text to be analyzed. The writer works backward from the meaning or point of focus to see all that leads up to it.

- *Look for patterns.* Meaning is constructed of relationships. One thing leads to another. Look for those connections, the map of meaning the writer has drawn.

- *Be skeptical.* Use your common sense. Question. Doubt. Check the evidence the writer uses to support the meaning. Double-check the sources. Examine the author's chain of logic for weak links. Remember what Ernest Hemingway said: "The most important essential gift for a good writer is a built-in, shock-proof shit detector."

- *Look at the context.* A piece of writing does not float free like a birthday balloon. Study what is written against the context in which it is written, the world in which the writing exists.

- *Write in an appropriate voice.* In most cases of analysis this means a professional, somewhat detached voice. The voice of a fair judge who is looking at the subject with a stern impartiality and analyzing in a way that is speaking to the subject, not the person or people behind the subject.

ANALYSIS IN THE BOOK REPORT

The book report is a common form of analytical writing, and the biggest mistake students make is to leave out the critical analysis. They limit their book reports to simply informing the reader that the book exists while the real purpose of the book—or article or short story—review is critical analysis. The reader wants an informed opinion of the information in the book, and the writer's success depends on presenting that information.

TIPS ON WRITING A BOOK REPORT

- *Include publication information.* The reader may want to buy the book or order it from the library. List the title and subtitle if there is one, the author, the publisher with principal city of publication, and the year of publication.

- *Be critical.* That does NOT mean being negative. It means evaluating the content and the presentation within the book.

- *Document each point with quotations.* The reader wants evidence to support what the reviewer says.

- *Compare.* Look at the book in the context of other books that have been published on the same subject, evaluating their strong and weak points.

- *Include biographical information about the author.* This background is helpful if it will help the reader to understand the basis of the writer's authority—or question it.

THE REFLECTIVE ESSAY

The reflective essay is a more sophisticated form of analysis. It often begins with a personal experience—the death of a loved one, the coach's instructions to cheat to win a game, the decision to get—or not get—an abortion. The essay finds meaning in its subject.

It is a common misconception that analysis is a cold, detached, scientific process in which the writer analyzes the thoughts, experiences, or writing of others. Of course, this assumption often holds true, but in reflective essays the writers analyze their own thoughts, feelings, reactions. A classic case of such an essay is George Orwell's "A Hanging" in which the real subject is Orwell's reflection upon his reaction to the event.

The personal experience is analyzed in much the same way as it is in the academic paper, but that experience is written about in a much more reflective manner as the writer focuses on a personal experience and finds meaning in it. The finding of meaning or significance is important. People who tell stories often just ramble on. The writer of an effective essay reflects, ruminates, considers, reconsiders, and takes the reader along on the adventure of thought.

That meaning may be thought out in considerable detail before the first draft is written. This is likely to happen when the writer attempts to explore a traumatic subject, such as the death of a loved one, because that topic has been rehearsed, thought over and over in the writer's mind.

The meaning, however, may be discovered entirely in the writing. The writer may be obsessed with a subject and have no understanding of it until the shape of the draft, what is in the act of being said, and how it is in the act of being said, reveals the meaning to the reader. This often happens to me. I plunge in, hoping that meaning lies on the blank page—or the blank screen—and it usually does, revealed in the words I do not expect to write. Most times meaning comes in a combination of prethinking and drafting. I have a hint, a clue, a sense of what I may discover, and then the writing defines and redefines, qualifies and clarifies that idea, gives it fullness and meaning.

In writing the reflective essay, you discover and develop the skills of critical thinking. You move in close and then stand back. There is immediacy and detachment, close examination and the placing of an event in perspective. There is compassion and judgment, feeling and thought.

An effective reflective essay is often personal, but it is not private. The reflective essay allows the reader to discover the subject—and the meaning of the subject—with the writer. The reader is invited to think along with the writer and to think against the writer, discovering in the act of reading the reader's own meaning in the essay.

TIPS ON WRITING THE REFLECTIVE ESSAY

- *Be personal.* The more personal you are, the more universal your readership. You should speak to the human condition—in specific terms. Your strength is your difference, your own peculiar vision of the world.
- *Allow your mind to run free.* Write fast so that you will discover what you didn't know you remembered, what you didn't know you thought and felt, what patterns and connections lay hidden in the experience.
- *Be critical.* The function of writing the personal or reflective essay is to find meaning in experience, not just to record experience. Be skeptical and critical, challenge your own prejudices, beliefs, your own knowing.
- *Put your vision in context.* Describe your vision of the world then place it in a context—historical, scientific, sociological, psychological, political. The personal experience should connect with a larger meaning.
- *Take the reader along.* Invite the reader to accompany you as you reflect upon experience. Allow the experience and the meaning that arises from it to unfold at a pace that encourages the reader to follow.

Write to Inform

One of the reasons to write is to report, to make others understand our knowing and our living, to explain. As the old hunter came back to the cave and described the mastodon, where it could be found, how it could be trapped, so we as citizens and scholars report back to the community so that what we each learn is shared with others, and the collective community knowing exceeds the knowledge of each individual.

To inform, you have to attract listeners by quickly showing them how what you have to say affects them. You have to make a connection with the reader, so that person has a personal stake in hearing what you have to say.

This is a tricky business. If you are too sure of yourself, too full of your own knowing, you will offend and put off potential listeners. You will call attention to yourself, not to what you have to say. On the other hand, if you are too modest, too shy, too unsure of what you have to say, no one will pay attention.

The best way to steer a middle course is not to say too much about oneself and not to say too much directly to the reader, telling the reader how valuable one's information may be for him or her. Instead, deliver the message, focus on the material itself, allowing its importance to grow in the reader's mind as he or she is informed by the facts.

Humans enjoy learning—and perhaps as much enjoy being authorities and informing others. You will be well read if you give the reader information the reader can put to use—and can share with others.

TIPS ON WRITING TO INFORM

- *Write with information.* Give specific, revealing details, concrete facts, accurate information. Build the piece of writing from information not language. Be direct, informative.

- *Anticipate your reader's questions.* Role-play your reader and imagine what you would need and want to know—and when you would want to know it. Good writing is a conversation with the reader in which the writer hears the reader's unspoken questions: "How come?" "What do you mean?" "So what?"

- *Answer your reader's questions.* In writing, the reader has no stupid questions. The reader must be accepted where the reader is. It is the task of the informing writer to serve the reader who does not know.

- *Connect the information with the readers' experience.* Give readers information in a form and context they can use in their thinking, in their lives, in their work.

- *Write in an inviting voice.* Do not preach, condescend, patronize, talk up or down to the reader. Just share your delight in the information with the reader in a voice that focuses on the information to be shared.

THE RESEARCH PAPER

One common way of informing is to write a research paper. In writing, revising, and editing the research paper, you must conform to the style in which research is reported in your discipline. Each scholarly discipline has its own form for the research paper. Not only are there significant differences in the way the physicists, literary scholars, sociologists, historians, botanists report their findings, but a single discipline such as psychology may have different styles within the field with clinical psychologists, social psychologists, and laboratory psychologists all conforming to different traditions. Discover the traditions and forms of the research paper appropriate to the discipline in which you write a research paper.

There are, however, important similarities in all research papers.

THE RESEARCH QUESTION

Good research is usually the product of a well-focused question. The experienced researcher spends time narrowing that question until it is one that can be answered within the limited time of a course or a grant and with the resources available to the researcher. Research is a discipline of accumulation, with each researcher adding to the increasing knowledge within a field of study.

RESEARCH NOTE TAKING

The researcher must have a consistent system of note taking appropriate to the discipline. Note cards—3 × 5, 4 × 6, 5 × 8—are still popular because each card can be ordered and reordered during research as the scholar explores the subject.

The biggest problem for the inexperienced researcher is knowing the difference between a direct quote and a paraphrase. A direct quote is precisely what is said or written. It is enclosed in "quotation marks." Paraphrasing is the technique of putting what you have read or heard in your own words; a paraphrase can never be put in quotation marks, but it should have an attribution so the reader can follow the quotation back to the source.

As the note cards are reordered, the information on the source of the information travels with the note. Write down ALL the details on where you found the information. For example, the title of the book, the author's name, the person quoted, the publisher of the book and the city where it was published, the edition or printing, the year of publication, the library where the material is stored, the chapter, page, paragraph, and line so that you can check the source, and so that other scholars can go to the source of your information.

PLAGIARISM

If you use another writer's words as your own, you have committed a major—perhaps the major—intellectual crime. I have been plagiarized, and I know what it feels like. A high school student won a national writing contest with a short story of mine until someone recognized it; a nun who ran workshops for writing teachers used almost one hundred pages of one of my books, distributing it as her own text, until another nun read it and identified it as mine. In both cases, the plagiarists had not changed a word. I felt as though they had broken into my mind and stolen my ideas and my language.

Plagiarism is a felony. Where I taught, students who plagiarized were given Fs and made to take the courses over. I thought they should have been driven from the campus and banned from ever returning; or hung by their writing hands from the university flagpole for a month; or put in stocks in front of a dining hall so students could pelt them with old salad parts; or used as human football tackling dummies; or charged with theft in a court of law, as they would have been if they had stolen the computers on which they had plagiarized.

The responsible writer—student or professional—gives credit for the specific words, information, and ideas that belong to someone else.

THE FORM OF THE RESEARCH PAPER

As I said at the beginning of this section, you must conform to the style required by your discipline. This is not a time for creativity. The form is designed to serve readers; they expect to find the information they need in a familiar form and place.

Footnotes

The research paper serves other researchers, and so you provide the sources of specific information at the time you use that information through a footnote system. A footnote tells the reader where you discovered the fact or quote you are using at the moment the reader reads it. This is easy if your notes are in order.

Bibliography

At the end of a research paper, you should provide other scholars with a list of your sources according to the style of the field in which you are working. Your note cards, if properly kept, make this a simple task.

Follow the golden rule: Serve your reader as you would want to be served yourself.

TIPS ON WRITING THE RESEARCH PAPER

- *Attribute. Attribute. Attribute.* The reader of a research paper not only wants to know the evidence you have to back up each point, but also where it came from. You should have a system of footnotes and bibliography that the reader can use to research the same area.
- *Define your terms.* Each discipline or profession has its own language or jargon that others may not understand. It is important to define any term that the reader may not understand, that others in a different branch of the same discipline may not understand, or that has a different meaning in normal, nonprofessional speech.

- *Use graphics.* Make charts, maps, illustrations that will clarify your research. Use typographical designs and type styles that emphasize what you have to say. If you have a list format, you may want to use a list, as I have here, rather than running information entirely in normal sentences.
- *Explain your methods.* Other researchers will want to know the procedures you followed to get your results. This part of the presentation may incorporate a review of the literature, or that review may be a separate section of the paper in which you reveal what you read and comment on how helpful particular articles or books were.

There are many forms of writing we use to inform: speeches and presentations, letters and brochures, advertisements and book reports. Each form has a similar purpose: to teach the reader the subject.

Write to Persuade

One of the principal reasons we write is to persuade. In the academic world, this form of writing is often called argument, but most students hear that tone and imagine a fight. I use the term persuasion, which more accurately describes the form—and voice—of appropriate intellectual discourse in which writers attempt to persuade readers through a process of reason to reconsider their views on a topic.

In fact, I believe, academic argument is a term and a process left over from the days when the academic world was exclusively male. The training I received from my male professors—and all my professors were men—was similar to the training I received on the football field and in the paratroops. Truth was found by two men taking completely opposite sides and each trying to destroy the other. It must be a direct descendant from the tournament practice of two knights trying to knock each other off their horses.

When I taught a course in argument, I found the male students comfortable with this term to describe a form of writing that is designed to cause the reader to rethink a position. They had been socialized on the playground or hockey rink to appear as if they enjoyed battle: hurt and do not reveal your own hurt.

But the majority of students in the class were women, most of them far brighter than the males in the class (and the male who taught the class). They hated *argument* which they told me was a male activity. I think we need far more development of forms of persuasion which are not built on the concept of the knights with lances hurtling toward each other on horseback. I reject the term *argument* and use *persuasion* to describe the form of writing in which the writer attempts to make readers reconsider their views on a topic.

Persuasion is the basic form of intellectual discourse; it is the way that new ideas are introduced, that old ideas are discarded, and old ideas are adapted to new trends of thought.

TIPS ON WRITING PERSUASION

- *State your position.* This is no place for suspense. Make it clear what you intend to advocate. Define and establish your own issues and the context in which they are to be discussed.

- *Establish your credentials.* Let the reader know up front what experience you have had, what research you have done that should convince the reader to listen to your position.

- *Anticipate your reader's points.* You should be able to empathize with your opponent. Read that person's mind by imagining you are taking the other side, then make the best persuasive points you can.

- *Counter your opponent's points.* Now that you know your opponent's views, you can counter them right away, answering them before presenting your own views.

- *Appeal to reason.* Readers are rarely persuaded—at the least in the intellectual world—by emotion. Appeal to reason, base your position on documented evidence presented in a logical order.

There are many other forms of persuasion. A letter applying for a job or a grant tries to persuade others that you should be given a job or financial support. Again, you should role-play those people so that you will know what appeals to them, what questions they will ask, what information they will want to know, what tone of voice will persuade them.

TIPS ON WRITING A LETTER APPLYING FOR A JOB

- *Research the application process.* Talk to your college placement office for counsel in writing job-seeking letters. Study books and articles that describe the strategies and techniques of successful job seekers.

- *Research the company.* Look up the company at which you are applying in the business references in the library. Read the company's annual report and brochures, interview people who work and have worked there, who supply the company and are supplied by the company. Make sure you know what the firm does—provide advertising services or manufactures ball bearings—and how it does that job—specializing in mail-order advertising or selling ball bearings in the international market.

- *Say specifically what skills you offer a potential employer.* "I'm willing to do anything" doesn't entice an employer, but "I learned to get along with a great variety of people working as a waiter, then the head waiter, at a resort that attracted many tourists from overseas" or "I tested my courses in accounting against my experience in summer jobs, in serving as treasurer of the student union, and in spending a semester internship with the Internal Revenue Service."

- *Be specific about your goals.* Tell the employer what you hope to learn from the job, what additional skills you hope to develop, so that you may better serve your employer.

- *Anticipate and answer the prospective employer's questions.* Remember that the reader is looking for someone who fills the company's needs. Read the advertisement or job announcement carefully and respond to the specifics of the position.

- *Sound professional.* Write in a professional manner that demonstrates that you are someone who will do a good job and represent the company well. When you are given a writing task you have never done before, jump at the chance to learn a new skill for your writer's tool box.

Explore Creative Nonfiction

I had known I wanted to be a writer from the fourth grade on, but when I graduated from college as an English major, I had been taught there was a grand Literary Pyramid. At the top was poetry, so I wanted to be a poet. Then one step—but a long one—down was fiction and drama and so I wanted to write a novel or two. Then far down at the bottom was nonfiction, mostly essays of literary criticism, so I did *not* want to write nonfiction.

But I wanted to eat and pay my rent and since openings for great poets and novelists were limited, I took a job as a copy boy on a metropolitan newspaper. This would embarrass my teachers and classmates. I did not live up to their expectations or, worse still, they may have known all along that I was not a poet or a novelist but, at best, a journalist.

I did the work my job required, but back in my room, I wrote short, tight poems in a secret code of compressed profundity, or short stories in which I cleverly left out the names of the characters, the place the story took place, and the story itself—no plots for me. I was a great artist.

It amazes me how long I believed in this literary aristocracy. I published newspaper and magazine articles, even nonfiction books, but I did not really feel I was a writer. Now things are different—and better. The richness of nonfiction is recognized as creative nonfiction—memoir, essay, profile, journalistic events around the world. As the genre of creative nonfiction became respected, more and more writers turned to nonfiction, and a rich variety of writing forms were published, and these writers inspired other writers to participate in the exciting "new" form of truth writing.

When I write nonfiction I can employ the compression and explosive power of poetry. When I tell a true story I can use all the techniques of narrative—dramatic conflict, dialogue, dramatic action, character—and I can steal techniques from film and drama and even attempt techniques I have never seen published anywhere else. The only requirement is that my story be true. I do not make up a story as I do when writing fiction; I build a story from the bricks of documented information. I do not feel any different when I write poetry and fiction than I do when writing nonfiction. Good writing is not a matter of genre and neither is bad. Writing is writing.

When we tell a story in traditional nonfiction form, we usually tell *about* the story. The narrative is filtered through our own reactions which, in turn, tell readers how we think they should react.

> Our daughter, Lee, who died of Reye's Syndrome at the age of 20, is now longer dead than she lived, but we still have mail addressed to her that offer credit cards or classes in hair dressing. She is with us every day, perhaps every hour, but we have achieved a degree of acceptance and then one of those letters or a phone call insisting she has won a free rug cleaning or a trip to Bermuda strips away our hard won acceptance. It is always a stab in the heart, always causes us the feel the old anger, our frustration and feeling of inadequacy that we could not protect her.

When I told this true story in my book *The Lively Shadow—Living with the Death of a Child,* I used fictional techniques, showing not telling, so that the reader would experience this story.

> The phone rings and I grab it quickly as is my habit, made immediate each time because of that phone call to Vermont so few, so many years ago.
> "I'd like to speak to Lee Murray."
> It is always a surprise, always unexpected. I am never prepared. I usually just hang up, but tonight I hear my voice, tight tense, carefully controlled, "So would I. She died 24 years ago."
> I hate the cold cruelty of my words and feel the anger rising. I tell myself it is not the telemarketer's fault. She may have lost her own child.
> "Is Lee Murray home?"
> The voice didn't hear what I said. I let my voice rise, make myself speak slowly. Minnie Mae hears my tone and turns to look at me.
> "Lee Murray is not at home. My daughter died twenty-four years ago."
> "She has won a chance for a trip to the Bahamas."
> I am yelling, "My daughter is dead! Didn't you hear? My daughter is dead."
> The slight burning across my chest will increase if I do not make myself calm. I gently put the phone in its cradle.

This worked in the book, but now I wonder what would happen if I pushed it further toward dramatic writing. I am surprised as I read this piece over that I did so much telling. Although it is near the end of the memoir, it was the first story I told, the anger forcing me to write on. Let's see what I could have done, using the third person rather than the first.

> The phone rings and he grabbed it quickly to protect his wife, wishing he had been able to protect her from that phone call to Vermont years ago.
> "I'd like to speak to Lee Murray."
> "So would I. She died 24 years ago."
> "Is Lee Murray home?"
> "Lee Murray is not at home. My daughter died twenty-four years ago."
> "She has won a chance for a trip to the Bahamas."
> "My daughter is dead! Didn't you hear? My daughter is dead."
> He gently put the phone in its cradle.

Dialogue is what people do to each other. It is action not speech.

This same story could be used in an essay of warning to those who have lost a child.

> The phone will ring for your child years after she is buried. Mail will come, a hat of hers will appear on a closet shelf, a sheaf of oboe music in the piano bench. Brace yourself. It will happen and there is nothing you can do about it.

We stretch the conventional limits of the nonfiction story so that we can better discover what we have to say and communicate the experience more clearly to the reader. The only limits are factual truth—we were away in Vermont, we had a 20-year-old daughter Lee, she died of Reye's Syndrome—and that the technique we use is appropriate for the story and effective for the reader. Each literary form can be employed to communicate significant meaning. Many poems are nonfiction. I could use this material in a poem.

> When your daughter is buried
> her ghost life begins. The credit
> card offers will come by mail,
> the prize trip to the Bahamas
> by phone. And you will call
> her at college, making a
> phone in an empty room
> ring and ring and ring
> until you put the phone
> in its cradle as gently
> as you placed her in
> her cradle so few years
> ago.

All forms merge. This poem, unfortunately, is autobiography, a form of nonfiction. It is also narrative, the story of a parent who has lost a child. It is an essay of comfort or explanation. Step across the boundaries between forms of writing as you practice your craft, always learning that what can't be said, can be said so that the readers' silent feelings and thoughts can be heard.

A Lifetime Apprenticeship

I invite you to join the Guild of Writers. There are no master writers in our guild, just apprentices facing the ever-new challenge of the next draft. Eudora Welty, who wrote until she was 92 years of age, said, "The writer himself studies intensely how to do it while he is in the thick of doing it; then when the particular novel or story is done, he is likely to forget how; he does well to. Each work is new. Mercifully, the question of *how* abides less in the abstract, and less in the past, than in the specific, in the work at hand . . . ."

Of course there are some writers who are better than others, but like Eudora Welty, they die still learning their craft. Writing the eighth edition of *Write to Learn* I have instructed myself and so will the next book, and so will the next one.

You and I have explored a craft that can never be learned. Be grateful—writing will bring you a lifetime of discovery and surprise. Each morning at my writing desk, I still face the page with enough fear to make it exciting and enough confidence that I will write what I do not expect.

Writing has allowed my voice to be heard. I have been able to participate in our society, arguing for new ways to teach writing, arguing against old ways of resolving differences, speaking out against war, speaking out on the satisfactions and concerns of my generation.

At my writing desk, I have discovered and explored the mysteries of life. I have also survived the tragedies that enter each life—hurt and loss, sickness and death. I have been able to complain and to celebrate, mourn and laugh, imagine, and learn. Writing has also brought me the gift of concentration as I become lost in my craft, searching for the right word, creating the phrase that gives off sparks of meaning, constructing sentences that flow and paragraphs that satisfy, tuning the music of my voice to my evolving meaning. Writing has been my therapy and my craft.

Writing began as play for me and it remains play. I hope you will be as fortunate and find a lifetime of play, fooling around with language, and finding yourself surprised by meanings that clarify your many lives life.

■ SHOPTALK ■

I'm not planning on getting a job where I have to write. Besides, I'll probably have a secretary who can write for me. Why should I think about ways to adapt my process to other writing tasks and forms?

Many jobs do not require writing. But just as many do. Because so many companies are in the process of downsizing and reorganizing, you may find yourself performing a variety of tasks, including writing.

Keep in mind too that the personal computer has replaced support staff in many organizations. Because it is so easy and quick to compose, revise, and edit on computers, employers have cut back on clerical help who take dictation and write up reports and letters. Usually one person does it all. That means you.

Won't I have to worry only about the forms of writing for my particular position?

You might want to consider the advantage of good writing skills if you decide to change jobs or seek a promotion. Most people no longer stay in one job for life but change careers several times before retirement. The more multi-skilled you are, the better prepared you are to meet any job demand. If you end up starting your own business, your writing skills will be all the more valuable. As your own employer, you may need to write grant requests, issue publicity statements, and correspond with clients all at one time.

If you learn now to adapt your process to various writing tasks, you will be prepared for whatever employment opportunity comes your way.

Why don't we learn how to write memos and reports in college instead of critical essays or personal narratives? It seems to me that learning these forms would prepare us more effectively for the "real" world.

You very well may write reports, memos, applications, letters, and other kinds of business forms in a business communications class or another writing class. But it's important not to lose sight of what writing's all about; it helps us communicate, and it helps us think.

Many top companies do not necessarily recruit students who come equipped with specific skills such as report or memo writing. They hope instead to find students who have learned how to think critically in college and can transfer their analytical skills to the work arena. They want workers who can analyze and solve problems as well as communicate. Your writing process will help you develop the analytical skills these employers seek.

> You've stressed the importance of finding your own voice and topics when you write. Yet now you're saying that I have to fit my voice and ideas into a particular form or genre. How can I write like that and still be original?

It's true that certain academic disciplines or fields of work have established accepted forms of writing. But this does not mean that you have to give up hope of working creatively. Scientists have always written their findings in a strict format. First they state a problem and a hypothesis for solving the problem; then they describe the methodology they intend to use in their study; finally they write about their findings and conclusions. But no one accuses them of being unoriginal. In fact, we are most likely to classify scientists as creative problem solvers.

Besides, no matter what form you use when you write, and no matter what your task, you will decide what details and information you will include in your piece. Your word choice and style of composing will enhance a sense of your own voice and perspective in whatever you write.

Don't give up on originality when you must write within the parameters of a particular genre. Make the genre work for you.

> You haven't talked about length. Isn't that part of form?

It is. As you study the traditional forms used to solve specific writing tasks, you will get a sense of the expected length, but that doesn't mean you have to meet it. You should give the reader all the information the reader needs and no more.

In general, remember: Shorter is better. I have never had to cut a piece of writing without making it better. One famous writer said to "kill all your darlings." I don't entirely agree. Some of the writing you especially like may be effective, but there is a danger that many of the paragraphs we like really don't carry their weight of meaning to the reader. When that occurs, cut them. If you have writing that you really like, you can always save it for another piece.

This is just as true for literary writing as business writing. Poetry is the highest form of literary art, in part, because it says the most with the fewest words.

Peter DeVries said, "When I see a paragraph shrinking under my eyes like a strip of bacon in a skillet, I know I'm on the right track."

> What if I mix forms? Can you write reflectively and still do research? Or be persuasive and still write reflectively?

Absolutely. It's good to be aware of the different features for each form, but you can certainly mix them if the draft leads you in that direction.

If you are writing formal reports from another class, check with your teacher first to see if it's okay to mix forms. Some teachers will want you to follow a particular genre in order to learn certain things about a topic.

■ IN THE WRITER'S WORKSHOP ■

ON YOUR OWN

1. Ask a professor to suggest a journal in your field of interest, or go to the library and ask the reference librarians to direct you to one. Copy an essay, study, or report from the journal and then outline it in your daybook. Notice how the author moves through the piece, what kinds of information he or she uses, and how it is arranged.

2. Collect at least three editorials, opinion pieces, or other kinds of persuasive writing from magazines and newspapers. Read each piece twice. After the first reading, write down your immediate responses: Did the piece persuade you? Did it help you change your mind about a particular issue or topic? During your second reading, jot down the author's major points. How does the writer establish himself or herself as an authority? How does he or she use evidence and information? In what ways does the writer account for opposing viewpoints? Decide from this reading which of the three pieces you found most persuasive and why.

3. Compare and contrast two pieces of writing in different forms—a researched essay with a persuasive essay, for example; or a reflective essay with an analytical essay. Draw a line down a page in your daybook and outline the main features of the first essay on the right, the second on the left. Discuss your findings in class.

4. Select a piece of writing, and rewrite the opening in a form suitable for at least three of the following genres—the reflective, persuasive, analytical, research, or narrative essay. Then write a couple of paragraphs describing the differences between the openings, the tone of voice you established, and what information you included in each. How do your different openings foretell the kind of writing that will follow?

5. If you had to write a college application essay, pull it out and review it. Recall the process of writing it and the kind of advice parents, teachers, friends, school counselors, or writing tutors gave you. What specific details did they want you to concentrate on? What did they think was appropriate to include or omit? What difference did the perceived readers of the piece make in the way

you wrote it? How did you revise it? What features characterize this kind of essay as a particular genre?

6. Try your hand at a writing form you are unfamiliar with. If you have never written an analytical essay, for example, plan one from beginning to end, and take it through the steps of your writing process. Keep track of your progress with your daybook, and make sure to note what you had to do differently with this piece of writing than with others you have done. Refer to the tips in Chapter 28 on writing the form of essay you have chosen.

7. Keep a notebook of writing you do for other classes. Include whatever instructions your teachers may give you, the pieces of writing themselves, and any notes and drafts. Insert a blank piece of paper after each piece and write a short but detailed analysis of how you approached the assignment and wrote it.

8. Think of a writing assignment that proved to be particularly challenging to you. Pretend that your writing partner must complete the same assignment. Define the assignment, the form of writing it required, and how you completed it. Then write up a list of tips, similar to the ones in Chapter 28, that will help your partner.

9. Gather sample essay questions from exams you have taken or that other students in similar classes may have taken. Determine the amount of time you are allowed to answer each question and then practice planning, writing, and editing the answers. In the margins of the draft or on a separate piece of paper, give yourself time to sketch out a thoughtful outline before you begin. Then write your answer and edit it. Work to complete all steps of the process within the allotted time. Keep practicing until you feel comfortable with the process and meet your time goal.

10. Choose one of the essay forms featured in Chapter 28, and find a published essay that is most like that form. Using the writing tips I've given for each form, analyze the essay and describe how the writer incorporates these steps into his or her piece. Note also where the writer deviates from the "tips" or combines different forms.

11. Choose a letter to the editor from your school or local newspaper. Analyze the letter and discuss why you think it is or is not effective. Make a list of suggestions for the writer that might help him or her write a more effective piece.

12. Ask a teacher in your major or field of interest what constitutes good student writing in that discipline. Have him or her give examples of successful student papers, or ask if you may have copies. What details of writing did the successful student writer pay attention to? Why are these details particular to that field or discipline?

13. Take a piece of writing, and draw up a plan for turning it into a research paper. You might, for example, study a letter to the editor in the school newspaper.

WITH A WRITING PARTNER

14. Brainstorm a list of all the writing tasks you've had to do over the past two to four weeks. Don't leave anything out; include application essays, exam essay answers, school excuse notes for children or siblings, memos, reports, lab observations, and so on. Then with a partner, talk about the context or setting for each form of writing. Where or why did you compose each? Who did you expect your readers to be? In what ways did the forms differ from one another? What might be appropriate to one form of writing and not to another? Did you feel that you were a novice with some forms and an expert with others?

WITH A GROUP

15. Split up into groups of three or four and visit different offices on campus. Have each group member interview an employee in the office about the kinds of writing he or she is expected to do at work. Ask if you can get copies of various reports, letters, or memos that the employee is likely to write. Then come back together as groups and discuss the main features of the different forms or genres. Do some of them have standard openings, use formal language? Do any include pictures or graphics? How do they begin and end? Who is the audience for each piece of writing?

16. Have each member of your group select a piece of writing that represents a particular genre, and imagine the process the writer went through. Pretend you are that writer and plan the piece—what information you'll need, the kind of readership you anticipate, how you intend to focus, when you expect to have a draft, what kind of feedback you will get, how you will revise and edit it.

17. Join a group of classmates to study three or four genres of television shows (a sitcom, a drama, a detective or cop show, a documentary, a mystery, a made-for-TV suspense film, a magazine news show, etc.). Assign one kind of show to each person. Take notes as you watch. Think of the writer's role and what features of the genre he or she must emphasize. What kinds of elements characterize certain kinds of shows? Get together as a group and write up an analysis comparing and contrasting the different features of particular television genres.

18. Write a persuasive essay that's not so persuasive. In other words, disregard the tips for writing such an essay. Ignore your opponent's arguments, and don't back up your points with evidence. Ignore reason, and make only emotional appeals. Then read your essay aloud to a group and have them "workshop" the essay to make it better. Ask the group to give you specific details and to talk about their responses to the essay as you read it.

WITH WRITING MENTORS

19. Think of a career you might like to enter after college, and brainstorm a list of the forms of writing you think you would do in that field. Then arrange an interview with employees in the field, and ask them to describe in detail their writing tasks. Ask to see copies, and write down the main features of particular genres.

ON THE INTERNET

20. Talk with someone who has created a home page on the World Wide Web. Study other home pages and note the features of this particular genre. What kind of writing is expected on a home page? What kind of writing would not be expected? How much of the writing is dictated by the technical perimeters of the home page itself? How much does text interact with pictures or graphics in these pages? What other forms of writing does home page text resemble? Design your own home page. You might want to look at information on a study done by Stanford University and the Poynter Institute for Media Studies at <http://poynterextra.org/et/i.htm> about how people read news on the Web, or at a site such as Webnovice.com, which offers advice on writing for the Web. The Journalist's Toolbox at <http://www.journaliststoolbox.com> has links to other sites dealing with writing for the Web on its Writing Resources page. And of course there are other sites out there dealing with this topic.

21. Subscribe to an online discussion group that discusses controversial topics, maybe one concerning politics or government or an issue such as free speech. Save and print out a bunch of the postings to the group and alone or with your class or a writing partner, go through them and determine which posters make the best arguments, which make the worst, and why. What elements or qualities do the successful arguments embody?

22. Check out a Web site dealing with writing in a discipline you aren't familiar with. You can find these by going to Web sites listing resources for writers or doing searches with Web search tools. Check out the Purdue University online writing lab Web site listing writing resources by going to <http://owl.english.purdue.edu/internet/resources/>.

If you choose the link on this page for Genres of Writing, you'll find links to online resources for business and technical writing, creative writing and non-academic writing, and writing in special fields.